YOUR...
THE OBSC...
AND...

Here is the most comprehensive collection of categories you've ever seen—and ever had to answer to! From **Airplane Crashes** to **Babies,** from **Clocks and Watches** to **Idiosyncrasies,** from **Mascots, Phobias, Record Labels,** to **Saints, Scholars,** and **Vitamins,** the questions in *Questions* give you the answers you need to make your trivia competition truly trivial.

One of the leading experts in the field today, FRED WORTH is the co-founder of *Trivia Unlimited,* the major newsletter of trivia afficionados; and the author of *The Complete Unabridged Super Trivia Encyclopedia* (volumes I and II), *World War II Superfacts, Thirty Years of Rock 'n' Roll Trivia,* and *Hollywood Trivia.*

Answers to the front cover trivia quiz:

Park Street.

Benito Mussolini.

Mickey Rooney.

Lacrosse.

Humans and pigs.

Answers to the back cover trivia quiz:

1. Elizabeth of York.
2. 220 yards.
3. Red, blue, and green.
4. *Exiles*
5. Robert Redford. The movie was *Ordinary People.*
6. Herbert George.
7. Alaska.
8. Tokyo Rose.
9. Orange, purple, and silver.
10. Chang—there are 85 million of them!

QUESTIONS:
The Perfect Companion To Your Trivia Games

FRED WORTH

WARNER BOOKS

A Warner Communications Company

Dedicated to my editor Brian Thomsen

Acknowledgments

I wish to thank my editor Brian Thomsen, my lady Missi Missildine, and my friends Don McCombs and Steve Tamerius for their help.

Contents

Introduction

Chances are this is probably not the first quiz book you have ever read. This is, however, one of the largest question-and-answer books, with over 425 different subjects contained within.

As you can see by perusing the chronological list that follows, quiz books have been around for quite a while. My collection goes back to 1926.

"Information Please" became a popular radio series in 1938, with the original panel members being the popular Oscar Levant, Franklin P. Adams, and John Kieran. "Dr. I.Q." was another popular radio series. It gave away silver dollars to members of the audience who could answer "not too difficult" questions. It was "Take It or Leave It" that gave a top prize of $64 to the winner. This inspired the TV spin-off "The $64,000 Question." To date there have been over 300 different game or quiz shows on TV.

The latest generation of the question-and-answer formula is represented by the popular board games, which combine quizzes with the fun of playing a table game with others.

Following is a list containing the majority of question books that have been published since 1926. If I have omitted any book, please let me know so that I can add it to the list.

I hope you have fun playing *Questions!*

Any questions?

F.L.W.

A Chronology of Quiz Books

1926

☐ *Answers To Questions*, Frederic J. Haskin, Grosset and Dunlap

1927

☐ *Ask Me Another*, Justin Spafford and Lucien Esty, preface by Robert Benchley, Blue Ribbon
☐ *Ask me Another!* Series 2, Justin Spafford and Lucien Esty, Viking Press
☐ *Now You Quiz Me!*, J. Perling, Samuels Printing
☐ *The Quiz Book*, The Inquisitors, Brentano's

1932

☐ *Ask Me Again*, J. N. Leonard, Blue Ribbon

1938

☐ *The Giant Quiz Book*, Rosejeanne Slifer and Louise Crittenden, Crown
☐ *The Quiz-and-Answer Book*, Frederic J. Haskin, Grosset and Dunlap
☐ *What Do You Know*, Sabina Hart Connolly, David McKay

1939

☐ *Ely Culbertson's Quiz Book*, Ely Culbertson, John C. Winston Co.
☐ *Information, Please!*, Dan Golenpaul, Simon and Schuster
☐ *What's the Answer*, Fred Garrigus, Books, Inc.

1940

☐ *Information Please* (1941 Edition), Dan Golenpaul, Random House

1941

☐ *The Experts Quiz Book*, Blue Ribbon
☐ *The 1941 Quiz Book*, Clement Wood and Gloria Goddard, Arcadia
☐ *The Pocket Quiz Book*, Rosejeanne Slifer and Louise Crittenden, Pocket

1942

☐ *Modern Events Quiz Book*, Neil MacNeil, Blue Ribbon
☐ *The Pocket Entertainer*, Shirley Cunningham, Pocket

1946

☐ *Coronet Quiz Book*, Coronet Magazine, A. S. Barnes
☐ *How Much Do You Know?*, Sylvan Hoffman, Farrar, Straus and Co.
☐ *Quiz Book of the Seven Arts*, Jo Ranson and Richard Pack, Summit Press

1952

☐ *Questions and Answers From the Book of Knowledge*, Cardinal

1955

☐ *The $64,000 Question*, Dell

1958

☐ *Modern Science Quiz Book*, Anne and Lewis Epple, Platt and Munk
☐ *The Second Perma Quiz Book*, Joseph Nathan Kane, Perma
☐ *The TV Quiz Book*, Literary Press
☐ *Twenty-One*, Pyramid

1963

☐ *Tom Harmon's Sports Information Book*, Tom Harmon and Jim Benagh, J. Jowell Pratt
☐ *Who Did It?*, Virginia Coigney, Collier

1965

☐ *Questions, Anyone?*, Robert Thomsen, Doubleday

1966

☐ *More Trivial Trivia*, Edwin Goodgold and Dan Carlinsky, Dell
☐ *The Sports Answer Book*, Bill Mazer, Grossett and Dunlap
☐ *Trivia**, Edwin Goodgold and Dan Carlinsky, Dell

1967

☐ *Party Fun Quiz Book*, Neil Farber and Ira M. Josephs, Lancer

1969

☐ *Geography Quiz Book*, Gilbert W. Davies, Funk and Wagnalls

---

*First use of the word *trivia* in a quiz book title.

☐ *The Nostalgia Quiz Book*, Martin A. Gross, Signet

1970

☐ *Ask Me Another*, George S. Phyllides, Dover
☐ *The Movie Quiz Book*, Malcolm Frederick Vance, Paperback Library
☐ *The Quiz Book*, Raymond J. Healy, Golden Press
☐ *Rock 'n Roll Trivia*, Edwin Goodgold and Dan Carlinsky, Popular Library
☐ *So You Think You Know Movies*, Donald Kennedy, Ace

1971

☐ *Dr. I. Q. Quiz Book*, Lee Segall, Ace
☐ *Pop/Rock Question and Answer Book*, David Dachs, Scholastic
☐ *So You Think You Know Rock 'n Roll*, Len Brown and Gary Friedrich, Tower
☐ *So You Think You Know T.V.*, Donald Kennedy, Ace

1972

☐ *Questions from the Rockpile*, Arthur L. Devlin and Thomas McInerney, Bantam
☐ *Sports Quiz Book*, Gilbert W. Davies, A. S. Barnes

1973

☐ *The Encyclopedia Britannica Quiz Book*, Pocket
☐ *Questions and Answers About Baseball*, Bill Hongash with Bruce Weber, Scholastic
☐ *Tons of Trivia*, Cally Comenos and Mary-Ann Ballenberg, Scholastic

1974

☐ *The Baseball Quiz Book*, Ted Misa, Hawthorn
☐ *Mindbenders Quizbook*, Sarah and Martin Clifford, Drake
☐ *Mindbenders Quizbook* Vol. 2, Sarah and Martin Clifford, Drake
☐ *Mindbenders Quizbook* Vol.3, Sarah and Martin Clifford, Drake
☐ *The Nostalgia Quiz Book #2*, Martin A. Gross, Signet
☐ *Pro Sports Trivia*, Lee Prentner, Stadium Sports
☐ *A Quarry of Quizzes*, Antony Lake, Hart
☐ *The Roger Caras' Nature Quiz Book*, Roger Caras, Bantam
☐ *Screen Test*, Peter Brown, Martin Hayden, and Frank Riess, Penguin
☐ *The Sherlock Holmes Quiz Book*, Albert J. Menendez, Drake
☐ *The World's Greatest TV Quiz*, Tom Bornhauser and Dennis Palumbo, Berkley

☐ *Zingers from Hollywood Squares,* Gail Sicilia, Popular Library

1975

☐ *The American Political Quizbook,* Albert J. Menendez, Drake
☐ *The Bantam Trivia Quiz Book,* Donald Saltz, Bantam
☐ *The Compleat Beatles Quiz Book,* Edwin Goodgold and Dan Carlinsky, Warner
☐ *The Compleat Motion Picture Quiz Book,* Harry D. Trigg and Yolanda L. Trigg, Doubleday
☐ *The Dugout Quiz,* Al Goldberg, Drake
☐ *52 Great Quizzes,* Antony B. Lake, Hart
☐ *The Football Quiz Book,* Al Goldberg, Drake
☐ *The Nostalgia Quiz Book #3,* Martin A. Gross, Signet
☐ *The Official TV Trivia Quiz Book,* Bart Andrews, Signet
☐ *Peoples Bicentennial Commission Quiz Book of the American Revolution,* Bantam
☐ *The Pro Football Quiz Book,* Bruce Weber, Scholastic
☐ *The Sports Nostalgia Quiz Book,* Zander Hollander and David Schulz, Signet
☐ *Tandem's 1st Quiz Book,* S. Mason, Tandem
☐ *The Trivia Quizbook,* Gilbert Davies, Drake
☐ *The World's Greatest Monster Quiz,* Dan Carlinsky and Edwin Goodgold, Berkley-Medallion

1976

☐ *The Agatha Christie Quiz Book,* Andy East, Pocket
☐ *The Bantam Trivia Quiz Book #2,* Donald Saltz, Bantam
☐ *The Baseball Trivia Book* (Originally titled *Who Was Harry Steinfeld and Other Baseball Trivia Questions*), Bert Randolph Sugar, Playboy
☐ *The Booker Quiz,* Christopher Booker, BBC/RKP
☐ *Car Quiz,* Chuck Wozney, Scholastic
☐ *The Complete Movie Quizbook,* Malcolm Vance, Drake
☐ *The Official Movie Trivia Quiz Book,* Martin A. Gross, Signet
☐ *The Official TV Trivia Quiz Book #2,* Bart Andrews, Signet
☐ *The Pop Quiz Book,* Maurice Kinn, Warner
☐ *The Rock Trivia Quiz Book,* Jon Allan, Drake
☐ *The Science Fiction Quiz Book,* Martin Last and Baird Searles, Signet
☐ *The Show Biz Trivia Quiz Book,* Thomas W. Moore, editor, Pocket
☐ *The Sports Nostalgia Quiz Book #2,* Zander Hollander and David Schulz, Signet

☐ *Thirty Years of Television? A Quizbook*, Bruce Nash, Drake
☐ *The World Championship Boxing Quizbook*, Bruce Nash and Julian E. Compton, Drake

1977

☐ *The Absolutely Most Challenging Baseball Quiz Book Ever*, David Nemec, Collier
☐ *The All-Star Turnabout Quiz Book*, Mark Tan, Price/Stern/Sloan
☐ *Book of Quizzes*, Bob and Betty Sanders, Great Lakes
☐ *The Country and Western Book*, Fred L. Worth, Drake
☐ *Everything You Always Wanted To Know About Sports*, Mickey Herskowitz and Steve Perkins, Signet
☐ *The Fifties Nostalgia Quizbook*, Bruce Nash, Drake
☐ *The Great American Baseball Trivia Book*, Jeffrey Feinman, Manor
☐ *Halliwell's Movie Quiz*, Leslie Halliwell, Penguin
☐ *The Official Rock and Roll Trivia Quiz Book*, Marc Sotkin, Signet
☐ *Once Upon a Question*, Warren E. Siegmond, Bantam
☐ *The Pow! Wham! Zap! Comic Book Trivia Quiz*, Michael Uslan and Bruce Solomon, William Morrow
☐ *The Princeton Trivia/Quiz Book*, Thomas Epstein, Pinnacle
☐ *The Quiz Show Quiz Book*, Frank W. Chinnock, Berkley Medallion
☐ *The Soap Opera Quiz Book*, Bill Adler and Alice Edmunds, Pocket
☐ *The Soap Opera Trivia Book*, Jeffrey Fienman, Manor
☐ *Son of the Compleat Motion Picture Quiz Book*, Harry D. Trigg and Yolander L. Trigg, Doubleday
☐ *Stan Fischler's Sports Stumpers*, Stan Fischler, Tempo
☐ *Star Trek Quiz Book*, Bart Andrews with Brad Dunning, Signet

1978

☐ *And the Envelope, Please*, Richard Altram, Lippincott
☐ *The Beatles Trivia Quiz Book*, Helen Rosenbaum, Signet
☐ *The Country Music Quiz Book*, Don and Barbara Humphreys, Doubleday Dolphin
☐ *The Elvis Presley Quizbook*, Bruce M. Nash, Warner
☐ *The Elvis Presley Trivia Quiz Book*, Helen Rosenbaum, Signet
☐ *The Even More Challenging Baseball Quiz Book*, David Nemec, Collier
☐ *The Fabulous Fifties Quiz Book*, Bart Andrews with Brad Dunning, Signet
☐ *The Great 1960's Quiz*, Dan Carlinsky, Harper & Row

- [ ] *More Stan Fischler's Sports Stumpers*, Stan Fischler, Tempo
- [ ] *More Zingers from Hollywood Squares*, Gail Sicilia, Popular Library
- [ ] *The Official Movie Trivia Quiz Book #2*, Martin A. Gross, Signet
- [ ] *The Official Rock and Roll Trivia Quiz Book #2*, Marc Sotkin, Signet
- [ ] *The Official Superman Quiz Book*, Bruce M. Nash, Warner
- [ ] *The Official TV Trivia Quiz Book #3*, Bart Andrews, Signet
- [ ] *Oscar Quiz Book*, Stanley Hopman, Dale/Caroline
- [ ] *The Rock 'n Roll Trivia Quiz Book*, Michael Uslan and Bruce Solomon, Fireside
- [ ] *Sports Question and Answer Book*, Bill Adler, Grosset and Dunlap
- [ ] *The Superhero Movie & TV Quiz Book*, Jeff Rovin, Signet
- [ ] *The TV Guide Quiz Book*, Stan Goldstein and Fred Goldstein, Bantam
- [ ] *The UFO Movie Quiz Book*, Jeff Rovin, Signet
- [ ] *Whatever Happened to Blue Suede Shoes?*, Bruce M. Nash, Grosset and Dunlap
- [ ] *The World's Greatest Comics Quiz*, Jerry Robinson, Tempo
- [ ] *The World's Most Challenging TV Quiz*, Joe Walders, Dolphin

1979

- [ ] *Bill Burrud's Animal Quiz*, Bill Burrud with Allen Rich, Tempo
- [ ] *Count Dracula's Vampire Quiz Book*, Jeff Rovin, Signet
- [ ] *The Great Sports Question and Answer Book*, Michael J.Pellowski, Moby
- [ ] *The Illustrated Rock Quiz*, Rob Burt, Exeter
- [ ] *The Quintessential Quiz Book*, Norman G. Hickman, St. Martin's Press
- [ ] *The Rolling Stones Trivia Quiz Book*, Helen Rosenbaum, Signet
- [ ] *The Sports Nostalgia Quiz Book #3*, Zander Hollander and David Schulz, Signet
- [ ] *The Super Sixties Quiz Book*, Bart Andrews with Brad Dunning, Signet
- [ ] *Teen Superstars Trivia Quiz Book*, Helen Rosenbaum, Signet
- [ ] *The Tolkien Quiz Book*, Bart Andrews, Signet
- [ ] *The TV Picture Quiz Book*, Bart Andrews, Signet
- [ ] *The TV Trivia Quiz Book*, Michael Uslan and Bruce Solomon, Harmony

1980

- [ ] *The Big Book of Amazing Facts*, Malvina G. Vogel, Moby Books

American Grab Bag

Academies

1. George Bancroft founded what military academy in 1845?
2. What well-known author was thrown out of West Point in 1831, (it is alleged) because he showed up at an inspection stark naked (except for belt and gloves)?
3. Prior to moving to its present location at Colorado Springs in 1958, where was the original site of the U.S. Air Force Academy?
4. Ulysses S. Grant and Dwight D. Eisenhower both graduated from what academy?
5. What President was General Omar Bradley's classmate in the class of 1915 at West Point?
6. In 1980, Elizabeth Belger became the first female graduate from what U.S. Academy?
7. Bunker Hill Academy was the featured boys military school in what 1981 movie, starring George C. Scott and Timothy Hutton?
8. Jean Marie Butler became the first female graduate of what U.S. military academy, on May 21, 1980?
9. Kings Point, New York, is the location of what academy?
10. What is the name given to the man who scores the lowest in marks in the graduating class at Annapolis?

Ambassadors

1. In 1933, William Christian Bullitt became the first U.S. ambassador to what country?
2. Who was the U.S. ambassador to South Vietnam from 1964 to 1965?
3. What is the official title of the U.S. ambassador to Great Britain?
4. Which President's father served as the ambassador to Great Britain from 1937 to 1940?

Academies (Answers)

1. Annapolis
2. Edgar Allan Poe
3. Lowry Air Force Base
4. West Point
5. General Dwight D. Eisenhower
6. Annapolis
7. *Taps*
8. Coast Guard Academy
9. United States Merchant Marines
10. Anchorman

Ambassadors (Answers)

1. U.S.S.R.
2. Maxwell Taylor
3. Ambassador to the Court of St. James
4. Kennedy

5. What red flower was named after a U.S. minister to Mexico?
6. What Confederate Army general, defeated at Gettysburg, later served as U.S. minister to Turkey in 1880?
7. On November 4, 1979, Ambassador Ken Taylor and his staff hid six Americans in his embassy in Tehran, Iran, until they were safely led out of the country. What country was Taylor the ambassador of?
8. Who was the Japanese admiral/ambassador who was in Washington, DC, when the Japanese attacked Pearl Harbor on December 7, 1941?
9. What world-favorite American author was appointed as American ambassador to Spain in 1842?
10. Benjamin Franklin served as the U.S. minister to what country from 1776 until 1795?

American Indians

1. Who won a Gold Medal in the 100-yard dash in the 1960 Olympics?
2. Nicknamed the Bird Woman, who was the Shoshone Indian guide who helped lead Meriwether Lewis and William Clark's expedition to the Pacific Northwest in 1804–1806?
3. Her Christian name was Rebecca but her Indian name was Matoaka. It was her father Powhatan who gave her the nickname that we know her by. What is it?
4. What Nez Percé Indian leader finally surrendered in 1877, with the famous quote "I will fight no more"?
5. After the settling of the Wild West what Hunkpapa Sioux chief traveled with Buffalo Bills's Wild West Show?
6. What was the name of the Shawnee Indian chief who joined the British forces against the colonists in the War of 1812?
7. What tribes belonged to the Five Civilized Tribes?
8. What tribes belonged to the Five Nations of the Iroquois?
9. This Apache chief, whose real name was Goyathlay, "One who yawns," was more commonly known as what?
10. Who was the leader of the Apaches?

5. Poinsettia (named for Joel Poinsett)
6. James Longstreet
7. Canada
8. Kichisaburo Nomura
9. Washington Irving
10. France

American Indians (Answers)

1. Billy Mills
2. Sacajawea
3. Pocahontas
4. Chief Joseph
5. Sitting Bull
6. Tecumseh
7. Cherokees, Choctaws, Chickasaws, Creeks, and Seminoles
8. Seneca, Mohawk, Oneida, Onondaga, and Cayuga
9. Geronimo
10. Cochise

Americana

1. What is the most common street name in the cities of the United States?
2. Excluding the Library of Congress, where is the largest library in the United States?
3. What was the original title of the painting *Whistler's Mother?*
4. Everyone knows 1600 Pennsylvania Avenue is the address of the White House—what was the address of the first official residence of the President?
5. Name the state with the smallest population.
6. What company is the largest producer of wine in the United States?
7. What is the oldest honor society in the United States?
8. What state has the highest number of automobiles registered?
9. Who was selected as *Time* magazine's first Man of the Year in 1927?
10. At what age do the most deaths occur in the United States?
11. What is the largest retail chain in the United States?
12. What do American insurance companies list as the most dangerous sport?
13. What city has the largest subway system of any American city?
14. What is the oldest female university in the United States?
15. What has the highest circulation of any American magazine?
16. Who was the first male to appear on the cover of *Playboy* magazine?
17. Who was the first woman elected to Congress?
18. What is the most expensive square in the game of Monopoly?
19. What were the names of the three ships involved in the Boston Tea Party?
20. What was the first stop of the *Mayflower* when it reached the New World?

Americana (Answers)

1. Park Street
2. Harvard University
3. Arrangement in Gray and Black
4. #1 Cherry Street, New York—home of George Washington
5. Alaska
6. Gallo
7. Phi Beta Kappa, founded in 1776
8. California
9. Charles Lindbergh
10. First year after birth
11. Sears and Roebuck
12. Football
13. New York
14. Vassar, founded in 1861
15. *TV Guide*
16. Peter Sellers in 1964
17. Jeanette Rankin, 1917
18. Boardwalk ($400)
19. *Beaver*, *Dartsmouth*, and *Eleanor*
20. Cape Cod to take on water

Astronauts

1. Who, on May 5, 1961, became the first U.S. astronaut to travel into space?
2. On July 20, 1969, he became the first person to set foot on the moon. Name him and what he said as he stepped onto the lunar surface.
3. What astronaut made an appearance on the TV quiz show "Name That Tune"?
4. Who was the first astronaut to return to space?
5. On April 12, 1981, the U.S. space shuttle *Columbia* made its maiden flight. What two astronauts piloted the craft through 36 orbits?
6. On July 20, 1969, he became the second man to walk on the moon. He also authored the book *Return to Earth*. Who is he?
7. Which U.S. astronaut was born in Rome, Italy?
8. Who became the first female astronaut to go into space (in 1983)?
9. What *Apollo 11* astronauts mother's maiden name is Moon?
10. This veteran of the *Apollo 8* flight later became the president of Eastern Airlines. Who is he?

Banks

1. Name the American financier who helped to build the Central Pacific Railroad, served as the president of the Southern Pacific Railroad, and today has a banking institute named for him?
2. Originally called the Bank of Italy, what large banking firm was founded by Amadeo P. Giannini in 1904?
3. As the first secretary of the treasury, he created the Bank of the United States in 1791. Who was he?
4. By what other name is the International Bank for Reconstruction and Development known?
5. What individual (with three members of what radical group) robbed a San Francisco Hibernia Bank on April 15, 1974?
6. What banker was the personal friend President Richard M. Nixon often visited in Key Biscayne, Florida?

Astronauts (Answers)

1. Alan Shepard
2. Neil Armstrong. "That's one small step for man, one giant leap for mankind."
5. John Glenn
4. Virgil "Gus" Grissom
5. Robert Crippen and John Young
6. Edwin "Buzz" Aldrin
7. Michael Collins
8. Sally Ride
9. Buzz Aldrin
10. Frank Borman

Banks (Answers)

1. Charles Crocker (Crocker Bank)
2. Bank of America
3. Alexander Hamilton
4. World Bank
5. Patty Hearst and the Symbionese Liberation Army
6. Charles "Bebe" Rebozo

7. The Dalton gang was almost wiped out when they over-ambitiously decided to rob two banks at once in what Midwestern town on October 5, 1892?
8. The First Brooklyn Savings Bank was the setting for an incident in 1972 that later inspired what 1976 Al Pacino movie?
9. What is known as "The Old Lady of Threadneedle Street"?
10. What was the first commercial bank to open its doors in the United States?

Clubs

1. Name the "club," founded in 1950 by Ralph Schneider, that introduced the use of credit cards?
2. In this self-help organization, which was founded on June 11, 1935, none of the members' last names are given. It was founded by Doctor Bob and Bill. What is it?
3. What do the initials L.O.O.M. stand for?
4. What is Harvard University's dramatic society (established in 1848) called?
5. What organization in known by the initials B.P.O.E.?
6. What was the 52-20 Club?
7. What are the names of the two rival gangs in the musical play and motion picture *West Side Story?*
8. In what U.S. city would you find the home of such private clubs as The Hells Angels Motorcycle Club and The Black Panthers Party?
9. Kappa Alpha Theta was the first sorority formed in 1870 at what university?
10. What club was formed to support actor Errol Flynn at his trial for rape?

Colleges

1. What Ohio college did President John Garfield once serve as president?
2. What university did Woodrow Wilson once serve as president?
3. What university did Dwight Eisenhower once serve as president?
4. The *Dove* is the yearbook for what university?

7. Coffeyville, Kansas
8. *Dog Day Afternoon*
9. The Bank of England
10. Bank of Pennsylvania

Clubs (Answers)

1. Diners Club
2. Alcoholics Anonymous
3. Loyal Order of the Moose
4. Hasty Pudding Club
5. Benevolent and Protective Order of Elks
6. Unemployed World War II G.I.'s were entitled to $20 for 52 weeks
7. Sharks and Jets
8. Oakland, California
9. DePaul University (formerly Indiana Asbury University)
10. ABCDEF (American Boys Club for the Defense of Errol Flynn

Colleges (Answers)

1. Hiram College
2. Princeton University
3. Columbia University
4. Notre Dame

5. What institute of learning was originally known as King's College?
6. What Macon, Georgia, college is the site of the first female sorority—the Adelphians (later Alpha Beta Pi), founded on May 15, 1851?
7. What California institution was the center of the free speech movement begun in the 1960s?
8. Name two Virginia colleges, both named for two people. The first was established in 1693, the second in 1749.
9. What is the British military college equivalent to West Point?
10. Where are the nine campuses of the University of California located?

Companies

1. The Warner Brothers Corset Company became the first company to manufacture what female undergarment?
2. Dog lover Carl E. Wickman founded what transportation company in Hibbling, Minnesota, in 1914?
3. Columnist Ann Landers's husband Jules Lederer borrowed $5,000 and turned it into a $10 million business when he founded what company?
4. What do the initials IBM and AT&T stand for?
5. What whiskey company did Col. Edmund Haynes Taylor, Jr., establish in 1887?
6. What is the largest black-owned business in the United States?
7. What company introduced nylon?
8. What is the theme song of Mary Kaye Cosmetics?
9. What large monopoly was broken up on January 1, 1984?
10. Shell Oil is a company with its home offices in what country?

Department Stores

1. What presidential candidate was shot at the Laurel shopping center in Wheaton, Maryland, on May 15, 1972?
2. What New York City department store sponsors the city's annual Thanksgiving Day parade?

5. Columbia University
6. Wesleyan College
7. Berkeley
8. William and Mary, Washington and Lee
9. Sandhurst
10. Berkeley, Davis, Irvine, Los Angeles, Riverside, San Diego, San Francisco, Santa Barbara, and Santa Cruz.

Companies (Answers)

1. Bras
2. Greyhound Bus Company
3. Budget Rent-A-Car
4. International Business Machines and American Telephone and Telegraph, respectively
5. Old Taylor Kentucky Straight Bourbon Whiskey
6. Motown Records
7. Dupont
8. "I've Got That Mary Kaye Enthusiasm"
9. AT&T
10. The Netherlands

Department Store (Answers)

1. George Wallace
2. Macy's

3. On Jack Benny's radio series what Los Angeles department store did his girlfriend, Mary Livingston, work for? (In reality Jack Benny met her there.)

4. What large department store chain was founded on September 16, 1893, by two men with the first names Richard and Aluah?

5. Utica, New York, was the site on February 22, 1879, of the opening of what chain store?

6. What is the largest department store chain in the Soviet Union?

7. What department store is mentioned in the lyrics of the classic Jimmy Dorsey Orchestra's hit "Tangerine," sung by Bob Eberle and Helen O'Connell?

8. What is the name of the large New York City sporting goods store that went out of business in 1977?

9. What department store chain began in Kemmerer, Wyoming, in 1902, in a small store named Golden Rule?

10. What New York City department store was Macy's chief rival? (The daughter of its founder married baseball great Hank Greenberg.)

First Ladies

1. What President often called his young wife Frances by the nickname of Frankie?

2. Lemonade Lucy was the nickname of the wife of what President, because she refused to serve alcoholic beverages at the White House?

3. Who is the only woman to have been both a First Lady and the mother of a President?

4. What First Lady did not have to change her name when she married her husband-president?

5. What was Lady Bird Johnson's real first name?

6. What First Lady would have made a bit appearance in the 1935 film *Becky Sharp*, had her role not been edited out?

7. Who was Varina Davis?

8. What First Lady christened the nuclear submarine U.S.S. *Nautilus?*

9. Who is the only First Lady to appear in a movie with her husband President? Name the film.

10. What First Lady used the CB handle of First Mama?

3. May Company
4. Sears and Roebuck
5. F. W. Woolworth
6. GUM
7. Macy's
8. Abercombie and Fitch
9. Penneys (J. C. Penney)
10. Gimbel's (founded by Bernard F. Gimbel)

First Ladies (Answers)

1. Grover Cleveland
2. Rutherford Hayes
3. Abigail Adams
4. Eleanor Roosevelt
5. Claudia
6. Pat Nixon
7. Jefferson Davis's wife
8. Mamie Eisenhower
9. Nancy Davis Reagan in *Hellcats of the Navy* (1957)
10. Betty Ford

Flags

1. What saying appeared on colonists' flags during the Revolutionary War?
2. Admiral Perry may have been credited with discovering the South Pole in 1909, but what black explorer, with him, placed the first U.S. flag there?
3. A new U.S. flag is flown over what place each day?
4. What South American country is the only country to have different faces on each side of its flag?
5. When is Flag Day celebrated?
6. What naval flag is hoisted when the vessel is to set to sail?
7. Name the six flags that have flown over the state of Texas (if that's not tough enough, give their chronological order)?
8. What symbol is on the Canadian flag?
9. The U.S. flag is authorized to fly day and night at what four locations?
10. What state has never had a foreign flag?
11. What are two affectionate names for the United States flag?
12. What are two affectionate names for the Confederate flag?
13. How many stripes did the American flag have that flew over Fort McHenry the night that Francis Scott Key wrote "The Star-Spangled Banner"?
14. Where was the 50-star flag raised for the very first time at 12:01 A.M. on July 4, 1960, the day that Hawaii became the 50th state?
15. Why are the interlocking Olympic rings the colors of black, blue, green, red, and yellow?
16. Great Britain's Union Jack, which was created on May 1, 1707, is actually made up of what three flags?
17. What island country has a depiction of itself on its national flag?
18. What is the message if a flag is flown upside down?
19. What are the three things on the red Soviet Union national flag?
20. Dating back to approximately 1219, what country has the oldest national flag (called the Danebrog)?

Flags (Answers)

1. "Don't Tread On Me"
2. Matthew Henson
3. The White House
4. Paraguay
5. June 14th
6. Blue Peter
7. French, Spanish, Mexican, Republic of Texas, Confederacy, and the United States (in that order)
8. Maple leaf
9. Capitol Building; home of Francis Scott Key (Frederick, Maryland); World War Memorial (Worcester, Maryland); and Fort McHenry (Maryland)
10. Idaho
11. "Old Glory" and "Stars and Stripes"
12. "Stars and Bars" and "the Southern Cross"
13. 15
14. Fort McHenry National Monument
15. They represent the colors that are present in every national flag
16. English flag of St. George, Scottish flag of St. Andrew, and the Irish flag of St. Patrick
17. Cyprus
18. Distress
19. Hammer, sickle, and a five-pointed star
20. Denmark

Folklore

1. Who was the steel-driving man who died trying to beat Captain Tommy's track-laying machine?
2. What was the name of Lumberjack Paul Bunyon's blue ox?
3. Who was the world's greatest oil-well driller in American folklore?
4. What town did the Pied Piper chase the mice from in 1284?
5. How much did the hammer weigh that John Henry swung?
6. In American folklore, who dug the Grand Canyon?
7. What are the little people of Ireland called whose job it is to help others?
8. The Irish Rovers recorded a song in 1968 about what animal of folklore?
9. What did the American Indians refer to as an Iron Horse?
10. Who is the only person that can capture a Unicorn?

Government Agencies

1. "Fidelity, Bravery, Integrity" is the motto of what government agency?
2. What was the previous name of the Department of Defense?
3. When it was created in 1953, what replaced the Federal Security Agency?
4. What government department does the U.S. Coast Guard come under?
5. Who was the first director of the Peace Corps?
6. Who, in 1933, was the first female director of the U.S. Mint?
7. In 1862 Jeannie Douglas became the first female hired by the Federal Government. What was her job?
8. President Franklin D. Roosevelt appointed Frances Perkins as the first woman to hold a cabinet post. What department did she head?
9. What executive department was established in August 1977?
10. What executive department head, in 1982, redesigned its departmental seal from a buffalo facing left to one facing right?

Folklore (Answers)

1. John Henry
2. Babe
3. Kemp Morgan
4. Hamlin
5. Nine pounds
6. Pecos Bill
7. Leprechauns
8. The unicorn
9. Train engine
10. A virgin

Government Agencies (Answers)

1. FBI (Federal Bureau of Investigation)
2. National Department Establishment
3. Department of Health, Education, and Welfare
4. Department of Transportation
5. Sargent Shriver
6. Nellie Ross
7. She cut and trimmed minted currency
8. Department of Labor
9. Department of Energy
10. James Watt (Secretary of the Interior)

Governments

1. What is the name of the Israeli Parliament?
2. The British Parliament is made up of what two houses?
3. What is the name of the Japanese Parliament?
4. What country's Parliament is made up of Seanad Eireann and Dail Eireann?
5. What are the names of the two Canadian Houses of Parliament?
6. What is the Parliament of Poland called?
7. What are the three branches of government of the United States?
8. According to the *World Almanac* what type of government does the Soviet Union have?
9. What type of government is the United States?
10. The Althing is the parliament of what country?

Governors

1. What Massachusetts governor played guard for Harvard and is a member of the Football Hall of Fame?
2. Barbara Blount became the first female college student in the United States. As the governor's daughter she attended what university, in 1794, the year it opened?
3. What former Alabama governor used the CB handle "Blue Bonnet"?
4. What Louisiana governor was shot to death by Dr. Carl A. Weiss on September 8, 1935?
5. What explorer was selected as the first governor of the newly purchased Louisiana Territory in 1807?
6. When he was elected governor of Massachusetts on May 18, 1631, he became the first known elected official in America. Name him.
7. In 1924, Nellie Taylor Ross became the first woman governor in U.S. history. To which state was she elected?
8. Miriam Ferguson became the first female governor of what state in 1924? (She ran for office to clear her husband's name.)
9. What father and son both served as governor of California?

Governments (Answers)

1. Knesset
2. House of Commons and House of Lords
3. Diet
4. Ireland's
5. House of Commons and the Senate
6. Seym
7. Executive, judiciary, legislature
8. Federal Union
9. Constitutional republic
10. Iceland

Governors (Answers)

1. Endicott "Chub" Peabody
2. University of Tennessee
3. Cornelia Wallace
4. Huey Long
5. Meriwether Lewis
6. John Winthrop
7. Wyoming
8. Texas
9. Edmund "Pat" Brown and Edmund "Jerry" Brown

10. Name the Arkansas governor who holds the record of serving in that position for six terms—1955 until 1967.

11. This Massachusetts governor was the first person to sign the Declaration of Independence. Name him.

12. Confederate General Robert E. Lee's father Henry Lee was the governor of what state from 1792 until 1795?

13. What restaurant owner was elected governor of Georgia because of his strong stand against integration?

14. What Indiana governor coined the expression "What this country needs is a good five-cent cigar?"

15. Who served as governor of Tennessee from 1827 until 1829 and then governor of Texas from 1859 to 1861?

16. Who was the governor of South Dakota from 1955 to 1959? (He was awarded the Medal of Honor during World War II.)

17. What New York governor was called the Happy Warrior?

18. Brothers Levi and Enoch Lincoln both served as governors of what New England states at the same time?

19. Ireland-born baseball pitcher John Kinley Tener, who played in the majors from 1885 to 1890, became the governor of what state in 1909?

20. What governor of Louisiana composed the classic song "You Are My Sunshine" in 1940, which served as his campaign song?

Halls of Fame

1. Where is the Jockey's Hall of Fame?
2. What city is the home of the Trivia Hall of Fame?
3. Who was the first inductee in 1980 into the hall of fame for famous legs?
4. Milwaukee, Wisconsin, is the location of this ABC-sanctioned hall of fame?
5. Ozzie Nelson, Nigel Bruce, and Robert Young were the first three inductees into what hall of fame, founded in Carroll, Iowa?
6. What sports hall of fame is located one block from Madison Square Garden?
7. Who is the member of the Pro Football Hall of Fame who has both a father and a grandfather in the Boxing Hall of Fame?
8. Where is the Hall of Fame Of Great Americans located?
9. Who is the only white member of the Black Athlete's Hall of Fame?

10. Orval Faubus
11. John Hancock
12. Virginia
13. Lester Maddox
14. Thomas Marshall
15. Sam Houston
16. Joe Foss
17. Al Smith
18. Massachusetts (Levi) and Maine (Enoch)
19. Pennsylvania
20. Jimmie Davis

Halls of Fame (Answers)

1. Pimlico, Maryland
2. Lincoln, Nebraska
3. Cyd Charisse (dancer)
4. Bowling Hall of Fame
5. Dull Men's Hall of Fame
6. Boxing Hall of Fame
7. Art Donovan, Jr. His father is Mike Donovan and his grandfather is Arthur Donovan, Sr.
8. New York University
9. Branch Rickey

10. The Baseball Hall of Fame is located in Cooperstown, as just about every one should know, but in what state?

Law Enforcement

1. Prior to J. Edgar Hoover's taking over as chief of the F.B.I., the young organization already had a chief. Name this former detective?

2. Who was in charge of the U.S. Treasury Department officers nicknamed "The Untouchables"?

3. When Edward B. Shanahan was shot and killed in 1929, he became the first employee of what agency to be killed in the line of duty?

4. After founding his own detective agency in 1850, who founded the secret service of the U.S. government, in 1861?

5. Civilian Curtis Sliva founded what New York City volunteer group, in order to cut down on street crime?

6. The first western book ever read by Louis L'Amour was written by what western sheriff?

7. What is the name of the F.B.I. agent who headed the agents who killed Public Enemy Number One, John Dillenger?

8. Who was the Attorney General who used the federal marshals to enforce desegregation in the South during President John F. Kennedy's administration?

9. "Maintain the Right" is the official slogan of what law enforcement agency?

10. What was the name of the Texas Ranger who tracked down Bonnie and Clyde after they publicly humiliated him?

Laws

1. What is the only state of the union with laws not based on the British system?

2. What is the limitation on the President of the United States's power to pardon people?

3. On May 20, 1899, a New York City cab driver became the first person arrested for breaking what law?

10. New York

Law Enforcement (Answers)

1. William J. Burns
2. Elliot Ness
3. F.B.I.
4. Allan Pinkerton
5. Guardian Angels
6. William Tilghman
7. Melvin Purvis
8. Robert Kennedy
9. Royal Canadian Mounted Police
10. Frank Hammer

Laws (Answers)

1. Louisiana (which is based on the Napoleonic code of France)
2. They must have been convicted of a Federal crime.
3. Speeding (he was traveling at 12 mph)

4. Whose name is attached to the unwritten law "If anything can go wrong it will"?
5. In 1942, President Franklin D. Roosevelt signed executive order No. 9066, which had an effect on Japanese Americans. What was it?
6. What unpopular law did the Volstead Act introduce?
7. Laurence J. Peter, was the father of what law? Recite it.
8. What are the archaic sabbath laws that are still on the books in many small towns and counties in the United States called?
9. What is Newton's third law?
10. What King of Babylonia set up the first set of recorded laws?

Mayors

1. San Diego's first mayor, Joshua Bean, was the older brother of what famous Texas judge?
2. Bob Hope portrayed what New York City mayor in the 1957 movie *Beau James?*
3. What San Francisco mayor was assassinated by Dan White in 1978?
4. When Carolyn Farrell was elected mayor of Dubuque City, Iowa, in 1980 she established what first in American history?
5. What Boston mayor was nicknamed "Honey Fitz"?
6. Who is the author of the bestselling autobiography *Mayor?*
7. What New York City mayor was nicknamed the Little Flower?
8. What Chicago mayor was killed by assassin Giuseppe Zangara, who on February 15, 1933, in Miami attempted to shoot President-elect Franklin D. Roosevelt, but hit the mayor instead?
9. What is the official residence of the mayor of New York City?
10. What popular dancer was affectionately nicknamed the Mayor of Harlem?

Organizations

1. Confederate general Nathan Bedford Forrest founded what organization in Pulaski, Tennessee, in December 1865?
2. On November 28, 1775, what organization was founded in a pub called the Tun Tavern?

4. Murphy
5. They were to be incarcerated in detention camps during the war with Japan
6. Prohibition
7. The Peter Principle—"In a hierarchy, every employee tends to rise to their level of incompetence."
8. Blue Laws
9. Every action has an equal and opposite reaction.
10. Hammurabi

Mayors (Answers)

1. Judge Roy Bean
2. Jimmy Walker
3. George Moscone
4. She became the first nun to be elected mayor of a U.S. town
5. John Fitzgerald (grandfather of John F. Kennedy)
6. Ed Koch, mayor of New York City
7. Fiorello LaGuardia
8. Anton J. Cermak
9. Gracie Mansion
10. Bill "Bojangles" Robinson

Organizations (Answers)

1. Ku Klux Klan
2. The United States Marine Corps

3. "When youth learns the business of business" is the slogan of what young people's business organization?

4. During World War I, Robert Baden-Powell served as a British spy against both Russia and Germany. Back in 1908, however, he was the founder of what worldwide organization?

5. What anticommunist organization was named after an intelligence officer who was killed in China in 1945?

6. Civil War General Ambrose Burnside served as the first president of what organization that today has built up a large political lobby?

7. In 1955, two trade unions merged, forming a six-letter abbreviation. Give its full title.

8. What was the name of the "colorful" mob led by Abe Bernstein during the Roaring Twenties?

9. Wells Hawk was what private club's first abbot when it was founded in June 1907?

10. This organization, in Harlington, Texas, restores and fixes vintage World War II aircraft. What is it called?

11. What home for wayward boys is located near Omaha, Nebraska? (It is where one of Spencer Tracy's Oscars is kept.)

12. Founded in 1914 by Melvin Jones, this organization's motto is "Liberty, Intelligence, Our Nation's Safety". Name it.

13. In 1897, Mrs. Phoebe Hearst and Mrs. Alice Birney organized what parental group that wanted to work with their children's schoolteachers?

14. SPEBSQSA is the abbreviation of what musical group?

15. What organization was founded in Holmes County, Mississippi, in 1907?

16. What government organization did William Donovan help to organize in 1942?

17. What organization whose sole purpose was the assassination of its enemies was organized by Louis Buchalter?

18. Who was the sportswriter who organized the first Golden Gloves Boxing Tournament?

19. Margaret "Maggie" Kuhn organized what lobby group in 1970 that seeks help for the senior citizens in our society?

20. Who founded the American Nazi party in 1959, which was originally called the Union of Free Enterprise National Socialists?

3. Junior Achievement
4. Boy Scouts
5. The John Birch Society
6. The National Rifle Association
7. AFL/CIO
8. The Purple Gang
9. Friar's Club
10. Confederate Air Force
11. Boy's Town
12. Lion's Club
13. P.T.A. (Parents Teachers Association)
14. Society for the Preservation and Encouragement of Barber Shop Quartet Singing in America
15. 4-H Club
16. OSS (Office of Strategic Services)
17. Murder Inc.
18. Paul Gallico
19. Gray Panthers
20. George Lincoln Rockwell

Political Figures

1. What Democratic representative from Arizona previously played pro basketball for the Denver Nuggets?
2. This Rhodes scholar and one-time member of the New York Knicks basketball team became a senator for New Jersey in 1978. Name him.
3. For what political position did both Norman Mailer and William F. Buckley unsuccessfully run?
4. In 1967, what congressman and orator made *Billboard*'s Hot 100 record chart with a speech titled "Gallant Men"?
5. What Georgia state senator appeared in an acting role in the 1977 Richard Pryor film *Greased Lightning?*
6. Who was the U.S. secretary of war from 1853 to 1857, and held the office immediately prior to becoming President?
7. Name the two Dulles brothers. One was the director of the C.I.A.; the other was the secretary of state.
8. Who served as governor of Ohio, U.S. treasury secretary, and Chief Justice of the Supreme Court?
9. Who was the special prosecutor fired by President Richard M. Nixon on October 20, 1973?
10. What U.S. secretary of war and later secretary of state coined the expression "To the victor belong the spoils of the enemy"?

Political Parties

1. What party nominated General Benjamin Franklin Butler for the Presidency of the United States in 1884?
2. What political party did President George Washington belong to?
3. Who founded the Know-Nothing Party (AKA the American Party)?
4. Who was the first Democratic President?
5. Who was the first Republican President?
6. On what political party ticket did George Wallace run for the 1968 Presidency?
7. Who was Wallace's running mate for Vice-President?
8. What does G.O.P. stand for?

Political Figures (Answers)

1. Morris K. Udall
2. Bill Bradley
3. Mayor of New York City (1969 and 1965, respectively)
4. Senator Everett McKinley Dirksen
5. Julian Bond
6. Jefferson Davis (President of the Confederate States of America)
7. Allen and John Foster respectively
8. Salmon Chase
9. Archibald Cox
10. William Marcy

Political Parties (Answers)

1. Anti-Monopoly Party/Greenback Party
2. Federalist
3. Dime Novelist Ned Buntline (Edward Judson)
4. Andrew Jackson
5. Abraham Lincoln
6. American Independent
7. Curtis LeMay
8. Grand Old Party

9. Who was the Peace and Freedom Party's candidate for President in 1968?
10. What Socialist party candidate received six percent of the popular vote in the 1920 campaign while he was in prison?

Presidential Advisers/Programs

List the Presidents who were served by the following advisers:
1. Brain Trust
2. Medicine Ball Cabinet
3. Tennis Cabinet
4. Kitchen Cabinet
5. Poker Cabinet

List the Presidents who started the following programs:
6. Square Deal
7. Fair Deal
8. New Freedom
9. New Frontier
10. Great Society

Presidential Middle Names

Give the middle names for the following Presidents:
1. Chester A. Arthur
2. James A. Garfield
3. Herbert C. Hoover
4. John F. Kennedy
5. Richard M. Nixon
6. Gerald R. Ford
7. Ulysses S. Grant
8. William H. Taft
9. Franklin D. Roosevelt
10. Rutherford B. Hayes

9. Dick Gregory
10. Eugene V. Debs

Presidential Advisors/Programs (Answers)

1. Franklin D. Roosevelt
2. Herbert Hoover
3. Theodore Roosevelt
4. Andrew Jackson
5. Warren G. Harding
6. Teddy Roosevelt
7. Harry S Truman
8. Woodrow Wilson
9. John F. Kennedy
10. Lyndon B. Johnson

Presidential Middle Names (Answers)

1. Alan
2. Abram
3. Clark
4. Fitzgerald
5. Milhous
6. Rudolph
7. Simpson
8. Howard
9. Delano
10. Birchard

Presidents

1. Who was the first President to be born in a hospital?
2. Who was the first President to be a veteran of the U.S. Navy?
3. Name the first President to be awarded the Nobel Prize.
4. What American President was described by a predecessor as having played football without a helmet?
5. What President chalked his initials on the side of the world's first nuclear submarine, the *Nautilus,* when it was launched in 1953?
6. Who was the only President to campaign for a single term, saying he would accomplish his goals in that time?
7. Who was the first President to live in the White House?
8. Who was the first President to ride in an automobile?
9. Who was the first President to have been a professional male model in his younger days?
10. Who was the only U.S. President to be impeached?
11. What was the significance of John F. Kennedy's middle name?
12. What is the name of Jefferson's home, pictured on the back of a nickel?
13. Who was the first President someone attempted to assassinate?
14. Who was the first President to leave the country in time of war?
15. What son of a President, whose father was assassinated, witnessed the assassination of another President?
16. What President, known for his inactivity, prompted some wag to comment on his death: "How do they know?"
17. What President had the shortest term in history?
18. Who was the first President of the United States to not have a middle name?
19. Who was the youngest man to become President of the United States?
20. Who was the youngest man elected President of the United States?

Senators

1. In 1932, who became the first woman *elected* to the U.S. Senate (after which she was re-elected twice)?

Presidents (Answers)

1. Jimmy Carter
2. J. F. Kennedy
3. Teddy Roosevelt
4. Gerald Ford
5. Harry Truman
6. James Polk
7. John Adams
8. Teddy Roosevelt
9. Gerald Ford
10. Andrew Johnson
11. It was his mother's maiden name.
12. Monticello
13. Andrew Jackson
14. Franklin Roosevelt, when he went to North Africa in 1943
15. Todd Lincoln, who was with Garfield in 1901 when he was shot
16. Calvin Coolidge
17. William H. Harrison, who died one month after inauguration
18. George Washington
19. Theodore Roosevelt (42 years, 322 days old at inauguration)
20. John F. Kennedy (43 years, 236 days old at inauguration)

Senators (Answers)

1. Hattie Caraway (wife of Senator Thaddeus Caraway)

2. Prior to the person in question one, what female served in the U.S. Senate, being appointed to that position in October 3, 1922?

3. What U.S. senator was married to an Academy Award-winning actress?

4. Who was elected to succeed U.S. Senator L. Wisconsin Robert La Follette as senator in 1925?

5. As a Republican for Mississippi, who became the first black U.S. senator in 1870?

6. What is the length of a term of office of a U.S. senator?

7. How many senators are there in the U.S. Senate?

8. Who presides over the U.S. Senate?

9. What is the minimum age for becoming a U.S. Senator?

10. The son of what heavyweight boxing champion became a U.S. senator from California?

11. Who is the only man to serve as U.S. senator for three different states?

12. What was the previous occupation of New Mexico Republican Senator Harrison Schmitt, who in 1983 died of cancer?

13. What state did Senator Joseph McCarthy represent?

14. What U.S. senator for Arizona and later U.S. secretary of the interior authored the best-selling book *The Quiet Crisis*, which appeared in 1963?

15. John F. Kennedy was a senator for what state?

16. Robert F. Kennedy was a senator for what state?

17. Edward Kennedy is a senator for what state?

18. What Vice-President previously served as both a representative and a senator for California?

19. What U.S. senator from Missouri previously had served as the secretary of the Air Force from 1947 to 1950?

20. Name both the father and the son who served as senators for Louisiana.

Taxes

1. What amendment to the U.S. Constitution addresses itself to income taxes?

2. What is the number of the most popular IRS long form for individuals?

3. What was the battle cry of the Stamp Act Congress that met in New York in October 1765?

2. Rebecca Felton
3. John Warner (once married to Elizabeth Taylor)
4. His son, Robert LaFollette, Jr.
5. Hiram Revels
6. Six years
7. 100 (two from each state)
8. The Vice-President
9. 30 years old
10. John Tunney (son of Gene Tunney)
11. James Shields—Illinois (1849–1855), Minnesota (1850–1859), and Missouri (1879)
12. Astronaut
13. Wisconsin
14. Stewart Udall
15. Massachusetts
16. New York
17. Massachusetts
18. Richard M. Nixon
19. Stuart Symington
20. Huey P. Long (1932–1935) and Russell Long (1948–   )

Taxes (Answers)

1. 16th Amendment
2. 1040
3. "No taxation without representation"

4. In what year were federal taxes (income) collected for the first time?
5. In what year did income tax withholding begin?
6. What British prime minister introduced the first income tax?
7. On July 20, 1868, what product was taxed for the first time and is still being taxed today?
8. What was Excedrin Headache No. 1040 on TV commercials?
9. What proposition led to a reduction of property taxes in California?
10. In 1955, April 15 became the date on which federal and state taxes are due. Prior to 1955, what had previously been the deadline?

Unions

1. COYOTE (Call Off Your Old Tired Ethics) was a union founded in San Francisco in 1972 by Margo St. James. What was the occupation of its members?
2. What was the name of the Air Traffic Controllers' union broken by the Federal Government in 1982?
3. What is the largest truck drivers' union in the United States called?
4. What union leader was killed in an airplane crash near Pellston, Michigan, in 1970?
5. What was the name of the U.S. labor leader who disappeared from a Michigan restaurant parking lot on July 30, 1975?
6. What first did New York's Journeymen Printers Union establish when they went out on strike in 1776?
7. Sally Field portrayed this union labor organizer in the 1979 *Norma Rae* movie as Norma Rae Webster, but what is her real name?
8. As president of the United Mine Workers of America, who built the union into one of the most powerful in the country?
9. What labor leader served as president of the AFL/CIO in 1955 until 1979 and was awarded the Presidential Medal of Freedom in 1964?
10. What do the initials AFL/CIO stand for?
11. Who served as president of the Actors Guild from 1947 until 1952?

4. 1914
5. 1943
6. William Pitt
7. Cigarettes
8. The tax audit
9. Proposition 13
10. March 15th

Unions (Answers)

1. Prostitutes
2. PATCO
3. Teamsters (International Teamsters Union)
4. Walter Ruther
5. James Hoffa
6. They became the first union in the United States to go on strike.
7. Crystal Leeds
8. John L. Lewis
9. George Meany
10. American Federation of Labor and Congress of Industrial Organizations
11. Ronald Reagan

12. Who was the founder and first president of the United Farm Workers Union?
13. Who was both a founder and served as the first president of the AFL from 1886 until 1924?
14. What union uses the theme song "Look for the Union Label"?
15. What was the name of the first national labor organization in the United States?
16. What union is AFTRA?
17. What is the name of the worker's union in Poland?
18. What union leader went to prison in 1950 for perjury after he claimed that he was not a member of the Communist party?
19. What are the two biggest musical performing rights organizations?
20. Author Jack London coined what word to describe a strike breaker?

United Nations

1. What two colors are found on the flag of the United Nations?
2. What is the official language of the United Nations?
3. In what city was the charter for the United Nations drawn up in 1945?
4. Who are the five permanent members of the Security Council?
5. How many countries were members of the original United Nations in 1915?
6. How many members (countries) are there today?
7. In what city is the United Nations headquarters located?
8. Who was the first secretary general of the United Nations, serving from February 1, 1946, until April 10, 1953?
9. What Swedish-born secretary general (the second) was killed in an airplane crash in 1961?
10. What English poet had referred to a United Nations in his 1816 poem *Childe Harold's Pilgrimage?*

12. Cesar Chavez
13. Samuel Gompers
14. International Ladies Garment Workers Union
15. Knights of Labor
16. American Federation of Television and Radio Artists
17. Solidarity
18. Harry Bridges
19. ASCAP and BMI
20. Scab

United Nations (Answers)

1. Blue and White
2. French
3. San Francisco
4. China, France, the USSR, the United Kingdom, and the United States
5. 51
6. 151
7. New York City
8. Trygve Lie of Norway
9. Dag Hammarskjöld
10. Lord Byron

United States Representatives

1. What U.S. congressman was killed in Guyana at the start of the Jamestown massacre?

2. What congressman's ex-wife wrote the revealing book *My Capitol Secrets?*

3. What All-AFL quarterback of 1960 who played for the Buffalo Bills and San Diego Chargers was elected to the House of Representatives in 1970?

4. In 1923 former Speaker of the House Joseph "Uncle Joe" Cannon's portrait graced the cover (Vol. 1, No. 1) of what new magazine?

5. What is the minimum age for becoming a U.S. representative?

6. What St. Louis Cardinal's pitcher became a U.S. representative for North Carolina in 1963?

7. What California congressman was the only man to have won the Olympic decathlon twice?

8. What U.S. representative was the publisher of the largest chain of newspapers in the United States?

9. What first did 18-year-old Selda Looper represent in the House of Representatives?

10. Who was the only man to have been a representative from two different states, Vermont and Kentucky?

11. Clare Booth Luce was a representative from what state from 1943 to 1947?

12. Who was the female Democratic representative from New York from 1970 until 1976?

13. What black, female U.S. Democratic Representative from New York became a candidate for the Presidency in 1972?

14. Who was the black U.S. representative from Georgia who served as the U.S. ambassador to the United Nations from 1977 until 1979?

15. Who was a U.S. representative for Michigan from 1949 through 1973?

16. Who served as the U.S. representative for Arizona beginning in 1961, which was the last year his brother served as a senator for the same state?

17. What U.S Representative for New York and prominent black leader was excluded from the House in 1967 for his alledged improper acts?

United States Representatives (Answers)

1. Leo Ryan
2. John Jenrette's (his wife was Rita Jenrette)
3. Jack Kemp
4. *Time*
5. 25 years old
6. Wilmer "Vinegar Bend" Mizell
7. Bob Mathias
8. William Randolph Hearst
9. She became the first female page.
10. Matthew Lyon
11. Connecticut
12. Bella Abzug
13. Shirley Chisholm
14. Andrew Young
15. Gerald Ford
16. Morris Udall (his brother was Stewart Udall)
17. Adam Clayton Powell

18. Name the brothers who were both U.S. representatives, one for Kentucky from 1946 to 1952, and the other from Maryland from 1962 to 1971?
19. Who was elected to the House as a representative from Louisiana in 1973 to replace her husband, who had died?
20. Which one of the Kennedy brothers served as a U.S. representative?

Vice-Presidents

1. Who became, at age 36, the youngest man to serve as Vice-President? (He served under President James Buchanan.)
2. Name Franklin Delano Roosevelt's three Vice-Presidents.
3. Under what President did Alexander Hamilton Stephens serve?
4. What ex-Vice-President authored the novel *The Canfield Decision?*
5. What Vice-President was in 1942 the youngest commissioned pilot in the U.S. Navy, receiving his wings at the age of 18?
6. What Vice-President took his oath of office in Cuba, but died (1853) before he could ever take office?
7. Which Vice-President was awarded the Nobel Peace Prize?
8. What former Vice-President was tried and acquitted for treason in 1807?
9. Who is the only Vice-President to serve under two U.S. Presidents—John Quincy Adams and Andrew Jackson?
10. Who was the first Vice-President of the United States?

18. Thruston and Rogers Morton, respectively
19. Corinne Boggs
20. John F. Kennedy

Vice Presidents (Answers)

1. John Breckinridge
2. John Garner, Henry Wallace, and Harry S. Truman
3. Jefferson Davis (Stephens was the Vice-President of the Confederate States of America
4. Spiro T. Agnew
5. George Bush
6. William King
7. Charles Dawes (awarded in 1925)
8. Aaron Burr
9. John C. Calhoun
10. John Adams

Geography

Addresses

1. What is located at the following address: 4 Penn Plaza in New York City?
2. 453 Tenth Street in Washington, DC, is the address of a boarding house. What took place there on April 15, 1865?
3. What world-famous lead guitarist was born at 12 Arnold Grove in Liverpool, England, on February 25, 1943?
4. What famous tourist attraction is located at 350 Fifth Avenue in New York City?
5. What crime occurred at 92 Second Street in Fall River, Massachusetts, on August 4, 1892?
6. What name was given to the unusual supernatural occurrences at 112 Ocean Avenue on Long Island?
7. What is the apartment house address of fictitious detective Sherlock Holmes?
8. What is the London address of the British Prime Minister?
9. What cartoonist lives at 1 Snoopy Place in Santa Rosa, California?
10. What is the address of the White House in Washington, DC?

Airports

Name the cities served by the following airports (past and present):
1. Logan International
2. Lindbergh Field
3. Will Rogers
4. McCarran
5. O'Hare
6. Friendship (past)
7. Dulles

Addresses (Answers)

1. Madison Square Garden
2. President Lincoln was taken there after having been shot at Ford's Theater. He died there.
3. George Harrison
4. Empire State Building
5. Lizzie Borden's mother and father were hacked to death
6. The Amityville Horror
7. 221B Baker Street
8. 10 Downing Street
9. Charles Schultz
10. 1600 Pennsylvania Avenue

Airports (Answers)

1. Boston
2. San Diego
3. Oklahoma City
4. Las Vegas
5. Chicago
6. Baltimore
7. Washington, DC

8. General Mitchell
9. Stapleton
10. John Wayne

Australia

1. What are the native people called who were there before it was colonized?
2. What is the capital of Australia?
3. Who is the only member of the U.S. Football Hall of Fame to be born in Australia (his initials are P.O.)?
4. How many states and territories make up Australia?
5. Name the states of Australia.
6. What is the largest city in Australia?
7. Who, in 1770, first claimed Australia for the British Crown?
8. What are the two houses of the Australian Parliament?
9. What is the name of the 1250-mile-long reef, the largest in the world, that is located off the northeastern coast of Australia?
10. What is the national song of Australia?

Birthplaces

1. Where is the birthplace of both President Harry S. Truman and actress Ginger Rogers?
2. What famous college football coach was born in Voss, Norway, on March 4, 1888?
3. What television host and comedian was born in Corning, Iowa, in 1925?
4. Who is the only member of Baseball's Hall of Fame to be born in Cuba?
5. What U.S. steel company has the same name as the birthplace of a biblical figure?
6. The actor brother of Steve Forest was born in Don't, Mississippi on January 1, 1909. Name him.
7. In what country were the acting sisters Olivia de Havilland and Joan Fontaine born?
8. What two ballad singers, both of whom have had several #1 hit songs, hail from the same Pennsylvania town of Canonsburg?

8. Milwaukee
9. Denver
10. Santa Ana, California

Australia (Answers)

1. Aborigines
2. Canberra
3. Pat O'Dea
4. Six states and two territories
5. New South Wales, Victoria, Queensland, South Australia, Western Australia, and Tasmania
6. Sydney
7. Captain James Cook
8. House of Representatives and the Senate
9. Great Barrier Reef
10. "Waltzing Matilda" (the national anthem is "Advance Australia Fair")

Birthplaces (Answers)

1. Independence, Missouri
2. Knute Rockne
3. Johnny Carson
4. Martin DiHigo
5. Bethlehem, birthplace of Jesus Christ
6. Dana Andrews
7. Japan
8. Perry Como and Bobby Vinton

9. Lou Costello often mentioned his New Jersey birthplace in his films with Bud Abbott. Name the town founded in 1791 by Alexander Hamilton.

10. She was born in Hot Springs, Iowa, and her measurements are 70-30-32. Name her?

11. Who is the only U.S. President to be born in New York City?

12. Both actor Errol Flynn, at Hobart in 1909, and actress Merle Oberon, at Port Arthur in 1911, were born in this country. Name it.

13. Where was novelist Ayn Rand, author of *The Fountainhead* (1943) and *Atlas Shrugged* (1957), born on February 2, 1905?

14. In what country was romantic novelist Rosemary Rogers born, in 1933?

15. What performer was born in Tupelo, Mississippi, at 12:20 P.M. on January 8, 1935?

16. Who is the only person to have played James Bond who was actually born in England?

17. In what city was comedian Bob Hope born, in 1903?

18. In what country was British superstar Cliff Richard born, in 1940?

19. What noted screen and stage actor was born in Sakhalin, Japan, in 1930?

20. Actor Clint Eastwood and this book's author were both born in what West Coast city?

Boundaries/Borders

1. What famous name is given to the boundary between the states of Pennsylvania and Maryland?

2. The Cheviot Hills separates what two countries?

3. What 563-mile-long river separates East Germany and Poland?

4. What river forms the boundary between Romania and Bulgaria and Romania with Yugoslavia?

5. The Connecticut River is the boundary between what New England states?

6. The Khyber pass is located on the border between what two countries?

7. What countries have divided up the city of West Berlin into three different sections?

8. What three states have their *entire* eastern boundary made up of the Mississippi River?

9. Patterson
10. Miss Piggy
11. Teddy Roosevelt
12. Tasmania
13. St. Petersburg (Leningrad), Russia
14. Ceylon
15. Elvis Presley
16. Roger Moore (Sean Connery—born in Scotland, David Niven—born in Scotland, George Lazenby—born in Australia)
17. London
18. India
19. Yul Brynner
20. San Francisco

Boundaries/Borders (Answers)

1. Mason-Dixon Line
2. Scotland and England
3. Oder River
4. Danube River
5. Vermont and New Hampshire
6. Afghanistan and Pakistan
7. United States, Britain, and France
8. Iowa, Missouri, and Arkansas

9.   What lake is situated on the boundary between the states of California and Nevada?
10. Name the U.S. states whose land masses border against Canada?

Bridges

1.   What is the name of the bridge that Billie Joe McAllister jumped from in Bobbie Gentry's 1967 #1 hit song "Ode To Billie Joe"?
2.   What bridge is the subject of a children's nursery rhyme?
3.   What major bridge originally called the Great East River Bridge opened in 1883?
4.   What did young, frustrated, Cassius Clay throw off the Jefferson County Bridge into the Ohio River?
5.   Simon and Garfunkel have recorded two singles with the word "bridge" in the title. Name them.
6.   For years visitors have mistaken this beautiful London bridge spanning the Thames River, next to the Houses of Parliament, for the London Bridge. What is its real name?
7.   What bridge is mentioned in the lyrics of Frankie Vali's #1 hit song "My Eyes Adored You"?
8.   Johnny Maestro was the lead singer of what group named for a famous span?
9.   Where is the real London Bridge now located?
10. On the night of July 8, 1969, Edward Kennedy accidently drove his Oldsmobile off what bridge at Chappaquiddick Island? (His secretary Mary Jo Kopechne drowned in the incident.)
11. What is the name of the island through which the San Francisco Bay Bridge travels?
12. Thornton Wilder won the Pulitzer Prize in 1928 for a novel about five people killed when a bridge fell. Name the bridge?
13. What is the name of the 5-mile-long bridge that crosses the straits connecting the two land masses of Michigan?
14. What 29-mile-long bridge connects Mandeull and New Orleans?
15. When soul singer Little Richard renounced rock music in 1959, from what Australian bridge did he throw his jewelry?
16. In what state is the highest bridge in the United States located?
17. At 4,260 feet, what is the longest single bridge span in the United States?
18. What was the bridge that crossed the Rhine, referred to in Cornelius Ryan's book *A Bridge Too Far?*

9. Lake Tahoe
10. Maine, New Hampshire, Vermont, New York, Minnesota, North Dakota, Montana, Idaho, and Washington

Bridges (Answers)

1. Tallahatchie Bridge
2. London Bridge
3. Brooklyn Bridge
4. His Olympic Gold Medal
5. "Bridge Over Troubled Waters" and "59th Street Bridge Song (Feelin' Groovy)"
6. Tower Bridge
7. Bonnicut
8. Brooklyn Bridge
9. Lake Havasu City in Arizona
10. Dike Bridge
11. Yuba Buena
12. The Bridge of San Luis Rey
13. Mackinoe Bridge
14. Pontchartrain Causeway
15. Sydney Bridge
16. Colorado (Royal George)
17. Verrazano Narrows in New York
18. Arnhem Bridge

19. Name the two films in which William Holden appeared that featured bridges, one took place during World War II, the other during the Korean War?
20. What color is the Golden Gate bridge?

Canada

1. What is the national anthem of Canada?
2. What became the tenth province on April 1, 1949?
3. What is the highest mountain in Canada at 19,850 feet?
4. What is Canada's official name?
5. What is the longest river (2,635 miles) in Canada?
6. What is the federal capital of Canada?
7. What are the ten provinces and two territories in Canada?
8. Who is the head of state in Canada?
9. What are the two divisions of Parliament?
10. What is the currency in Canada?

Cities

1. North Beach is a section of what rather liberal city?
2. What is the largest city south of the equator?
3. Situated at 5,280 feet above sea level, this city is nicknamed the Mile High City. Name it.
4. Name the twin-cities of the United States.
5. What U.S. city is called the insurance city, because it is the home of approximately 50 insurance companies?
6. What city has been mentioned in the titles of movies by singers Frank Sinatra, Elvis Presley, and Frankie Laine?
7. What Oregon city was almost named Boston but for the flip of a coin?
8. What are the five boroughs of the city of New York?
9. Who were the two mythological founders of the ancient city of Rome?
10. To what city was Gertrude Stein referring when she once stated, "There's no there, there"?
11. What is the oldest city in the United States?

19. *Bridge on the River Kwai* (1957) and *The Bridges at Toko-Ri* (1955)
20. Orange

Canada (Answers)

1. "O Canada"
2. Newfoundland
3. Mt. Logan
4. Dominion of Canada
5. MacKenzie
6. Ottawa, Ontario
7. Alberta, British Columbia, Manitoba, New Brunswick, New-foundland, Nova Scotia, Ontario, Prince Edward Island, Quebec, Saskatchewan, North West Territories and Yukon Territory
8. Queen Elizabeth II (represented by a Governor-General)
9. Senate and House of Commons
10. Canadian dollar

Cities (Answers)

1. San Francisco
2. Buenos Aires, Argentina
3. Denver, Colorado
4. Minneapolis and St. Paul, Minnesota
5. Hartford, Connecticut
6. Las Vegas—*Las Vegas Nights* (1941), *Viva Las Vegas* (1964), and *Meet Me Las Vegas* (1956), respectively
7. Portland
8. Bronx, Brooklyn, Manhattan, Queens, and Richmond (Staten Island)
9. Romulus and Remus
10. Oakland, California
11. St. Augustine, Florida (founded September 1565)

12. What are the two cities in Charles Dickens's 1859 novel *A Tale of Two Cities*?
13. What is the southernmost city in the United States?
14. What (in altitude) is the highest city in the world?
15. Prior to Washington, DC, what city served as the capital for the United States?
16. What is the most populated metropolitan city in the world?
17. As the crow flies, what is the exact distance between Indianapolis, Indiana, and Boston, Massachusetts?
18. As the crow flies, what is the exact distance between Phoenix, Arizona, and Boston?
19. What city is called the Gateway to the West?
20. The nickname of Birmingham, Alabama, includes the name of another city. What is it?

City Nicknames

Identify the following cities by their nicknames:
1. Eternal City
2. Windy City
3. City of Light
4. Beantown
5. Railroad City
6. Music City
7. Motown
8. Birthplace of American Liberty
9. The Big Apple
10. City of Brotherly Love

College Locations

Name the state in which these colleges are located:
1. Kent State
2. Cornell University
3. Columbia University
4. Harvard University
5. Johns Hopkins University
6. Northwestern University

12. London and Paris
13. Honolulu
14. La Paz, Bolivia
15. New York City
16. Shanghai, China
17. 1,000 miles (according to the *Information Please Almanac*)
18. 2,300 miles (according to the *Information Please Almanac*)
19. St. Louis, Missouri
20. Pittsburgh of the South

City Nicknames (Answers)

1. Rome
2. Chicago
3. Paris
4. Boston
5. Indianapolis, Indiana
6. Nashville
7. Detroit
8. Lexington, Mass.
9. New York City
10. Philadelphia

College Locations (Answers)

1. Ohio
2. New York
3. New York
4. Massachusettes
5. Maryland
6. Illinois

7. Dartmouth
8. Yale University
9. Duke University
10. Tuskegee Institute

Countries' Previous Names

Give the previous names of the following countries:
1. Ethiopia
2. France
3. Thailand
4. Zaire
5. Zambia
6. Iran
7. Sri Lanka
8. Ghana
9. Belize
10. Botswana

Country Groupings

1. Name the six Balkan states.
2. Name the countries of Central America.
3. What countries made up the Axis powers during World War II?
4. What are the five Scandinavian countries?
5. What countries make up French Indochina?
6. What were the original 11 members of NATO?
7. Who were the ABCD powers during World War II?
8. What makes up the United Kingdom?
9. Aside from the island countries of the Caribbean, what countries are included in North America?
10. What three countries made up "the Triple Alliance" in 1882?

7. New Hampshire
8. Connecticut
9. North Carolina
10. Alabama

Countries' Previous Names (Answers)

1. Abyssinia
2. Gaul
3. Siam
4. Belgian Congo
5. Northern Rhodesia
6. Persia
7. Ceylon
8. Gold Coast
9. British Honduras
10. Bechuanaland

Country Groupings (Answers)

1. Albania, Bulgaria, European Turkey, Greece, Romania, and Yugoslavia
2. Costa Rica, Guatemala, Honduras, Nicaragua, British Honduras (Beliz), and Panama
3. Japan, Germany (includes Austria), Italy, Thailand, Bulgaria, Hungary, Romania, and Finland
4. Denmark, Finland, Norway, Sweden, and Iceland
5. North and South Vietnam, Laos, and Cambodia
6. Belgium, Canada, Denmark, Iceland, Italy, Luxembourg, the Netherlands, Norway, Portugal, United Kingdom, and the United States
7. America, Britain, China, Dutch Allies
8. Great Britain, Isle of Man, Channel Islands, and Northern Islands
9. Mexico, United States, Canada, and Greenland
10. Italy, Germany, and Austria-Hungary

France

1. What is celebrated annually on July 14 in France?
2. The French government jointly built the Concorde jet airliner with what other government?
3. What stands 984 feet high?
4. On July 3, 1962, France granted what North African country its independence?
5. What French statesman was nicknamed "The Tiger"?
6. In what year did France withdraw its troops from N.A.T.O.?
7. What title does the Head of State hold?
8. What title does the Head of Government hold?
9. Paris is the largest city in France. What is the second largest?
10. What was the period in French history from July 13, 1793, to July 28, 1794 known as?

The Globe

1. What English town does the prime meridian pass through?
2. Which is farther west, Reno, Nevada, or Los Angeles, California?
3. Which has a more temperate climate, Washington, DC, or Juneau, Alaska?
4. Is the Tropic of Cancer north or south of the equator?
5. What is the effect of the earth's rotation on the wind called?
6. Which direction does water drain in the northern hemisphere?
7. What name did ancient mariners give to areas of calm air north and south of the equator?
8. Where did the Greeks identify the edge of the earth to be?
9. What is the distance around the equator?
10. What is the primary gas in the earth's atmosphere?
11. What is the name of the belt of radiation around the earth?
12. At the equator, how far apart are lines of longitude?
13. Which imaginary line runs north and south, latitude or longitude?
14. At what time does a new calendar year begin?
15. What is the day called when the earth is nearest the sun?

France (Answers)

1. Bastille Day
2. British
3. The Eiffel Tower
4. Algeria
5. George Clemenceau
6. 1966
7. President
8. Prime Minister
9. Marseilles
10. The Reign of Terror

The Globe (Answers)

1. Greenwich
2. Reno
3. Juneau
4. North
5. Coriolis force
6. Counterclockwise
7. Horse latitudes or doldrums
8. The Pillars of Hercules or Gibraltar
9. Just over 24,000 miles
10. Nitrogen
11. Van Allen belt
12. 69 miles
13. Longitude
14. 12 o'clock precisely on the night of December 31, local time
15. Equinox

Geography

16. Name the zone between the polar circles and the poles.
17. What is the name of a tide with little variation between high and low tides?
18. Where is the International Date Line?
19. How high does the ozone layer go?
20. The atmosphere is the air surrounding the earth. What is the water portion of the earth called?

Highways and Roads

1. What is the name of the highway that connects Dawson Creek, British Columbia, and Fairbanks, Alaska?
2. Bobby Troup composed a song recorded by the Rolling Stones about what famous highway?
3. This 600-mile road, built in 1840, ran from Maryland to Vandalia, Illinois. What was the name of this road, named for its point of origin?
4. What road winds 23 miles through the hills overlooking Los Angeles?
5. The "Senders" was the working title of what 1960–1964 TV series starring Martin Milner?
6. Jesse Chisholm lent his name to the trail that ran from the Mexican border to Abilene. What traveled on the Chisholm Trail?
7. What frontiersman is credited with breaking the trail called the Wilderness Road in Eastern Kentucky in 1775?
8. When it was completed in 1913, what name was given to the first coast-to-coast paved road, which ran from New York to California?
9. Who is the only country singer to have a street named for him in Herderconville, Tennessee, his present residence?
10. What are the routes called that aircraft follow by using navigational aids?

16. Frigid zone
17. Neap tide
18. Roughly the 180 meridian through the Pacific
19. About 12 miles above the earth
20. Hydrosphere

Highways and Roads (Answers)

1. Alcan or Alaska Highway
2. Route 66
3. Cumberland Road
4. Mulholland Drive
5. Route 66
6. Cattle
7. Daniel Boone
8. Lincoln Highway
9. Johnny Cash (Johnny Cash Parkway)
10. Airways

Hills

1. The Parthenon in Athens, Greece, is situated on what famous hill?
2. The nation's capital building in Washington, DC, is situated on what hill?
3. What is the name of the small hill on the South Pacific island of Iwo Jima, where the U.S. Marines raised the U.S. flag on February 23, 1945?
4. On what hill in Jerusalem was Jesus Christ crucified?
5. What are the two look-alike small peaks in San Francisco from which one can see the entire city below?
6. On how many hills was the city of Rome originally built?
7. How many of the hills of Rome can you name?
8. What famous tourist attraction in San Francisco has a tower on it overlooking San Francisco Bay?
9. In what states are the Black Hills located?
10. In what state is Bunker Hill, a site of an American Revolutionary war battle, located?

Islands

1. What are the eight largest islands that make up the Hawaiian Islands?
2. What is the Argentine name for the British Falkland Islands?
3. Name the island situated off the Southeast coast of Africa.
4. At 839,800 square miles in area, what is the largest island in the world?
5. On what island was Napoleon born (1769)?
6. What island was Napoleon exiled to in 1814?
7. On what island did Napoleon die in 1821?
8. Name the island in the San Francisco Bay that was man-made for the Golden Gate Exposition and is now a U.S. Navy base.
9. What is the only island in the world divided into two countries?
10. Portuguese explorer Ferdinand Magellan was killed on what Pacific Island in 1521?

Hills (Answers)

1. The Acropolis
2. Jenkins Hill
3. Mt. Suribachi
4. Calvary or Golgotha
5. Twin Peaks
6. Seven
7. Aventine, Caelian, Capitoline, Esquiline, Palatine, Quirinal, and Viminal
8. Nob Hill
9. South Dakota and Wyoming
10. Massachusetts (the battle was actually fought on nearby Breed's Hill.)

Islands (Answers)

1. Hawaii, Kahoolawe, Kauai, Lanai, Maui, Molokai, Nilihaus, and Oahu
2. Malvinas
3. Madagascar
4. Greenland
5. Corsica
6. Elba
7. St. Helena
8. Treasure Island
9. Hispanola, which is part of Haiti and part Dominican Republic
10. Philippines

11. What is the name of the legendary island that Plato believed once existed in the Atlantic Ocean?

12. What three islands help to make up the City of New York?

13. Originally named Bedloe's Island, until June 1960, on what island is the Statue of Liberty located?

14. What three island divisions make up the Pacific Ocean islands?

15. What is the name of the very last island in the Florida Keys, which is but 90 miles from Cuba?

16. Name the two islands in the Bering Strait one owned by the United States and the other by the Soviet Union?

17. What island is second to Greenland as the largest island in the world?

18. What is the largest Mediterranean island situated just below the south of Italy?

19. What is the island nation that is situated in the Indian Ocean off the Southeast coast of Africa?

20. What South Pacific Island was settled by the survivors of the H.M.S. *Bounty* mutineers?

Lakes

1. What large lake is situated on the border between California and Nevada?

2. Which one of the Great Lakes is the largest body of fresh water in the world?

3. Which one of the five Great Lakes lies entirely within the boundaries of the United States?

4. Lake Superior is the second-largest lake in the world, but the largest lake is five times as large. Name it.

5. This Oregon lake, which is situated on top of a volcano, is the deepest lake in the United States (1,932 feet deep). Name it.

6. What state has the most lakes, with approximately 30,000?

7. Minnesota's Lake Itasca is the source of what river?

8. Two of the world's largest lakes are pronounced the same but are spelled differently. One is located in Australia. Name them both.

9. What is the largest body of saltwater within the United States?

10. What is the name of the largest lake in Florida?

11. Atlantis
12. Manhattan Island, Staten Island, and Long Island
13. Liberty Island
14. Micronesia, Indonesia, and Polynesia
15. Key West
16. Big Diomede (USSR) and Little Diomede (USA)
17. New Guinea
18. Sicily
19. Madagascar
20. Pitcairn

Lakes (Answers)

1. Lake Tahoe
2. Lake Superior
3. Lake Michigan
4. Caspian Sea
5. Crater Lake
6. Florida
7. Mississippi River
8. Eyre (Australia) and Erie (United States and Canada)
9. Great Salt Lake in Utah
10. Lake Okeechobee

Locations

1. Where was "Custer's last stand"?
2. Kettle Hill is the site of what actual charge in Cuba on July 1, 1898, miscredited to another location?
3. Where did Christopher Columbus and his crews land in 1492 believing that they had found a route to India?
4. Although Waterloo is credited as the location where Napoleon was defeated by the Duke of Wellington on June 18, 1815, where in Belgium did the final defeat take place?
5. Bay City is the setting of what TV soap opera?
6. Bay Port is the hometown of what fictional brothers?
7. On what California coastal town did the 1963 Alfred Hitchcock film *The Birds* take place?
8. What historical event took place at Boston's Griffin Wharf on December 16, 1773?
9. Bonanza Creek, Alaska, was the setting for what incident in 1897?
10. On what continents are the two battle locations mentioned in the U.S. Marine Corps's hymn?
11. Cleveland's intersection of Euclid Avenue and East 105th Street was the site of what first, on August 5, 1914?
12. A site near the small North Dakota town of Rugby is the center of what?
13. What San Francisco intersection most exemplified the center of the hippy community?
14. What town in Rhode Island manufactured quonset huts during World War II?
15. Where today is the site of the house in which Roy Rogers was born, in Cincinnatti on November 5, 1912?
16. In what western town was Wild Bill Hickok shot in the back and killed by Jack McCall on August 2, 1876?
17. In what California town is Disneyland located?
18. Where did King John sign the Magna Carta in 1215?
19. In what European country does the opera *Carmen* take place?
20. What occurred in Ujiji, Tanzania, on November 1871?

Locations (Answers)

1. On the shores of the Little Big Horn in Montana
2. San Juan Hill
3. San Salvador Island
4. La Belle—Alliance
5. "Another World"
6. Hardy Boys
7. Bodega Bay
8. The Boston Tea Party
9. Klondike gold rush
10. North American (Halls of Montezuma), Africa, (Tripoli)
11. First traffic light
12. North America
13. Haight and Ashbury
14. Quonset Point
15. It is located approximately where second base is situated in Riverfront Stadium.
16. Deadwood, South Dakota
17. Anaheim
18. Runnymede
19. Spain
20. Reporter Henry Stanley located Dr. Livingston, to whom he said, "Dr. Livingston, I presume."

Military Bases

1. The U.S. Navy has a base located on the island of Cuba. What is its name?
2. Name the U.S. Army post where the United States Gold Reserve is kept.
3. The aircraft of the president of the United States, *Air Force One*, is stationed at what military post?
4. Thousands of the U.S. Air Force's aircraft, from B-17s to B-52s are stored at what desert base?
5. What West Coast city is the hometown for a Marine Corps basic training base?
6. When the Confederacy fired upon this South Carolina fort, on April 12, 1861, it marked the beginning of the American Civil War. Name the fort.
7. This fort's bombardment by the British on the night of September 13, 1814, inspired Frances Scott Key to pen the "Star Spangled Banner". Name the fort.
8. Formerly named Bunker Hill Air Force Base, what is the only U.S. Air Force base named for an astronaut?
9. What California base was previously known as Muroc Field?
10. What was the name of the U.S. Cavalry fort in Dakota Territory from which George Armstrong Custer departed on May 17, 1876, for the Little Big Horn?

Mountains

1. Mount Blanc is the highest mountain in what European country?
2. At 20,270 feet high, what is the highest peak in North America?
3. What is the highest mountain in the 48 contiguous states?
4. Mount Logan, at 19,850 feet high, is the highest mountain found in what country?
5. On July 14, 1808, Maria Paradis became the first woman to climb what 15,771-foot European mountain?
6. Annie Smith Peck became the first woman to climb what European mountain that was first scaled in 1865 by Edward Whymper?

Military Bases (Answers)

1. Guantanamo
2. Fort Knox
3. Andrews Air Force Base
4. Davis Monthan Air Force Base in Arizona
5. San Diego
6. Fort Sumter
7. Fort McHenry
8. Grissom A.F.B.
9. Edwards A.F.B.
10. Fort Abraham Lincoln

Mountains (Answers)

1. France
2. Mt. McKinley (in Alaska)
3. Mt. Whitney (14,495 feet)
4. Canada
5. Mount Blanc
6. The Matterhorn

7. What often repeated quote did George Leigh-Mallony give when he was asked why he and Andrew Irvine decided to climb Mt. Everest?
8. What mountain range separates France from Spain?
9. At 19,565 feet high, what is the highest mountain in Africa?
10. What is the origin of the names of the West Coast mountains Mt. Helena, Mt. Hood, and Mt. Ranier?

Oceans

1. At what land point is the Atlantic Ocean West of the Pacific Ocean?
2. In order for vessels to go through the Panama Canal they must be raised or lowered by locks, according to their direction. Which ocean is higher at Panama?
3. Which ocean is saltier, the Atlantic or the Pacific?
4. Name the four oceans.
5. In what ocean can the greatest depth be found (36,201 feet)?
6. The International Date Line runs through what two oceans?
7. What oceans border Antarctica?
8. Who named the Pacific Ocean?
9. Name the oceans according to their sizes.
10. What song did Irving Berlin compose about the oceans in 1932?

Parks

1. What large recreational park, featuring playing fields as well as museums, is located in the western sector of San Francisco?
2. What large (363 acres) London park is well-known for the many soapbox orators who give speeches there?
3. Which national park (our first, established in 1872) is the home of the famous geyser "Old Faithful" that erupts on an average of once every 64.5 minutes?
4. What large park, named after a motion picture figure, contains the Los Angeles Zoo and Observatory?
5. In what state is Zion National Park located?
6. The 13,000-acre South Mountain Preserve is the largest city park in the United States. In what city is it located?

7. "Because it is there."
8. Pyrennes
9. Kilimanjaro
10. They are all named for British Admirals

Oceans (Answers)

1. Panama
2. Atlantic Ocean
3. Atlantic Ocean
4. Atlantic, Pacific, Indian, and Arctic
5. Pacific Ocean
6. Pacific and Arctic
7. Pacific, Atlantic, and Indian
8. Vasco Balboa
9. Pacific, Atlantic, Arctic, and Indian
10. "How Deep Is the Ocean"

Parks (Answers)

1. Golden Gate Park
2. Hyde Park
3. Yellowstone National Park
4. D. W. Griffith Park
5. Utah
6. Phoenix, Arizona

7. Chicago's Jackson Park was the site of what event in 1893?
8. What park was the title of a #1 hit song, and whose version reached that position?
9. What Hollywood actor had a mountain peak named after him in Yosemite National Park?
10. Rock Creek is the name of the park that cuts through what U.S. city?

Previous Names of Cities and Towns

1. Fort Dearborn was the previous name of what major U.S. city?
2. Which Canadian city was once known as Fort York?
3. The Vietnamese city of Saigon is known today by what name?
4. What is the Russian city of Volgograd's previous name?
5. What was the previous name of the City of New York?
6. Christiana was the previous name of what European capital?
7. What Pennsylvania town was previously named Mauch Chunk until they changed it in 1954 to honor an Olympic champion?
8. What foreign capital city was once known as Tenochtitlan?
9. By what name was the People's Republic of China capital city once known?
10. In November 1941, the Oklahoma town of Berwyn changed its name to that of what popular movie star and singer?

Rivers

1. What river runs through the city of London?
2. The longest river in Europe empties into the Caspian Sea. Name it.
3. What is the longest river in South America?
4. Gold was discovered at Sutter's Mill in 1848 along the banks of what California river?
5. On what river is 727-foot-high Hoover Dam located?
6. What river runs through hell in Greek mythology?
7. What is the source of Africa's Blue Nile river?
8. What is the source of Africa's White Nile river?
9. What river carries more water in it than any other in the world?

7. Chicago World's Fair
8. "MacArthur Park" by Donna Summer in 1978 (Richard Harris's version went to #2 in 1968)
9. Douglas Fairbanks
10. Washington, DC

Previous Names of Cities and Towns (Answers)

1. Chicago
2. Toronto
3. Ho Chi Minh City
4. Stalingrad
5. New Amsterdam
6. Oslo, Norway
7. (Jim) Thorpe
8. Mexico City
9. Peiping
10. (Gene) Autry

Rivers (Answers)

1. Thames
2. Volga
3. Amazon
4. American
5. Colorado River
6. Styx
7. Lake Tana in Ethiopia
8. Lake Victoria in Uganda
9. Amazon

10. George Washington crossed what river on Christmas 1776 to attack the British and capture Trenton?
11. According to legend George Washington threw a dollar across what river?
12. The highest waterfall in the world falls into Venezuela's Carrao River. Name this 3,212-foot drop.
13. What river runs through the Hungarian capital city of Budapest, which at one time was made up of three towns named Pest, Obuda, and Buda?
14. What is the longest river in Asia?
15. What U.S. river is nicknamed Big Muddy?
16. Oscar Hammerstein II and Jerome Kern wrote their 1927 classic song "Ol' Man River" about what U.S. river?
17. There are six rivers that have the same name as the state they traverse. Name them.
18. What river runs through Liverpool, England?
19. What river runs through Rome, the capital city of Italy?
20. What Stephen Foster song is also known as "Swanee River"?

Russia

1. Who is the patron saint of Russia?
2. What state name is common to both Russia and the United States?
3. What was the exact date of the start of the Russian Revolution?
4. What is the official name of Russia?
5. Who was the last czar to rule Russia (from 1894 until 1917)?
6. On what two continents does Russia lie?
7. What are the two most populous cities in Russia?
8. With what country did Russia go to war in 1904?
9. What is the closest distance that Russian soil is to U.S. soil?
10. Who was the first premier of Russia, who served from 1917 until 1924?

Seas

1. What is the largest sea in the world?
2. This sea, which Moses once crossed, separates Asia from the continent of Africa. Name it.

10. Delaware River
11. Potomac
12. Angel Falls
13. Danube
14. Yangtze
15. Missouri
16. Mississippi
17. Colorado, Connecticut, Delaware, Missouri, Mississippi, and Ohio
18. Mersey
19. Tiber
20. "Old Folks at Home"

Russia (Answers)

1. St. Nicholas
2. Georgia
3. November 7, 1917
4. Union of Soviet Socialist Republics
5. Nicholas II
6. Europe and Asia
7. Moscow and Leningrad
8. Japan
9. 15 miles (the distance between Big Diomede and Little Diomede islands)
10. Nikolai Lenin

Seas (Answers)

1. Mediterranean
2. Red Sea

3. Located between Europe and Asia, what is the world's largest inland sea?
4. What two seas are connected by the Suez Canal?
5. The Aleutian Islands separate what sea from the Pacific Ocean?
6. What sea separates Great Britain from the European mainland above the English Channel?
7. What sea separates Korea from Japan?
8. What sea is situated between Vietnam and the Philippines?
9. What sea is to the east of Central America?
10. Where is the Sea of Tranquillity?

South America

1. What is the native language of Brazil?
2. What is the largest oil-producing country in South America?
3. What is the name of the cape on the southern tip of the continent?
4. What country touches both the Pacific Ocean and the Atlantic Ocean?
5. What is the name of the largest freshwater lake in South America (and the highest in the world)?
6. In 1960, the capital of Brazil was changed from Rio de Janeiro to what city?
7. Ecuador is named for the equator, which runs through the country. What two other South American countries have the equator running through them?
8. Name all 13 countries of South America.
9. What is the chief export of Brazil?
10. What wife succeeded her husband as the first head of state in the western hemisphere?

State Capitals

1. What two state capitals begin with the same six letters?
2. What four state capitals have the word "city" in their name?
3. Which is the only state capital that doesn't share a single letter with the name of the state?
4. Name the four state capitals that begin with the same letter as their state?

3. Caspian Sea
4. Mediterranean Sea and Red Sea
5. Bering Sea
6. North Sea
7. Sea of Japan
8. South China Sea
9. Caribbean Sea
10. On the moon

South America (Answers)

1. Portuguese
2. Venezuela
3. Cape Horn
4. Chile
5. Lake Titicaca
6. Brasilia
7. Brazil and Columbia
8. Argentina, Bolivia, Brazil, Chile, Colombia, Ecuador, Paraguay, Peru, Uruguay, Venezuela, Guyana, Surinam, and French Guiana
9. Coffee
10. Eva Peron

State Capitals (Answers)

1. Columbus (Ohio) and Columbia (South Carolina)
2. Carson City, Nevada; Jefferson City, Missouri; Oklahoma City, Oklahoma; and Salt Lake City, Utah
3. Pierre, South Dakota
4. Dover, Delaware; Honolulu, Hawaii; Oklahoma City, Oklahoma; and Indianapolis, Indiana

5. Which state capital is closest to the equator?
6. Name the four state capitals named after U.S. Presidents?
7. What is the only state capital to be named for the state it is in?
8. What is the only state capital made up of two words that is in a state made up of two words?
9. Alphabetically what is the last state capital?
10. Not including Oklahoma City, what is the only state capital that has the name of the state included within its name?

State Facts

1. What is the smallest county in the United States?
2. After whom was the state of Pennsylvania named?
3. What is the only U.S. state that touches just one other state?
4. Tennessee borders more states than any other U.S. state. Name the eight states that Tennessee borders?
5. What are the 19 states that end in the letter *a?*
6. What state was named after a British monarch?
7. At 242 feet below sea level, where is the lowest geographical point in the United States?
8. Averaging a height of 60 feet above sea level, what is the lowest state in the U.S.?
9. The U.S. government owns close to 90% of what state's land?
10. In 1780 what became the first state to abolish slavery?

State Nicknames

Name the states with the following nicknames:
1. Wolverine State
2. Hawkeye State
3. Hoosier State
4. Sunshine State
5. Empire State
6. Buckeye State
7. Golden State
8. Show-Me State
9. Keystone State
10. Bluegrass State

5. Honolulu, Hawaii
6. Madison, Wisconsin; Jackson, Mississippi; Jefferson City, Missouri; and Lincoln, Nebraska
7. Oklahoma City
8. Sante Fe, New Mexico
9. Trenton, New Jersey
10. Indianapolis, Indiana

State Facts (Answers)

1. New York, New York (22 square miles)
2. Admiral Sir William Penn (father of the states founder William Penn)
3. Maine (borders New Hampshire)
4. North Carolina, Georgia, Alabama, Mississippi, Arkansas, Missouri, Kentucky, and Virginia
6. Virginia (after Queen Elizabeth the Virgin Queen)
7. Death Valley, California
8. Delaware
9. Nevada
10. Massachusetts

State Nicknames (Answers)

1. Michigan
2. Iowa
3. Indiana
4. Florida
5. New York
6. Ohio
7. California
8. Missouri
9. Pennsylvania
10. Kentucky

States

1. Which two states did not ratify the 18th Amendment (Volstead Act), which introduced prohibition in 1919?
2. Name the 48th, 49th, and 50th states of the Union.
3. Which state has no official nickname?
4. How is the state of Louisiana divided?
5. How is the state of Massachusetts divided?
6. Which U.S. states have the longest and second-longest coast lines?
7. What state was previously known as Franklin, named for Benjamin Franklin?
8. What states admission to the Union was finally ratified by Congress and signed into law by President Eisenhower on August 7, 1953?
9. The only diamond mine in North America is located in what state?
10. In 1869, what state first granted suffrage to women?
11. What was the first state admitted to the Union in 1791, following the original 13?
12. What state still reserves the right to divide itself into five states if it so desires?
13. New Connecticut is the previous name of the only New England state without a seacoast. Name it.
14. What was the first state to abolish slavery, in 1780?
15. What four states are officially designated as commonwealths?
16. Deseret is the former name of what state?
17. What four states come together at Four Corners. List them in clockwise order.
18. What was the first state to secede from the Union on December 20, 1860?
19. Name the eight states that border Missouri.
20. What was the first state of the United States and the first state to ratify the Constitution on December 7, 1787?

States (Answers)

1. Rhode Island and Connecticut
2. Arizona (1912), Alaska (1959), and Hawaii (1959)
3. Alaska
4. Parishes
5. Townships
6. Alaska and Florida
7. Tennessee
8. Ohio
9. Arkansas
10. Wyoming
11. Vermont
12. Texas
13. Vermont
14. Massachusetts
15. Pennsylvania, Kentucky, Massachusetts, and Virginia
16. Utah
17. Colorado, New Mexico, Arizona and Utah
18. South Carolina
19. Arkansas, Illinois, Iowa, Kansas, Kentucky, Nebraska, Oklahoma, and Tennessee
20. Delaware

Streets

1. What is the main street that runs through downtown San Francisco that once featured four sets of streetcar tracks?
2. What street, which runs through Los Angeles in a north-south direction, is the longest street in the world?
3. Beal Street was once the scene of jumping music for what southern city?
4. What world-famous thoroughfare is nicknamed the Great White Way?
5. On what famous street in New York is the New York Stock Exchange located?
6. Name the beautiful main street in Paris that begins at the Arc de Triomphe?
7. The street names in the popular Monopoly board game were taken from the names of what city?
8. What is the name of the fashion-center street in London?
9. On what Pasadena street does the Tournament of Roses Parade take place each year?
10. On January 15, 1983, Los Angeles's Santa Barbara Blvd. changed its name in honor of what man?
11. What San Francisco street is called the crookedest street in the world, making eight turns within one block?
12. On what New York City street does the annual Easter Parade take place?
13. What is located where Manhattan Island's 42nd Street, 7th Avenue, and Broadway meet?
14. What is London's equivalent to Wall Street?
15. In what U.S. city are the names of streets limited to eight letters?
16. What London street, in 1807, became the first street ever equipped with gas lights?
17. What Chicago intersection is called the busiest in the world?
18. What New York street is the center of the garment district?
19. In what southern city can one find Peachtree Street?
20. In what European country is Kaerntner Strauss located?

Streets (Answers)

1. Market Street
2. Figueroa
3. Memphis
4. New York City's Broadway
5. Wall Street
6. Avenue des Champs Elysées
7. Atlantic City, New Jersey
8. Carnaby Street
9. Colorado Blvd.
10. Martin Luther King (it became Martin Luther King Blvd.)
11. Lombard Street
12. Fifth Avenue
13. Times Square
14. Lombard Street
15. Salt Lake City
16. Pall Mall
17. Madison and State
18. Seventh Avenue
19. Atlanta, Georgia
20. Vienna

Towns

1. Actress Betty Hutton was born in what Michigan town that is famous for its cereal manufacturing and nicknamed "Breakfast Food City"?
2. In what town did the 1940 Errol Flynn-Olivia DeHavilland movie *Santa Fe Trail* make its world premiere?
3. What name did astronaut John Glenn's New Hampshire home-town change its name to?
4. What New Mexico town named itself, in 1950, after a radio program?
5. What is the significance of The Dalles in Oregon and The Plains in Ohio?
6. Film director-producer George Lucas set his 1973 movie *American Graffiti* in the California town in which he grew up. Name it.
7. Name Sherwood Anderson's 1919 novel about small-town life in America.
8. Ripcon is the Wisconsin town in which what political party was born in 1828?
9. What major city of the South is now located where Fort Dallas once stood in 1895?
10. What steel town of the United States did Billy Joel record a hit record about in 1983?

World Capitals

1. What is the southernmost world capital on the globe?
2. What South American country has two capitals?
3. What capital city was named for a U.S. President in 1822?
4. Name the three European capitals that are situated on the Danube River.
5. What is the capital of the alphabetically first member of the United Nations?
6. What is the name of the capital of both Hong Kong and Seychelles?
7. Name the six countries that use the national name for their capital?

Towns (Answers)

1. Battle Creek
2. Santa Fe, New Mexico
3. Spacetown
4. Truth or Consequences
5. They are the only two towns in the United States that begin with the word "The."
6. Modesto
7. *Winesburg, Ohio*
8. Republican Party
9. Miami, Florida
10. Allentown

World Capitals (Answers)

1. Wellington, New Zealand
2. Bolivia with Sucre (legal) and LaPaz (de facto)
3. Monrovia, Liberia (named for President James Monroe)
4. Belgrade (Yugoslavia), Budapest (Hungary), and Vienna (Austria)
5. Kabul (Afghanistan)
6. Victoria
7. Kuwait, Luxembourg, Monaco, Panama, San Marino and Singapore

8. What are the capitals of the two Germanys?
9. What is the northernmost world capital on the globe?
10. What is the capital city of the Philippines?

8.　Bonn (West Germany) and East Berlin (East Germany)
9.　Reykjavick, Iceland
10.　Quezon City

Math, Science, and

Technology

Airlines

1. World War I aviator Juan Terry Trippe founded what large U.S. airline in 1928?
2. Prior to being known as Trans World Airlines, when Howard Hughes owned it, what was TWA known as?
3. What is the national airline of the Soviet Union?
4. What is the national airline of Spain?
5. What West Coast airline painted a smile on the front of their airplanes in the late 1970s?
6. What Boeing 747 airliner did the Soviets shoot down in 1983?
7. What Greek airline was owned by Aristotle Onassis?
8. El Al is the national airline if what country?
9. KLM is the national airline of what country?
10. When Howard Hughes bought Air West Airlines what did he rename it?

Anatomy

1. How many permanent teeth should an adult have?
2. What is the colored portion of the human eye called?
3. What are the five known senses of the human body?
4. On Christmas Eve 1888, what part of his body did painter Vincent Van Gogh cut partly off in frustration?
5. How many bones are there in the human body?
6. What is the longest bone in the human body?
7. How many pints of blood are there in the average human body?
8. What is the heaviest organ in the human body?
9. What are the four taste areas of the tongue?
10. What is a male's largest laryngeal cartilage projection better known as?

Airlines (Answers)

1. Pan American Airways
2. Trans Western Airlines
3. Aeroflot
4. Iberia
5. PSA
6. Korean Airlines flight 007
7. Olympic
8. Israel
9. The Netherlands
10. Hughes Air West

Anatomy (Answers)

1. 32
2. Iris
3. Hearing, sight, smell, taste, and touch
4. Left ear
5. 206
6. Thigh bone (femur)
7. 12
8. Liver (approximately 3½ pounds)
9. Bitter, salty, sour, sweet
10. Adam's apple

Architects

1. What building did Benjamin Latrobe redesign after it had been destroyed in 1812?
2. What residence did James Hoban design in Washington, DC?
3. Name the French engineer who designed France's highest monument as well as the frame for the Statue of Liberty?
4. William LeBaron Jenney is credited with developing what architectual first in Chicago, in 1885?
5. Julie Morgan became the first graduate of the University of California College of Civil Engineering. What famous California estate did she design?
6. Who designed the Tokyo Imperial Hotel, which was built between 1915 and 1922, as the world's first earthquake-proof building?
7. What city did surveyor Benjamin Banneker help to design, beginning in 1789?
8. Who was Adolf Hitler's chief architect who was going to redesign Berlin after the war?
9. What architect and engineer built a 20,000-foot-long tunnel into California's Mt. Davidson in order to reach the Comstock Lode? (He later served as mayor of San Francisco from 1894 to 1896.)
10. What famed architect did Harry K. Thaw murder at Madison Square Garden in 1906 over a dispute concerning showgirl Evelyn Nesbit?

Astronomy

1. Name the nine planets in order from the sun.
2. What planet was originally called Georgium Sidus, after King George III?
3. What planet takes 687 days to orbit the sun?
4. What planet was discovered in 1930 by Clyde Tombaugh?
5. What galaxy are we a part of?
6. What are the magnetic storms that appear on the surface of the sun called?
7. What is the smallest planet?

Architects (Answers)

1. The Capitol building in Washington, DC
2. White House (He never lived to see it.)
3. Alexandre-Gustave Eiffel
4. The first skyscraper
5. Hearst Castle at San Simeon
6. Frank Lloyd Wright
7. Washington, DC
8. Albert Speer
9. Adolph Sutro
10. Stanford White

Astronomy (Answers)

1. Mercury, Venus, Earth, Mars, Jupiter, Saturn, Uranus, Neptune, Pluto
2. Uranus
3. Mars
4. Pluto
5. Milky Way
6. Sunspots
7. Mercury

8. What is the largest planet?
9. What is the first planet that a man-made object landed on?
10. What planet has three rings encircling it?
11. What is the biggest star of our solar system?
12. Name the largest moon of Saturn.
13. What is the name given to small planets that travel in orbits between Mars and Jupiter?
14. What is the brightest planet, which is often seen in daytime?
15. What planet has the most moons?
16. What is the only known satellite in the solar system that rotates faster than its central planet?
17. The majority of the planets appear yellow in space. What color would the earth appear to be?
18. Where is the largest reflector telescope in the world?
19. Which of the planets is known as the red planet?
20. What is the head of a comet called?

Automobile Manufacturers

1. What British firm manufactures sports cars under the initials *M.G.?*
2. What two automobiles were named after Ransom Eli Olds?
3. What two automobiles were named after Henry J. Kaiser?
4. What two American automobiles stopped production in 1960?
5. What U.S. automobile company manufactured only taxi cabs?
6. What American automobile began as a sports car but eventually was enlarged to a luxury automobile?
7. What automobile division manufactures the Corvette?
8. In what country did John DeLorean manufacture his DeLorean automobile?
9. At the end of World War II the German government offered to what U.S. automobile maker the Volkswagen Company, so they could build it back up?
10. What are the four biggest American manufacturers of automobiles?

QUESTIONS

Jupiter
Mars
Saturn
Sirius A
Titon
Asteroids
Venus
Jupiter with 12
Phobos, one of the two moons of Mars, which rotates two-thirds faster
Blue, because of the oceans
Mt. Palomar, California
Mars
Coma

Automobile Manufacturers (Answers)
Morris Garage
REO and Oldsmobile
Kaiser-Frazier and the Henry J.
Edsel and DeSoto
Checker Cab Company
Thunderbird
Chevrolet
Ireland
Ford
General Motors, Ford, Chrysler, and American Motors

Buildings

1. What New York City building, located at 1619 Broadway, has become world-famous for being the headquarters of numerous music publishing and record companies?
2. In what city is the unusual pyramid building located?
3. New York City's Baster Building is the fictional headquarters of what comic-book crime-fighting unit?
4. What New York City apartment complex was both the setting of the 1968 movie *Rosemary's Baby* and the home of John Lennon (in front of which he was shot and killed in 1980)?
5. What is the tallest building in the world, at 1,453 feet?
6. What record does the Palace of Governors in Santa Fe, New Mexico, hold?
7. What is the largest building in the United States?
8. What building in New York City is named for the U. S. airline that has offices there?
9. In what city is the largest palace building found?
10. What was the very top of the Empire State Building designed to be used for?

Chemistry

1. What common cooking ingredient has the chemical formula NaCl?
2. What is the Fahrenheit temperature corresponding to 0° Centigrade?
3. What is the most abundant chemical in the earth's crust?
4. What is the most abundant element in saltwater?
5. What is the most abundant mineral in the human body?
6. Name the three parts of the atom.
7. If you increase the pressure on a gas, what happens to the volume?
8. Name the three states of matter.
9. What mineral is a diamond made of?
10. What do the numbers 5-10-5 on a bag of fertilizer indicate?

Buildings (Answers)

1. Brill Building
2. San Francisco
3. Fantastic Four
4. The Dakota Apartments
5. Chicago's Sears Tower
6. It is the oldest public building in the United States (built in 1609)
7. Boeing 747 Manufacturing Plant in Everett, Washington
8. Pan Am Building
9. Peking (Imperial Palace)
10. A mooring mask for dirigibles

Chemistry (Answers)

1. Salt
2. 32°
3. Oxygen
4. Oxygen
5. Calcium
6. Proton, electron, neutron
7. It decreases
8. Gas, liquid, and solid
9. Carbon
10. 5% nitrogen, 10% phosphorus, and 5% potassium

Clocks and Watches

1. Brothers Charles and Robert founded what watch-manufacturing company in 1887?
2. What does the four look like on a Roman-numeral clock?
3. What U. S. Vice-Presidents' face appeared in a wristwatch?
4. Who sponsored the very first TV commercial on July 1, 1941, which aired over New York City's WNBT, at a cost of $9.00?
5. What brand of stopwatch is used on the TV series "60 Minutes"?
6. In 1787, Levi Hutchins invented what device that people have been cursing him over ever since?
7. On the *Apollo II* flight what watch did astronaut Gene Cernan wear?
8. What innovation did George Thiess introduce in 1968?
9. Many times clocks on display or in catalogues are set at 8:18. What is the reason for this?
10. What time is it on land if it is eight bells at sea?

Designers

1. Charles Thomson created what design on the back side of the U.S. dollar?
2. Name the English cabinetmaker best known for his chairs.
3. Cedric Gibbons designed what statuette that he himself won 11 times?
4. Who designed the University of Virginia?
5. Who designed the CETI plaques depicting the nude male and female attached to the *Pioneer 10* and *11* spacecraft?
6. What did attorney Francis Hopkinson design that Elizabeth Griscom Ross has been given credit for?
7. Who designed the uniforms worn by the Swiss guards at the Vatican in Italy?
8. Shah Jehau designed and built what monument for his wife?
9. From 1937 until 1965, C. Gary Clovell was the designer of the prizes that were included in what product?
10. Who designed the class B Air Force uniform for the Air Force Academy (it is the service outfit/general purpose uniform)?

Clocks and Watches (Answers)

1. Ingersoll
2. IIII
3. Spiro T. Agnew's (also Richard Nixon's, but not until he was President)
4. Bulova Watch Company
5. Heuver
6. The alarm clock
7. Mickey Mouse watch
8. Electronic digital wristwatches
9. It gives an even balance to the display of the clock face
10. Four o'clock, eight o'clock, or twelve o'clock

Designers (Answers)

1. The Great Seal
2. Thomas Chippendale
3. Oscar—the Academy Award statuette
4. Thomas Jefferson
5. Linda Sagan (wife of Carl Sagan)
6. The American flag
7. Michelangelo
8. Taj Mahal
9. Cracker Jacks
10. C. B. DeMille

Diseases

1. Cook Mary Mallon was nicknamed what after she spread her illness in New York City, eventually infecting 53 other people and causing their deaths?
2. What disease broke out in large numbers among the homosexual community in the 1980s?
3. In 1901, Dr. Emil Avon Behring won the first Nobel Prize for Medicine. What disease did he study?
4. What is the more popular name given to amyotrophic laterial sclerosis?
5. James Phipps on May 14, 1796, became the first person to be vaccinated by Dr. Edward Jenner against what disease?
6. What pathologist, who discovered the source of Rocky Mountain spotted fever, was portrayed by Errol Flynn in the 1937 movie *Green Light?*
7. After how many experiments did Dr. Paul Ehrlich finally discover salvarsan, the cure for syphilis, in 1908?
8. What doctor discovered the source of malaria in 1880?
9. What did U. S. Army surgeon Walter Reed study while stationed in Cuba?
10. What cancer did a London pathologist lend his name to when he first isolated it in 1832?

Doctors

1. What doctor of pediatrics was a oarsman member of the Yale crew that won a Gold Medal in the 1924 Olympics at Paris?
2. What is the last name of the quintuplets delivered by Dr. Alan Roy Dafoe on May 28, 1934?
3. On December 3, 1967, in New Johannesberg, South Africa, who performed the first successful heart transplant?
4. What was the name of the physician who treated John Wilkes Booth's broken leg? (Because of this he was assumed to have been involved in the assassination plot against Abraham Lincoln.)

Diseases (Answers)

1. Typhoid Mary
2. AIDS
3. Diphtheria
4. Lou Gehrig's disease
5. Smallpox
6. Dr. Howard Taylor Ricketts
7. 606
8. Charles Laveran
9. Yellow fever
10. Hodgkin's disease (Thomas Hodgkins)

Doctors (Answers)

1. Dr. Benjamin Spock
2. Dionne
3. Dr. Christian Barnard
4. Dr. Samuel Mudd

5. What was the nickname of Dr. William Abruzzi, who handled 5,000 cases during the Woodstock festival?

6. Who is known as the Father of Medicine?

7. What physician discovered the oral polio vaccine?

8. Who was the only U.S. President to be the son of a doctor?

9. Irish physician Dr. William Stokes invented what device in 1837, that is still used by doctors today?

10. Name the doctor who authored such best-sellers as *The Keys of the Kingdom* and *The Stars Look Down?*

Famous Aircraft

1. Country singer Kenny Rogers named his private BAC-111 jet aircraft after his beautiful wife. What is the name of the plane?

2. Elvis Presley named his private Convair 880 jet after his daughter, who was born in 1968. Name the aircraft.

3. When *Playboy* magazine publisher Hugh Heffner owned an all-black DC-9 aircraft with a white bunny on the tail, what did he name the aircraft?

4. The *Silver Phyllis*, a Boeing 707, belonged to what financier?

5. *Bataan* was the nickname of whose private B-17 aircraft during World War II?

6. *Columbine* was the name of what Presidential aircraft? It was named by the First Lady after the state flower of Colorado.

7. Who crashed his unsuccessful 1903 airplane *Aerodrome* into the Potomac River, thus losing out to the Wright brothers to fly the first heavier-than-air craft?

8. What is the nickname given to the Boeing 747 Presidential aircraft that will serve as an airborn command post in the event of a nuclear war?

9. What name was given to the U.S. Air Force DC-9 that brought the 52 American hostages home to Washington, DC, from Germany in January 1981?

10. What historical first did the aircraft nicknamed *Glamorous Glennis* make on October 14, 1947?

11. What was the name of the B-29 piloted by Major Charles Sweeney that dropped the A-bomb on Nagasaki on August 9, 1945?

5. Rock Doc
6. Hippocrates
7. Dr. Jonas Salk
8. Warren G. Harding
9. Stethoscope
10. Dr. Archibald J. Cronin

Famous Aircraft (Answers)

1. *Marianne*
2. *Lisa Marie*
3. *Big Bunny*
4. Robert Vesco
5. General Douglas A. MacArthur's
6. President Dwight D. Eisenhower
7. Samuel P. Langley
8. Doomsday Plane
9. *Freedom One*
10. It became the first Bell X-1 airplane to officially exceed the speed of sound.
11. *Bock's Car*

12. What nickname did President John F. Kennedy give to *Air Force One?*

13. What is the name of the man who invented the autopilot, the 8-track stereo, and became the manufacturer of a business jet?

14. What was the name of the B-50 Super Fortress that flew nonstop around the world in 1949?

15. What radio and television hero flew an aircraft called the *Song Bird?*

16. What type of aircraft did the Red Baron fly during World War I?

17. What type of aircraft does Snoopy often pretend his doghouse is?

18. What was the name of the aircraft that Wilbur and Orville Wright flew on Thursday December 17, 1903, at Kill Devil Hills, Kitty Hawk, North Carolina?

19. What is the designator of Russia's supersonic airliner?

20. On August 17, 1927 auto magnate Henry Ford made his first airplane flight ever. What was the name of that Ryan aircraft?

Formulas

What are the following formulas used to find?

1. Multiply the base by the height and divide by two. $A = \frac{Ab}{2}$

2. Multiply the diameter by 3.1416. $C = \pi d$

3. Multiply one side by itself. $A = A^2$

4. Multiply the length by the width by the height. $V = a^3$

5. Multiply the square of the radius by 3.14. $A = \pi r^2$

6. Add the two parallel sides, multiply by the height, divide by two. $A = \frac{h(a+b)}{2}$

7. $E = Mc^2$

8. Multiply the area of the base by the height and divide by three. $V = \frac{Ah}{3}$

9. Multiply four times pi, times radius cubed, divided by 3. $V = \frac{4\pi r^3}{3}$

10. Multiply 16 times time in seconds squared. $d = 16t^2$

Geology

1. Name the three major types of rocks.

2. What is the name given to the theory of continental drift?

12. *Caroline*, named after his daughter
13. William Lear
14. *Lucky Lady II*
15. Sky King
16. Fokker Triplane
17. Sopwith Camel
18. *Flyer*
19. TU-144 (Tupoleu)
20. *Spirit of St. Louis* (piloted by Charles Lindbergh)

Formulas (Answers)

1. Area of a right triangle
2. Circumference of a circle
3. Area of a square
4. Volume of a cube
5. Area of a circle
6. Area of a trapezoid
7. How to convert matter into energy
8. Volume of a pyramid
9. Volume of a sphere
10. Distance traveled by a falling body

Geology (Answers)

1. Igneous, sedimentary, and metamorphic
2. Plate tectonics

3. Name the line along which earthquakes occur.
4. What is the name of the fault from San Francisco to Los Angeles?
5. What is it called when a rock breaks along a specific plane?
6. What is the name given to molten rock while it is deep underground?
7. What would you be discussing if you talked about calving, quarrying, or rock flour?
8. What is the name given to the super-continent of all land masses that supposedly exploded 200 million years ago?
9. What era do we live in?
10. Name the branch of geology that studies fossils?
11. What are submerged volcanoes called?
12. Name the recognized scale used to measure the magnitude of an earthquake.
13. What is the point on the surface directly above an earthquake called?
14. Which cave projection hangs from the ceiling, stalagmites or stalactites?
15. What is a well called that flows naturally above ground?
16. What is the hardest mineral known to man?
17. What are you studying if you read about dikes, necks, and sills?
18. Name the outer layer of the earth.
19. Name the innermost layer of the earth.
20. Name a strip of sand offshore that parallels waterlines.

Inventors

1. What did Peter Goldmark introduce in 1948 that made possible Michael Jackson's "Thriller" album?
2. What female undergarment was invented by Caresse Corby (AKA Mary Phelps Jacobs) in 1914?
3. The Beatles dedicated their 1965 movie *Help!* to what inventor?
4. A DuPont chemist named Roy J. Plunkett discovered in 1938 polytetrafluoroethylene. What is it better known as?
5. Many years before the invention of the copy machine, Ralph Wedgewood invented what product in 1906?
6. Chester Carlson's invention eventually replaced Ralph Wedgewood's invention. What was it?
7. In 1885, Englishman J. K. Stanley introduced what variation on the bicycle?

3. Fault line
4. San Andreas Fault
5. Cleavage
6. Magma
7. Glaciers
8. Pangaea
9. Cenozoic
10. Paleontology
11. Seamounts
12. Richter scale
13. Epicenter
14. Stalactites
15. Artesian
16. Diamond
17. Volcanoes
18. The crust
19. The core
20. Barrier islands

Inventors (Answers)

1. The long-playing record
2. The bra
3. Elias Howe (inventor of the sewing machine)
4. Teflon
5. Carbon paper
6. Xerox copy machine
7. He made one with two equal-sized tires

8. Although he himself did not own a driver's license, he invented the first rotary combustion machine, manufactured by Masda. Name him.

9. In 1876, F. W. Thayer, a member of the Harvard Club, introduced what piece of equipment for baseball?

10. What table-sized game did Frank P. Beal introduce in the late 1940s?

Liquids

1. What liquid is known as the universal solvent?

2. What liquid comes in a Nebuchadnezzar?

3. How many times thicker is blood than water?

4. What popular drink was introduced at the World's Fair of 1904, which was held in St. Louis, Missouri?

5. What percentage of alcohol was included in near beer?

6. What liquid is found at the center of a golf ball?

7. What liquid would one be concerned with if one was asked to watch their P's and Q's?

8. What name was given to the popular children's drink made of ginger ale or 7-Up and a dash of grenadine, with a cherry?

9. What kind of poison did Socrates drink in 399 B.C.?

10. What additive does 7-Up claim that it never has had and never will have?

Mathematics

1. The numbers 28, 496, and 8,128 are called perfect, because they have a positive integer which is equal to the sum of its factors. What perfect number precedes 28?

2. What is the sum of the interior angles of a triangle?

3. Who is the Father of Geometry?

4. What British mathematician devised his theory of universal gravitation after watching an apple fall?

5. What is pi rounded off to two decimal places?

6. In 1859, what invention did Amedee Mannheim introduce to help mathematicians?

8. Felix Wankel
9. The catcher's mask
10. Table tennis

Liquids (Answers)

1. Water
2. Champagne (it's a bottle)
3. Six times
4. Ice tea
5. ½% (0.5%)
6. Castor oil
7. Beer (Pints and quarts)
8. Shirley Temple
9. Hemlock
10. Caffeine

Mathematics (Answers)

1. 6
2. $180°$
3. Euclid
4. Isaac Newton
5. 3.14
6. Slide rule

7. When 13 states seceded from the Union to form the Confederacy, how many states were left?
8. What mathematician developed the quantum theory of the atom?
9. What name is given to a triangle that has two equal sides?
10. If you multiply inches by 2.54, what measurement have you converted to?

Measurements

1. On February 4, 1983, Billy Olson became the first man to pole vault over how many feet?
2. What net is 32 inches high at its center?
3. On what yard line does a team kick off to their opponents in a pro football game?
4. How long is a standard football field from the end of one end zone to the end of the other end zone?
5. How many seconds are there in a day?
6. How many gallons are in a barrel of oil?
7. What linear measurement equals 5.5 yards, 5.03 meters, or 16.5 feet?
8. What is the width of a football field in yards?
9. What is the distance between consecutive bases in baseball?
10. What term is used for measuring the height of horses?

Medicine

1. Simon Bernard performed the first operation for appendicitis in the United States in 1888. Simon is the father of what businessman and Presidential adviser?
2. Dr. Emil Behring became, in 1901, the first recipient of what prestigious award in the field of medicine?
3. Novelists Louis Bromfield, W. Somerset Maugham, Sidney Howard, Dashiell Hammett, Ernest Hemingway, and John Dos Passos all did what same thing during World War I?
4. What English physician discovered the circulation of blood in the human body in 1616?

7. 22
8. Max Planck
9. Isosceles
10. Centimeters

Measurements (Answers)

1. 19 feet (19 feet ⅜ inches)
2. Tennis court net
3. From their 35-yard line
4. 140 yards—100 yards of playing field and 20 yards each for end zones
5. 86,400
6. 42
7. A rod
8. 53⅓ yards (160 feet)
9. 90 feet
10. Hand—which is equal to 4 inches

Medicine (Answers)

1. Bernard Baruch
2. Nobel Prize
3. Drove ambulances
4. William Harvey

5. In 1796, English physician Edward Jenner created a vaccine for the first disease conquered by modern medicine. What disease did he treat?

6. Polish American Casmir Funk discovered what complex organic substances occurring naturally in plant and animal tissue and necessary in small quantities for metabolic processes?

7. What is Elizabeth Blackwell's claim to fame?

8. Because John Merrick suffered from the physical ailment known as neurofibromatosis, he was nicknamed what?

9. Who held Medicare card #1?

10. What Cleveland osteopath was sent to prison in 1954 for the murder of his wife? (While in prison he became one of the first men to be inoculated with live cancer cells.)

Multiple Births

1. What is the birth of four babies called?

2. What is the birth of five babies called?

3. What are the first names of the Dionne quintuplets?

4. Who was the only left-handed one among the Dionne quintuplets?

5. What was the name of Elvis Presley's twin brother, who died at birth?

6. What great American Olympic pentathlon and decathlon champion had a twin brother?

7. Who are the only twin brothers to be selected to the college All-American football team?

8. What twin brothers finished first and second in the men's slalom at the 1984 Winter Olympics, winning the Gold and Silver Medals?

9. On June 6, 1981, what first did twins Stephen and Amanda establish when they were born in Australia?

10. On August 25, 1981, what actor's wife gave birth to triplet girls—Barbara, Gwyneth, and Pilar?

5.   Smallpox
6.   Vitamins
7.   On January 23, 1849, she became the first woman doctor, when she was granted her medical degree.
8.   The Elephant Man
9.   Harry S Truman
10. Sam Sheppard

Multiple Births (Answers)

1.   Quadruplets
2.   Quintuplets
3.   Annette, Cecile, Emilie, Marie, and Yvonne
4.   Marie
5.   Jessie Garon
6.   Jim Thorpe
7.   Mike and Marvin McKeever
8.   Phil and Steve Mahre
9.   First test tube twins
10. Richard Thomas's (wife's name is Alma)

Scientists

1. Who was the first woman scientist to be awarded a Nobel Prize?
2. Name the ship used by Charles Darwin on his around-the-world cruise of exploration.
3. Who was the Italian physicist who performed the first controlled nuclear chain reaction?
4. What scientist, instrumental in nuclear theory, could not get a security clearance from the U.S. government to work on the atom bomb?
5. Who discovered penicillin?
6. What British scientist is noted for his work with heat?
7. Who discovered "charmed quarks," and thus won a Nobel Prize for physics?
8. Who created the transistor component?
9. Name the Austrian monk who became famous for his work on heredity.
10. What physicist invented the wireless telegraph or radio?
11. What U.S. plant breeder developed the study of plants into a science of its own?
12. What British physicist discovered the nucleus of the atom?
13. Who is credited with being the Father of Modern Chemistry?
14. What British astronomer calculated the orbits of the planets and had a comet named after him?
15. Who was the director of Los Alamos nuclear research center for the development of the atom bomb?
16. Who introduced the Fahrenheit scale for thermometers?
17. Name the German engineer who pioneered the development of the automobile.
18. What U.S. electrical engineer developed the first electronic computer?
19. What Swiss psychiatrist is the founder of analytical psychology?
20. Name the British scientist/philosopher who posited the laws of gravity in motion?

Scientists (Answers)

1. Madame Curie
2. H.M.S. *Beagle*
3. Enrico Fermi
4. Albert Einstein
5. Alexander Fleming
6. William Kelvin
7. Burton Richter and Samuel Ting
8. William Shockley
9. Gregor Mendel
10. Marconi
11. Luther Burbank
12. Ernest Rutherford
13. Anton Lavoisier
14. Edmund Halley
15. J. Robert Oppenheimer
16. Gabriel Fahrenheit
17. Gottlieb Daimler
18. Vannevar Bush
19. Carl Jung
20. Issac Newton

Speed

1. What is the regulation speed of the U.S. Army's marching?
2. What is the speed of light?
3. How long did it take an SR-71 aircraft to fly New York to Paris with refueling en-route?
4. He has been called the fastest hockey player on ice, having been clocked on the ice once at 29.7 miles per hour. Name him.
5. Who was clocked throwing a pitch at 100.9 mph at Anaheim Stadium on August 20, 1974?
6. Who, in 1973, served up the fastest recorded tennis serve, which was clocked at 154 mph?
7. What is the fastest bird in the world?
8. What is the speed of mach 1?
9. What is the fastest mammal, having been clocked at over 60 mph?
10. Who is faster than a speeding bullet?

Temperatures

1. What is the average temperature on the planet Venus?
2. What reading is $-273.16°C$ or $-459.69°F$?
3. What is the average temperature of a human body?
4. Who had a #7 hit record in 1967 with the title of "98.6"?
5. What is the freezing point of water?
6. At what temperature should Saki be served?
7. At what temperature does the Fahrenheit and centigrade (Celsius) scales coincide?
8. At what temperature does book paper catch fire and burn? (It is also the title of a 1953 novel by Ray Bradbury.)
9. What is the constant regulated temperature of the Astro-dome?
10. What novel began with the opening line "The temperature hit ninety degrees the day she arrived"?

Speed (Answers)

1. 3 miles per hour
2. 186,272 miles per second (rounded off to 186,000 mps)
3. 1 hour, 56 minutes
4. Bobby Hull
5. Nolan Ryan
6. Michael Sangster
7. Spine-tailed swift
8. 760 mph at sea level/650 mph at 35,000 feet and above
9. Cheetah
10. Superman

Temperatures (Answers)

1. 800°F
2. Absolute zero
3. 98.6
4. Keith (James Berry Keefer)
5. 32°F
6. 98.5°F
7. −40°
8. Fahrenheit 451
9. 72°F
10. *Valley of the Dolls* by Jacqueline Susann

Vitamins

1. What movie character has a brand of vitamins manufactured by Squibb named after him?
2. Name the sunshine vitamin.
3. Name the two television cartoon characters who have vitamins named after them.
4. What vitamin that prevents scurvy can be obtained in great quantities by eating citrus fruits?
5. What vitamin is made of thiamine?
6. What vitamin, called phylloquinone, is concerned with the normal clotting of blood as well as functions of the liver?
7. Name the brand of vitamins that is a by-product of a video game?
8. Beriberi is caused by what vitamin deficiency?
9. What vitamin is made of ascorbic acid?
10. What vitamin is made of riboflavin?

Weather

1. What is the wettest state in the Union?
2. On July 10, 1913, a record high temperature was set in the United States. Where did it occur?
3. What is the name of the Pennsylvania groundhog who comes out of his hole on Ground Hog Day to see if winter is over?
4. Who is credited with the quote "Everybody talks about the weather, but nobody does anything about it"?
5. The tradition of naming hurricanes after females was begun in 1952 by the U.S. Weather Bureau. What book inspired this tradition?
6. According to the heads of the National Weather Service, what must the wind velocity be forecast at in order to establish a hurricane warning?
7. When a tornado occurs over water, what is it called?
8. What results when the temperature and the dew point are within 3° of each other?

Vitamins (Answers)

1. E.T.
2. D
3. Bugs Bunny and Fred Flintstone
4. C
5. B_1
6. K
7. Pac Man vitamins
8. B_1
9. C
10. B_2

Weather (Answers)

1. Hawaii
2. Death Valley
3. Punxsutawney Phil
4. Mark Twain
5. *Storm* by George Stewart
6. 74 knots or more
7. A waterspout
8. Fog

9. What is the scientific name given to both the Northern and Southern lights?
10. What is the scientific study of weather called?

Weights and Measures

1. How many tablespoons are in a cup?
2. How many quarts in a gallon?
3. What is measured by the Beaufort scale?
4. 29.92 is a typical reading for what instrument?
5. What is 550 foot-pounds per second equal to?
6. How many pounds does a British man weigh if he weighs 11 stone?
7. How many items are in a baker's dozen?
8. What two measurements appear in both degrees of a circle as well as in time?
9. What country measures road distances in versts?
10. What name is given to the unit of mass that weighs approximately 2.2046 pounds?

9.   Aurora Borealis and Aurora Australis
10.   Meteorology

Weights and Measures (Answers)

1.   16
2.   4
3.   Wind speed (knots)
4.   A barometer
5.   1 horsepower
6.   154 pounds (1 stone = 14 pounds)
7.   13
8.   Minutes and seconds
9.   Russia
10.   Kilogram

Music and Radio

Anthems

1. "Hatikvak" is the national anthem of what country that came into existence in 1948?
2. When Brooklyn's Ebbets Field ball park was officially opened on April 9, 1913, who sang "The Star-Spangled Banner"?
3. What was the original title of Francis Scott Key's poem that later became known as "The Star-Spangled Banner"?
4. "Ever Onward" is the anthem of what giant communications and electronics firm?
5. What is the name of the official Nazi anthem, which was composed by Horst Wessel and adapted by Joseph Goebbels?
6. What is the national anthem of Great Britain, which is even played at the end of a film in a movie theater?
7. "Lift Every Voice and Sing" is the unofficial national anthem of what group?
8. What two national anthems are played at every baseball All-Star Game?
9. "March On, March On" is the title of what country's national anthem?
10. A version of "The Star-Spangled Banner" peaked at #50 on the *Billboard* Hot 100 chart in 1968. Recorded live at the World Series in Detroit, who sang the song?

Big Bands

1. *Rumba Is My Life* is the 1948 autobiography of what band leader?
2. In the 1940s female band leader Ina Ray Hutton married another band leader. Name him.
3. The Cabaliers was the name of whose jazzy band?
4. What rock singer with two #1 hit records to his credit is the son of what big band leader?

121

Anthems (Answers)

1. Israel
2. Charles Ebbets, President of the Brooklyn Dodgers
3. "The Defense of Fort McHenry"
4. IBM
5. "Horst Wessel Song"
6. "God Save the King (or Queen)"
7. American blacks
8. Canadian and U.S.
9. People's Republic of China
10. José Feliciano

Big Bands (Answers)

1. Xavier Cugat
2. Randy Brooks
3. Cab Calloway
4. Rick Nelson—son of Ozzie Nelson

5. Whose band of the 1920s and 1930s was called the Connecticut Yankees?

6. Name the band leader who developed the radio giveaway show "Pot of Gold," which became so popular that it inspired a 1941 James Stewart movie?

7. Who led the big band called The Band of Renown?

8. The brother of a very popular singer led a band called The Bobcats. Name him.

9. Glenn Miller was the first artist to receive a solid gold record (awarded on February 10, 1942) for a million-selling single. What was the name of the song?

10. Name five of the eight big band leaders whose last name began with an *H?*

11. What band leader won the Gold Cup in 1946 for unlimited hydroplane racing?

12. What band was the first to appear on television?

13. Sexy singer Charo not only sang with an orchestra, but she married its leader. Name him.

14. Name the two bands that Doris Day sang with.

15. What 1930s band leader used the catch-line "Yow-suh, yow-suh, yow-suh"?

16. Although he died in 1956, his band had the 1958 hit song "Tea for Two Cha Cha." Name the band.

17. Singer Jo Stafford married what band leader?

18. Talk show host, Merv Griffin, was once the singer for whose orchestra?

19. Give both Benny Goodman's opening and closing theme songs?

20. Whose band was known as the Herd or Thundering Herd?

Big Band Theme Songs

Name the theme songs for the following leaders' big bands:

1. Ray Anthony
2. Fletcher Henderson
3. Harry James
4. Guy Lombardo
5. George Shearing
6. Lawrence Welk
7. Bunny Berrigan

5.　Rudy Vallee
6.　Horace Heidt
7.　Les Brown
8.　Bob Crosby
9.　"Chattanooga Choo Choo"
10.　Edgar Hayes, Earl Hines, Fletcher Henderson, Horace Henderson, Les Hite, Claude Hopkins, Woody Herman, and Teddy Hill
11.　Guy Lombardo
12.　Fred Waring and the Pennsylvanians
13.　Xavier Cugat
14.　Bob Crosby and Les Brown
15.　Ben Bernie
16.　Tommy Dorsey
17.　Paul Weston
18.　Freddy Martin's
19.　"Let's Dance" (opening) and "Good-bye" (closing)
20.　Woody Herman

Big Band Theme Songs (Answers)

1.　"Young Man with a Horn"
2.　"Christopher Columbus"
3.　"Ciribiribin"
4.　"Auld Lang Syne"
5.　"Lullaby of Birdland"
6.　"Bubbles in the Wine"
7.　"I Can't Get Started"

8.   Tommy Dorsey
9.   Vincent Lopez
10. Glenn Miller

Celebrity Recordings

1.   "Wand'rin' Star" from the 1969 motion picture *Paint Your Wagon* went to the #1 position on the British charts for whom in 1970?
2.   On the flip side of the above recording was another excerpt from the film score. A song titled "I Talk To The Trees." Who sang this song?
3.   In 1980 what 83-year-old comedian made the record charts with the song "I Wish I Were Eighteen Again"?
4.   In 1967 what actor made the Top 40 with the song "Little Ole Wine Drinker Me"? Another actor's version peaked at #96. Name him too.
5.   "Let's Do Something Cheap and Superficial" charted in Billboard's Hot 100, peaking at #88 in 1980. Who sang it?
6.   While in college, Jose Ferrer's college band backed up what future actor on his recording of "Love Comes But Once"?
7.   What comedian performed "The Pledge of Allegiance" on his TV show in 1969? A recording of the song made the Billboard charts that same year.
8.   To celebrate the birth of his daughter, Jennifer, in 1961, what actor made his singing debut with the song "Christmas Lullaby"?
9.   What was so unusual about the hit record "Back Home"—#1 in Britain in August 1970?
10. What Hollywood actress charted a minor hit in 1967 with "Felicidad"?

Classical Music

1.   To whom did Ludwig Beethoven dedicate his third symphony, "Eroica," when he wrote it in 1804?
2.   On what classical piece was Freddy Martin and his Orchestra's theme song "Tonight We Love" based?

8.   "I'm Getting Sentimental Over You"
9.   "Nola"
10. "Moonlight Serenade" and "Slumber Song"

Celebrity Recordings (Answers)

1.   Lee Marvin
2.   Clint Eastwood
3.   George Burns
4.   Dean Martin and Robert Mitchum, respectively
5.   Burt Reynolds
6.   James Stewart
7.   Red Skelton
8.   Cary Grant
9.   It was recorded by the English World Cup Squad (soccer)
10. Sally Field

Classical Music (Answers)

1.   Napoleon
2.   Tchaikovsky's First Piano Concerto

3. What classical ballet by Tchaikovsky can be heard over the opening credits of the 1931 Bela Lugosi film *Dracula?*
4. Who are the three *B*'s of classical music?
5. Who composed the ballets *The Firebird*, in 1910, and *The Rite of Spring,* in 1913?
6. What classical Russian composer was a graduate of the Naval Academy at St. Petersburg?
7. What opera was composed for the opening of the Suez Canal?
8. What Austrian musician composed the *Unfinished Symphony?*
9. What classical piece did Maurice Ravel compose for dancer Ida Rubinstein in 1928?
10. Who had the best-selling 1982 album titled "Hooked on Classics"?

Composers

1. What figure of history is credited with composing the traditional English ballad "Greensleeves"?
2. What popular composer titled his 1947 autobiography *Washboard Blues* after one of his hit songs?
3. Who composed the beautiful classic "White Christmas"?
4. C.A.P. are the initials of what composer (1893–1964)?
5. What Vice-President of the United States and Nobel Prize-winner wrote the tune on which the 1958 Tommy Edwards hit song "It's All in the Game" was based?
6. Clifford "Tippy" Gray, the composer of such songs as "If You Were the Only Girl in the World" and "Got a Date with an Angel," won a gold medal in 1932 Olympics. What was his event?
7. Who composed, in 1962, Freddie Cannon's hit rock 'n' roll record "Palisades Park"?
8. Harry Carmichael wrote the music, but who composed the lyrics for the evergreen "Stardust"?
9. Who composed the lyrics with Johnny Burke and Sammy Cahn to Frank Sinatra's 1944 hit record "Nancy with the Laughing Face"?
10. Who composed Johnny Carson's "Tonight Show" TV theme "Here's Johnny"?

3. "Swan Lake"
4. Bach, Beethoven, and Brahms
5. Igor Stravinsky
6. Rimsky-Korsakov
7. Verdi's *Aida*
8. Franz Schubert
9. *Bolero*
10. Royal Philharmonic Orchestra

Composers (Answers)

1. King Henry VIII
2. Hoagy Carmichael
3. Irving Berlin
4. Cole Albert Porter
5. Charles G. Dawes
6. He was a member of the U.S. four-man bobsled team.
7. Chuck Barris
8. Mitchell Parrish
9. Phil Silvers
10. Paul Anka

Concerts

1. St. Louis policeman Ralph Mcnail made many of the nation's papers when his photo with two bullets striking his ears was shown during a concert in 1982. Who was the featured artist?
2. While taping a CBS TV special at Pasadena's Ambassador Auditorium on March 3, 1977, what singer fell 20 feet into the orchestra pit, rupturing a disc?
3. What was the first rock group to play New York City's Carnegie Hall, in April 1971?
4. When the Beatles first appeared on the Ed Sullivan TV program in February 9, 1964, what two Presidential relatives were in the audience?
5. What two members of a one-time duet got together once again to perform in New York's Central Park in 1983?
6. Who were the featured performers at the Altamont festival in California in 1968?
7. Stephen Wozniak, the co-founder of Apple Computers, set up what rock concert over the Labor Day weekend of 1982?
8. In what city were 11 youths killed when they were trampled to death in a rush to get general admission tickets for a Who concert on December 3, 1979?
9. Where did the Beatles give their final live concert on August 29, 1966?
10. On what three days did the Woodstock Music Festival take place?

Conductors and Orchestras

1. What orchestra did John Williams conduct for the recording of his famous soundtrack for the 1977 movie *Star Wars?*
2. Who replaced the late Arthur Fiedler as the conductor of the Boston Pops?
3. Who led the U.S. Marine Corps band before he retired to write such classics as "Stars and Stripes Forever" and "Semper Fidelis"?
4. Comedian Dudley Moore played an orchestra conductor in what two movies?

Concerts (Answers)

1. Elton John
2. Bing Crosby
3. Chicago
4. Julie and Tricia Nixon
5. Paul Simon and Art Garfunkel
6. The Rolling Stones
7. US Festival
8. Cincinnati
9. Candlestick Park in San Francisco
10. August 15–17, 1969

Conductors and Orchestras (Answers)

1. The London Symphony
2. John Williams
3. John Philip Sousa
4. *Foul Play* (1978) and *Unfaithfully Yours* (1984)

5. What note does an orchestra conductor use to coordinate the adjustment of pitch for his musicians' instruments?

6. Sarah Caldwell founded and conducted what opera company that celebrated its 25th anniversary in 1984?

7. Who conducted the New York Philharmonic from 1958 to 1969? He also composed the musical *West Side Story*.

8. Who has been the conductor of the Pittsburgh Symphony since 1976?

9. Who directed the Cincinnati Symphony from 1909 to 1912 and the Philadelphia Orchestra from 1912 to 1936?

10. What are the four sections of an orchestra?

Country Music—Autobiographies

1. *Living Proof* is the 1979 autobiography of the son of what member of Country Music Hall of Fame?

2. Who authored the 1976 autobiography *Coal Miner's Daughter*?

3. What member of Country Music's Hall of Fame titled his 1969 autobiography *It's a Long Way from Chester County*?

4. *Country Gentleman* is the 1974 memories of what musician/producer member of Country's Hall of Fame?

5. What folksinger's 1968 autobiography was titled *Bound for Glory?*

6. *Sing Me Back Home* is the fascinating story of what popular country troubador?

7. Anne Murray's 1981 autobiography was titled *Anne Murray _____ _____*. What are the other two words in the title?

8. Who authored the 1978 soul-searching book *Disciple in Blue Suede Shoes*?

9. *From Harper Valley to the Mountain Top* is the title of whose 1981 story?

10. What country singer's 1979 autobiography has the same title as her biggest hit record, as well as a 1981 TV movie that was based on her life?

5. A
6. Opera Company of Boston
7. Leonard Bernstein
8. Andre Previn
9. Leopold Stokowski
10. Percussion, strings, brass, and woodwinds

Country Music—Autobiographies (Answers)

1. Hank Williams
2. Loretta Lynn
3. Eddy Arnold
4. Chet Atkins
5. Woody Guthrie's
6. Merle Haggard
7. *So Far*
8. Carl Perkins
9. Jeannie C. Riley's
10. Tammy Wynette's *(Stand by Your Man)*

Country Music—Male

1. What country singer has had more #1 hit songs on the country charts?
2. Randy Owen is the lead singer of what country supergroup?
3. What country singer suffered severe damage to his face and body when he fell off Montana's Ajax Mountain, on August 8, 1975?
4. To many people's surprise, when this country singer's *All My Best* album was advertised on TV in 1979 and 1980, it sold over a million and a half copies. Name him.
5. What was the country song composed and recorded by Al Dexter in 1943, which became the first country song to be sung on radio's *Your Hit Parade?*
6. What popular country singer has an acute case of stuttering when he speaks, yet it totally disappears when he sings?
7. What late country singer is a member of both the Cowboy Hall of Fame and the Country Music Hall of Fame and is also the father of a popular actor?
8. What country artist had the longest stay at #1 of any country hit?
9. What two country singers host the TV show "Hee Haw"?
10. What country artist had a #1 hit record on the pop charts in 1957 with "Young Love"?

Country Music—Nicknames

1. Cecil "Marty" Martin is more well-known by what nickname?
2. Who is nicknamed the Mother of Country Music?
3. What great country singer was nicknamed the Singing Brakeman?
4. What popular country singer, who has been recording since the 1950s, is known as the Southern Gentleman?
5. What Grand Ole Opry favorite was nicknamed the Texas Troubadour?
6. What country artist has been know as the Cherokee Cowboy, while his back-up band is called the Cherokee Cowboys?
7. Who is Whispering Bill?
8. The Country Gentleman is the nickname of what guitarist?

Country Music—Male (Answers)

1. Conway Twitty
2. Alabama
3. Hank Williams, Jr.
4. Slim Whitman
5. "Pistol Packin' Mama"
6. Mel Tillis
7. Tex Ritter (father of John Ritter)
8. Hank Snow (his record "I'm Movin On" stayed at #1 in 1950 for 21 weeks)
9. Buck Owens and Roy Clark
10. Sonny James

Country Music—Nicknames (Answers)

1. Boxcar Willie
2. Maybelle Carter
3. Jimmie Rodgers
4. Sonny James
5. Ernest Tubb
6. Ray Price
7. Bill Anderson
8. Chet Atkins

9. What rock singer turned country singer is nicknamed the Silver Fox?

10. What late country singer with a voice as smooth as silk was nicknamed Gentleman Jim?

Disc Jockeys

1. In 1957, Buffalo radio disc jockey, Tom Clay, was fired after he barricaded himself in the control room and played what record for 17 consecutive hours?

2. Who played a disc jockey in a Carmel, California, radio station in the 1971 movie *Play Misty for Me?*

3. His real name is Barry Hansen, but by what name is this zany syndicated player of novelty recordings from the present all the way back to the earliest days of recordings known?

4. He has been called the father of FM radio. This San Francisco disc jockey founded Autumn records, which recorded the Beau Brummels and Bobby Freeman, hiring Sly Stone as a producer. Name him.

5. Who plays the zany disc jockey Dr. Johnny Fever on the TV series "WKRP in Cincinnati"?

6. On October 12, 1969, Detroit WKNR-FM disc jockey Russ Gibb made a startling discovery, after studying a number of clues on both album jackets and on various songs. What misconception did Gibb create that day?

7. Although several people have been known as the Fifth Beatle, what New York City disc jockey held the title in 1964?

8. WAKY radio station's disc jockey Gary Guthrie created what hit duet recording when he spliced together two solo versions of what song?

9. Considered to have been the first disc jockey, he originated the "Make Believe Ballroom," on Los Angeles's KFWB radio in the 1930s. Name him.

10. Name the gruff-sounding disc jockey who hosted the TV series "Midnight Special". (His real name is Robert Smith.)

9. Charlie Rich
10. Jim Reeves

Disc Jockeys (Answers)

1. "That'll Be the Day" by the Crickets
2. Clint Eastwood
3. Dr. Demento
4. Tom Donahue
5. Howard Hesseman
6. That Paul McCartney of the Beatles was dead
7. Murray the K
8. "You Don't Send Me Flowers" by Barbra Streisand and Neil Diamond
9. Al Jarvis
10. Wolfman Jack

Girl Groups

1. What Sheboygan, Wisconsin, group became the first guests on the TV series "American Bandstand" in the 1950s?
2. Who established themselves as the best-selling female singing group of all time before their lead singer left to establish a solo career?
3. Belinda Carlisle is the lead singer of what all-female rock group?
4. What 1960s female rock group consisted of two sets of sisters?
5. Record producer Phil Spector was once married to the lead singer of what group?
6. Martha Reeves was the lead singer of what Motown girl singing group?
7. Which Phil Spector produced group had such hits as "He's a Rebel" and "Da Doo Ron Ron"?
8. The Harlots are the female back-up singers for what singer?
9. In the late 1970s, Rosemary Clooney, Rose Marie, Helen O'Connell, and Margaret Whiting formed a nightclub singing act named what?
10. What 1960s girl group had the #1 hit song "My Boyfriend's Back"?

Gospel Music Hymns

1. Who is called the Queen of the Gospel singers?
2. Who is called the Father of the English hymn?
3. Although it has been written that the crew and passengers sang the hymn "Nearer My God To Thee," as the *Titanic* sank, in reality they sang another hymn. What was it?
4. What is the hymn of the United States Air Force?
5. What is the hymn of the U.S. Marines?
6. What is the hymn of the U.S. Navy?
7. What is the hymn of the U.S. Army?
8. What is the hymn of the U.S. Coast Guard?
9. What popular song was sung by Maybelle Carter, Johnny Cash, and June Carter as the last performance at the Grand Ole Opry at Ryma's Auditorium on March 15, 1974?

Girl Groups (Answers)

1. The Chordettes
2. The Supremes (or Diana Ross and the Supremes)
3. The Go-Go's
4. The Shangri-las
5. The Ronettes
6. Martha and the Vandellas
7. The Crystals
8. Bette Midler
9. 4 Girls 4
10. The Angels

Gospel Music/Hymns (Answers)

1. Mahalia Jackson
2. Isaac Watts
3. "Autumn"
4. "Wild Blue Yonder" ("Off we go . . .")
5. "Marine Hymn"
6. "Anchors Aweigh"
7. "As the Caisons Go Rolling Along"
8. "Semper Paratus"
9. "Will the Circle Be Broken"

10. What composer of such songs as "This Ole House" and "Beyond the Sunset," ran for President of the United States on the Prohibition Ticket in 1952?

Jazz

1. Name four jazz greats who were named for royalty?
2. Count Basie, Cozy Cole, and Buck Johnson all have what same first name?
3. Who is called the Father of the Blues?
4. What jazz musician scored the 1959 movie *Anatomy of a Murder*, starring James Stewart and Lee Remick?
5. In 1961, The Dave Brubeck Quartet placed their only record in the Top 40 with what instrumental?
6. What was the first TV series to feature a jazz musical score?
7. What is the source of Louis Armstrong's nickname of Satchmo?
8. What type of music do Mel Torme and Benjamin Leroy Crothers sing?
9. Who was known as "Bird"?
10. Who were the members of the Benny Goodman Trio?

Musical Groups

1. Edwin P. Christy founded what musical group in 1842?
2. Bing Crosby, Harry Barris (father of Chuck Barris), and Al Rinker were known as what singing trio?
3. James Petrozelli, Patty Principi, Fred Tramburo, and Frank Sinatra sang together under what name in the mid-1930s?
4. Stephen Stills, John Sebastion, Paul Williams, Jerry Yester, Danny Hutton, and Paul Peterson all failed an audition to become a member of what musical assembly?
5. What U.S. President played trombone in a musical group called the Silver Cornet Band?
6. What comic and star of the 1979 musical *They're Playing Our Song* appeared on the Ted Mack Amateur Hour at age 14 with a vocal group called the Teen Tones?
7. Who was the lead singer of an unfamous rock 'n' roll group called Beaver and the Trappers?

10. Stuart Hamblen

Jazz (Answers)

1. Count Basie, King Oliver, Duke Ellington, and Earl Hines
2. William
3. William C. Handy
4. Duke Ellington
5. "Take Five"
6. "Peter Gunn" by Henry Mancini
7. It originally meant Satchel Mouth
8. Scat music (or Bebop)
9. Charlie Parker
10. Benny Goodman, Teddy Wilson, and Gene Krupa

Musical Groups (Answers)

1. The Christy Minstrels
2. The Rhythm Boys
3. Hoboken Four
4. The Monkees
5. Warren G. Harding
6. Robert Klein
7. Jerry Mathers

8. Name the singer for whom the back-up group was the Blue Moon Boys.
9. What Hollywood actor often plays banjo with the Beverly Hills Unlisted Jazz Band?
10. What was the name of Spike Jones's zany band?

Musical Instruments

1. How was Jerry Lee Lewis and the musical instrument he played credited on his early Sun Record releases?
2. Nero played what instrument while Rome burned?
3. When Paul McCartney played his instrument on Ringo Star's 1974 hit song "You're Sixteen" it became the first #1 hit song to feature this instrument. Name it.
4. What is the name of blues singer B. B. King's guitar?
5. What is the name of the guitar that Eric Clapton gave to his close friend Beatle George Harrison in 1968?
6. The Beatles and the Rolling Stones used what exotic Indian instrument on a few of their recordings in the 1960s?
7. What musical instrument did Glen Miller play?
8. Radio's Bob Burns created what musical instrument? Its name was later borrowed for the name of a World War II army weapon.
9. What musical instrument did Harpo Marx play in the zany Marx Brothers' films?
10. What instrument did Jack Webb's character play in the 1955 movie *Pete Kelly's Blues?*

Music Videos

1. What do the initials AVA stand for?
2. Who was the first inductee into the AVA's Hall of Fame in 1983?
3. Cable network MTV was created to show the latest music videos. What does MTV stand for?
4. Paul McCartney, Michael Jackson, and Linda Eastman-McCartney appeared in what video to promote the McCartney-Jackson hit?
5. In 1983, Dean Martin made a video based on a 1950s rhythm and blues song. What was it?

8. Elvis Presley
9. George Segal
10. The City Slickers

Musical Instruments (Answers)

1. Jerry Lee Lewis and His Pumping Piano
2. Lyre (not the fiddle, since it hadn't been invented yet)
3. Kazoo
4. Lucille
5. Lucy
6. Sitar
7. Trombone
8. Bazooka
9. Harp
10. Cornet

Music Videos (Answers)

1. American Video Awards
2. Paul McCartney
3. Music Television
4. "Say Say Say"
5. "Since I Met You Baby"

6. What actress appeared in Billy Joel's "Uptown Girl" video?
7. In 1984, Chad Stuart and Jeremy Clyde rejoined, after their split in 1969, to record "Bite the Bullet." What actress made a cameo on the video?
8. Who directed Michael Jackson's "Thriller" video?
9. What comedian made a cameo in Billy Joel's "Tell Her About It" video?
10. In Cindy Lauper's video of her song "Girls Just Want to Have Fun," who plays her father?

Original Song Titles

1. "Bright Mohawk Valley" is the original title of director John Ford's favorite song. Name it.
2. What Duke Ellington classic song was originally titled "Dreamy Blues"?
3. Paul McCartney originally titled what Beatles ballad "Scrambled Egg"?
4. Felicia Sanders introduced what song in 1954 as "In Other Words"?
5. "The Ocean Burial" was the original title of what popular folk song sung by cowboys out west?
6. "Daisy Hawkins" was the working title for which Beatles hit song?
7. "Alexander and His Clarinet" was the original title that Irving Berlin gave to which of his 1910 compositions?
8. Elvis Presley's beautiful 1956 ballad "Love Me Tender" was based on what traditional folk song?
9. What Andrew Sisters classic was originally titled "Anywhere the Bluebird Goes"?
10. When this song originally was sung in the 1932 play *The Great Magoo* it was titled "If You Don't Believe Me," but what is its more popular title?
11. "I Have No Words" was the original title of what Howard Dietz-Arthur Schwartz song.
12. What traditional folk song was originally known, in 1888, by the title "Frankie and Albert"?
13. What Bert Kalmar, Oscar Hammerstein II, and Harry Ruby song was originally titled "Moonlight on the Meadows"?

6. Christine Brinkley
7. Lauren Hutton
8. John Landis
9. Rodney Dangerfield
10. Lou Albano

Original Song Titles (Answers)

1. "Red River Valley"
2. "Mood Indigo"
3. "Yesterday"
4. "Fly Me to the Moon"
5. "Bury Me Not on the Lone Prairie"
6. "Eleanor Rigby"
7. "Alexander's Ragtime Band"
8. "Aura Lee"
9. "Don't Sit under the Apple Tree (with Anyone Else but Me)"
10. "It's Only a Paper Moon"
11. "Something to Remember You By"
12. "Frankie and Johnny"
13. "A Kiss to Build a Dream On"

14. Written in 1939, what big band classic tune was originally titled "Tar Paper Stomp" by its composers Andy Razaf and Joe Garland?

15. What was the controversial original title of George M. Cohan's classic tune "You're a Grand Old Flag"?

16. "You're the Flower of My Heart, Sweet Rosalie" was the original title of what 1903 song?

17. "The Bad in Every Man" is the original title of what Rodgers and Hart song?

18. John Latouche, Ted Fetter, and Vernon Duke composed a 1940 hit titled "Fooling Around With Love." What is the tune better known as?

19. What popular song of the early 1940s did Jules Styne and Frank Loesser originally compose for evangelist Aimee Semple McPherson as "I Don't Want to Walk without You, Jesus"?

20. "Red River" was the working title of what hit song by Henry Mancini?

Radio

1. Who played the lead role of Judy Grimes on the radio series "Junior Miss"?

2. Where were the two Conelrad frequencies on the A.M. radio dial?

3. What was the nickname given to the buzzer on the radio program "Truth or Consequences"?

4. Walter Vaughn, who played Harold Sayers on the radio series "Crime Doctor," is the father of what actor?

5. What comedian actually married his wife, Marjorie, on an episode of the radio program "Bride and Groom"?

6. Who did *Time* magazine nickname, in 1939, the "First Lady of Radio"?

7. Who played the western hero Britt Ponset on the 1952 radio series "The Six-Shooter"?

8. Who played the role of Marshal Matt Dillon on radio's "Gun-smoke"?

9. James Melghan and who else played the role of Flash Gordon on radio?

10. Name the wife of the son of the orchestra leader who provided the music for the radio series "The Baby Snooks Show"?

14. "In the Mood"
15. "You're a Grand Old Rag"
16. "Sweet Adeline"
17. "Blue Moon"
18. "Taking a Chance on Love"
19. "I Don't Want to Walk without You, Baby"
20. "Moon River"

Radio (Answers)

1. Shirley Temple
2. 640 and 1240
3. Beulah
4. Robert Vaughn
5. Dick Van Dyke
6. Kate Smith
7. James Stewart
8. William Conrad
9. Gale Gordon
10. Toni Tennille (Her husband is Darryl Dragon, son of the show's orchestra leader, Carmen Dragon.)

Radio Stations

1. KSFO is a foremost radio station in what city?
2. In 1932, President Ronald Reagan began his sportscasting career on what Des Moines, Iowa, station?
3. What Pittsburgh radio station became a part of history when they broadcast the first election returns?
4. What Detroit radio station became the first commercial radio station in the United States when it began broadcasting on August 20, 1920?
5. What is the name of the Lubbock, Texas radio station where Buddy Holly and Bob Montgomery hosted a show and where Waylon Jennings worked as a disc jockey?
6. On what Detroit radio station did the Lone Ranger originate?
7. Who read the Sunday comics to the children of his city over WNYC radio when the newspapers went on strike in 1937?
8. What format did Mexico radio station XTRA introduce in 1961?
9. In 1924, Sears Roebuck and Co.-owned Chicago radio station WLS began broadcasting. What did WLS stand for?
10. Originally, radio call letters began with a different letter, depending on whether the station was east or west of the Mississippi River. What are the two letters?

Record Labels

1. "His Master's Voice" has been the motto of what large American record company?
2. For what British record label did the Beatles record before forming their own label?
3. What record label did the Beatles form in 1968?
4. Both Okeh and Epic records are a subsidiary of what larger label?
5. What rock group founded their own Brother Record label?
6. After Clive Davies was fired from Columbia Records, he founded what label for which Barry Manilow and Dionne Warwick recorded?
7. In the 1970s Decca Records and its subsidiaries, Coral and Brunswick labels, became what larger label?

Radio Stations (Answers)

1. San Francisco
2. WHO
3. KDKA
4. WWJ
5. KDAV
6. WXYZ
7. Mayor Fiorello H. La Guardia
8. All news
9. World's largest store
10. W (east of Mississippi) and K (west of Mississippi)

Record Labels (Answers)

1. RCA Victor
2. Parlophone Records
3. Apple Records
4. Columbia Records
5. Beach Boys
6. Arista Records
7. MCA Records

8. What was the name of the first record label?
9. For what small Memphis record label did Elvis Presley record prior to recording for RCA Victor beginning in 1956?
10. What was the name of the record label founded by Frank Sinatra in the 1960s?

Singers' Autobiographies

1. What is the title of singer/actor Gene Autry's autobiography? The title is also the name of one of his hit recordings.
2. *Call Me Lucky* was the 1953 autobiography of what singer?
3. Her own story published in 1976 was titled *Her Own Story*. Name the singer?
4. What singer took the title of one of his hit records, *Laughter in the Rain,* as the title of his 1982 autobiography?
5. In 1965, with the help of Jane and Burt Boyal, Sammy Davis, Jr., penned his huge autobiography. Name it.
6. What black singer wrote her memoirs in 1956, titled *Thursday's Child?*
7. *Vocal Refrain* is the title of the autobiography of what British female singer who was popular during World War II?
8. This singer's 1956 autobiography is titled *Who Can Ask for Anything More?*
9. *A View from a Broad* is the 1980 title of a book by what singer/comedienne?
10. *This for Remembrance* was the title of the 1977 autobiography of what popular female singer of the 1950s?

Singing Brothers

1. Name the country group made up of Larry, Rudy, and Steve.
2. This singing brothers group of the 1950s consisted of Ed, Gene, Joe, and Vic. Their real last name is Urick. Name them.
3. Although these two characters were not related, they still billed themselves as the Blues Brothers. Name them.
4. Bobby Hatfield and Bill Medley, singers of blue-eyed soul, are better known by what name?

8. Edison Victrola Company (actually they originally made cylinders)
9. Sun Records
10. Reprise Records

Singers' Autobiographies (Answers)
1. *Back in the Saddle Again*
2. Bing Crosby
3. Doris Day
4. Neil Sedaka
5. *Yes I Can*
6. Eartha Kitt
7. Vera Lynn
8. Ethel Merman
9. Bette Midler
10. Rosemary Clooney

Singing Brothers (Answers)
1. Gatlin Brothers
2. Ames Brothers
3. Dan Aykroyd and John Belushi
4. Righteous Brothers

5. What brothers duet was consistently on the record charts until its popularity declined after both members joined the U.S. Marines?

6. When they originally began recording, they were billed as Two Boys and a Guitar. Who were they?

7. Their first names are Mark, Brett, and Bill. Bill has been married to both Cindy Williams and Goldie Hawn. Name the brothers.

8. Name the six Jackson brothers.

9. What Mormon family found great success beginning as a barbershop quartet?

10. Tom and Dick are the first names of the members of what brothers team of comic musicians and singers?

Singing Sisters

1. What is the last name of the sisters group of Connie, Vet, and Martha?

2. These young singers, who sang on the vaudeville circuit, were named Judy, Virginia, and Suzanne. Who were they?

3. Sisters Christine, Dorothy, and Phyllis had such hit records as "Sincerely" and "Sugartime." Name the group.

4. What are the first names of the beautiful and talented Mandrell Sisters?

5. What is the last name of the singing sisters Lily, Mary, and Ann?

6. Their first names were Maxene, LaVerne, and Patty. What was their group's name?

7. They are the daughters of not one but two minister parents, and their first names are Bonnie, Anita, June, and Ruth. Name the group.

8. What sisters group had members with the first names Geri, Bea, and Marge?

9. Who not only sang together with Fred Waring's orchestra, but appeared together in a series of films beginning with *Four Daughters* (1938)?

10. What sweet-looking sisters named Diane, Peggy, Kathy, and Janet sang together on TV's "The Lawrence Welk Show"?

5. Everly Brothers (Don and Phil)
6. Mills Brothers
7. Hudson Brothers
8. Jackie, Jeramaine, Maron, Michael, Randy, and Tito
9. Osmonds
10. Smothers Brothers

Singing Sisters (Answers)

1. Boswell Sisters
2. Gumm Sisters (Judy Garland was the "Judy" of the group.)
3. McGuire Sisters
4. Barbara, Louise, and Irlene
5. DeMarco Sisters
6. Andrew Sisters
7. Pointer Sisters
8. Fontane Sisters
9. Lane Sisters
10. Lennon Sisters

Song Lyrics

1. What two New York restaurants are mentioned in the lyric of the 1935 Al Dubin-Harry Warren song "Lullaby of Broadway"?
2. In the Glen Miller song "Chattanooga Choo Choo," from what track does the passenger train leave?
3. What is the cafe mentioned in the lyric of Barry Manilow's 1983 hit "Some Kind of Friend"?
4. What Hollywood actor is mentioned in the lyric of the 1929 Irving Berlin song "Puttin' on the Ritz"?
5. Fourth and Grant is an intersection mentioned in the lyric of what 1950 country song made popular by both Red Foley and Bing Crosby?
6. What actor and two actresses are mentioned in the lyric of the Frank Sinatra 1944 song "Nancy with the Laughing Face"?
7. What two planets are mentioned in the lyric of the 1954 hit song "Fly Me to the Moon"?
8. What motion picture studio is referred to in the lyric of the 1936 song "I Can't Get Started with You"?
9. Father McKenzie is a character featured in the lyric of what song?
10. What is the name of the small boy mentioned in the lyric of the British World War II song "The White Cliffs of Dover"?

Songs

1. What 1948 song composed by Buddy Kaye, Fred Wise, and Sidney Lippman is also known as "The Alphabet Song"?
2. Whenever a home run is hit by a Texas Astro in Houston's Astrodome, what song is played?
3. Originally titled "Good Morning to You," this 1893 composition by sisters Mildred and Patty Hills is still sung thousands of times each day. Name it.
4. What Christmas song originally began with these lyric "I'm sitting here in Beverly Hills . . ."
5. Who wrote the song "I Write the Songs"?
6. What is the unofficial anthem of the musical theater?

Song Lyrics (Answers)

1. Angelo's and Maxi's
2. Track 29
3. Beachwood Cafe
4. Gary Cooper
5. "Chattanoogie Shoe Shine Boy"
6. (Clark) Gable, (Dorothy) Lamour, and (Lana) Turner
7. Jupiter and Mars
8. Metro Goldwyn
9. "Eleanor Rigby"
10. Jimmy

Songs (Answers)

1. "A, You're Adorable"
2. "The Eyes of Texas"
3. "Happy Birthday to You"
4. "White Christmas"
5. Bruce Johnson
6. "There's No Business like Show Business"

7. Who is the only member of royalty to have appeared on a million-selling recording?

8. As an inside joke what song did comedian Peter Sellers have played at his funeral?

9. What song, written by Eben Alabez, became the first song to enter radio's *The Hit Parade* at the #1 position?

10. In 1960, what became the first song from a foreign-made movie to win an Oscar for Best Song?

Songs in History

1. What ballad was Nat "King" Cole singing at the time that he was attacked by a group of white men in Birmingham, Alabama, on March 10, 1956?

2. What song were the Rolling Stones in the process of playing during their famous Altamont Speedway free concert when one of the Hell's Angels security force knifed a member of the audience (an act that was captured on film)?

3. Marilyn Monroe will forever be remembered for singing what song to President John F. Kennedy at Madison Square Garden on May 21, 1962?

4. When British General Charles Cornwallis surrendered to George Washington at Yorktown on October 19, 1781, what song was being played?

5. At the moment of impact of these two ocean liners on July 26, 1956, the ship's band on one of them was playing the song "Arrivederci Roma" in the ballroom. Name the ships.

6. What was the name of the song that President Gerald Ford asked Queen Elizabeth II to dance to at the Bicentennial Ball at the White House?

7. "See, the Conquering Hero" was played by a band welcoming a rider in San Francisco on April 14, 1861. What was the occassion?

8. What New York mayor used "Will You Love Me in December as You Do in May" as his campaign song, which he also co-wrote?

9. What American song composed by Francis Hopkinson was based on the British drinking song "Battle of the Kegs"?

10. Name one of the two songs played as Col. Armstrong Custer and the 7th Calvary left Fort Abraham Lincoln for the Little Big Horn.

7. Grace Kelly when she sang "True Love" in a duet with Bing Crosby
8. "In the Mood"
9. "Nature Boy"
10. "Never on Sunday"

Songs in History (Answers)

1. "Autumn Leaves"
2. "Under My Thumb"
3. "Happy Birthday to You"
4. "The World Turned Upside Down"
5. Italian liner *Andrea Doria* and the Swedish liner *Stockholm*
6. "The Lady Is a Tramp"
7. Arrival of first Pony Express rider
8. James Walker
9. "Yankee Doodle"
10. "Gary Owen" (regimental march) and "The Girl I Left Behind Me"

Song Subtitles

1. Written by Joni Mitchell, what 1968 hit song, sung by Judy Collins, was subtitled "Clouds"?
2. What is the subtitle of the 1919 comedy song "How Ya Gonna Keep 'Em Down on the Farm"?
3. "Means That You're Grand" is the subtitle to what 1937 Yiddish song with English lyrics?
4. "Keeps Rainin' All the Time" is the subtitle of what 1933 Ted Koehler-Harold Arlen song?
5. What is the subtitle to the Beatles song "Norwegian Wood"?
6. What Beatles ballad was given the unofficial subtitle of "Ringo's Theme," because Ringo sang lead?
7. "Bicycle Built For Two" is the subtitle of what song?
8. When the subtitle is included, what is the longest-titled song to have gone to #1 on *Billboard's* Hot 100 chart?
9. "Be Sure to Wear Flowers in Your Hair" is the subtitle of what 1967 hit by Scott McKenzie?
10. "To Everything There is a Season" is the subtitle of what 1960 hit by The Byrds?

Songwriting Teams

1. What composer along with lyricist Al Dubin wrote such classic tunes as "42nd Street," "Lullaby of Broadway," and "I Only Have Eyes for You"?
2. Joe Weber joined with what other composer to compose numerous Broadway musicals?
3. This brotherly songwriting team composed such classics as "I Got Rhythm" and "Love Walked In." Name them.
4. Who composed such hits as "Who's Sorry Now?" and "Three Little Words"?
5. Frederick Loewe teamed with what lyricist to compose many standards such as "Almost Like Being in Love"?
6. What is the most successful songwriting team, in record sales, of all time?

Song Subtitles (Answers)

1. "Both Sides Now"
2. "(After They've Seen Paree)"
3. "Beir Mir Bist Du Schoen"
4. "Stormy Weather"
5. "(This Bird Has Flown)"
6. "This Boy"
7. "Daisy Bell"
8. "(Hey, Won't You Play) Another Somebody Done Somebody Wrong Song" by B. J. Thomas
9. "San Francisco"
10. "Turn! Turn! Turn!"

Songwriting Teams (Answers)

1. Harry Warren
2. Lou Fields
3. George and Ira Gershwin
4. Bert Kalmar and Harry Ruby
5. Alan Jay Lerner
6. John Lennon and Paul McCartney

7. What pair composed *Oklahoma!*, *Carousel*, *South Pacific*, *The King and I*, *The Flower Drum Song*, and *The Sound of Music?*
8. Hal David joined forces with what composer to produce dozens of hit records in the 1960s, especially for Dionne Warwick?
9. Jerry Leiber and what other New Yorker were responsible for some of the most popular rock 'n' roll songs of the 1950s?
10. What are the first names of the songwriting trio of Henderson, DeSylva, and Brown?

State Songs

1. What is the only state song taken from a Broadway play?
2. When this song was adopted as a state song, Ray Charles sang it to the state assembly. What was the song?
3. President Harry S. Truman often played his state song on the piano. Name it.
4. What state uses "Yankee Doodle Dandy" as its official state song?
5. "Home on the Range" is the state song for which Midwest state?
6. What state song is named for a river within the state?
7. Which state song was composed by Paul Dresser, the brother of novelist Theodore Dreiser?
8. What is California's state song?
9. What two states do not have state songs?
10. Alma Gluck's version of what 1915 song was the first recording to sell a million copies?

Theme Songs

1. The son of what film director composed the lyric to the song "Suicide is Painless," theme song of the 1970 movie *M*A*S*H?*
2. What song does Christine Jorgensen, who underwent a sex change from male to female, feature as her theme in her nightclub act?
3. Both Gene Autry and Ray Whitley composed Autry's theme song. Name it.
4. Rimsky-Korsakov's "Flight of the Bumble Bee" was used as the theme for what radio/TV series?

7. Richard Rogers and Oscar Hammerstein II
8. Burt Bachrach
9. Mike Stoller
10. Ray, Buddy, and Lew

State Songs (Answers)

1. Oklahoma—"Oklahoma!"
2. "Georgia On My Mind"
3. "Missouri Waltz"
4. Connecticut
5. Kansas
6. "Swanee River"—Florida
7. "On the Banks of the Wabash"—Indiana
8. "I Love You California"
9. Pennsylvania and New Jersey
10. "Carry Me Back to Old Virginny"

Theme Songs (Answers)

1. Robert Altman (the film's director)
2. "I Enjoy Being a Girl"
3. "Back in the Saddle Again"
4. The Green Hornet

5. What is cowboy-actor Roy Rogers's theme song?

6. David Rose composed what song that was used as the theme for TV's "The Red Skelton Show"?

7. What song did Bert Parks sing for years as the contestants in the Miss America Pageant paraded before the audience?

8. What is the title of the opening theme song on the TV series "All In the Family" and "Archie Bunker's Place"?

9. Who used the theme song "When the Blue of the Night Meets the Cold of the Day"?

10. What singer used the theme song "Dream Along with Me" for his TV series?

5. "Happy Trails"
6. "Holiday for Strings"
7. "There She Is"
8. "Those Were the Days"
9. Bing Crosby
10. Perry Como

Verbiage

Abbreviations

What do the following abbreviations mean?
1. I.G.Y.
2. SST
3. ASCAP
4. C.A.R.E.
5. N.A.S.A.
6. SWAK
7. U.P.I.
8. RFD
9. YMCA
10. FAA

Animal Collectives

Give the name of a group of the following animals:
1. Frogs
2. Ferrets
3. Rhinoceroses
4. Lions
5. Oxen
6. Leopards
7. Elks
8. Moles
9. Bears
10. Fish

Abbreviations (Answers)

1. International Geophysical Year
2. Super Sonic Transport
3. American Society of Composers, Authors and Publishers
4. Cooperative for American Relief Everywhere
5. National Aeronautics and Space Administration
6. Sealed With a Kiss
7. United Press International
8. Rural Free Delivery
9. Young Men's Christian Association
10. Federal Aviation Administration

Animal Collectives (Answers)

1. Army
2. Business
3. Crash
4. Pride
5. Yoke
6. Leap
7. Gang
8. Labor
9. Sleuth
10. School

Animal Young

To what animal does the following young belong?
1.   Joey
2.   Cygnet
3.   Fry
4.   Squab
5.   Kid
6.   Gosling
7.   Poult
8.   Elver
9.   What is a young whale called?
10. What is a young zebra called?

Bird Collectives

Give the name of a group of the following animals:
1.   Quail
2.   Larks
3.   Geese
4.   Owls
5.   Turkeys
6.   Eagles
7.   Sparrows
8.   Chickens
9.   Peacocks
10. Swans

British Titles and Words

1.   What is the name of Herman Melville's 1851 novel that was titled *The Whale* when it was sold in Great Britain?
2.   *Everybody's Cheering* was the British title of what 1949 Busby Berkeley directed movie starring Frank Sinatra, Ester Williams, and Gene Kelly?

Animal Young (Answers)

1. Kangaroo
2. Swan
3. Fish
4. Pigeon
5. Goat
6. Geese
7. Turkey
8. Eel
9. Calf
10. Colt

Bird Collectives (Answers)

1. Bevy
2. Exaltation
3. Gaggle or skin
4. Parliament
5. Rafter
6. Convocation
7. Host
8. Peep
9. Master
10. Wedge

British Titles and Words (Answers)

1. *Moby Dick*
2. *Take Me Out to the Ball Game*

3. *Enemy of the People* was the title of what 1931 James Cagney-Mae Clarke film when it was released in Great Britain?
4. What is the British word for gasoline?
5. *One Born Every Minute* was the British title of what 1967 American movie starring George C. Scott and Michael Sarrazin?
6. What is the British word for an elevator? For a truck?
7. What British novel was given the title of *Too Hot To Handle* when first distributed in the United States in 1954? (It was feared that Americans could not pronounce the title.)
8. What word do the British use in lieu of *flashlight?*
9. What 1951 biographical American film was released in Britain under the title *Man of Bronze?*
10. What was the 1948 film *Abbott and Costello Meet Frankenstein* called when it was released in Britain?

Coined Words and Expressions

1. "Machine Gun" Kelly coined this word during a gun battle with FBI agents in 1933 when he yelled, "Don't shoot,_____"?
2. What expression is Canadian stagecoach robber Bill Miner credited with having created? (He was so polite when he held up a stage that he was nicknamed the Gentleman Bandit.)
3. The phrase "affluent society" came into existence after what economist titled his book with the two words in 1958?
4. What columnist coined the phrase "America—love it or leave it," back in 1940?
5. What word did entrepreneur Billy Rose coin to represent his water follies?
6. Who coined the phrase "The Beat Generation"?
7. Mike Eruzione introduced a word to describe how he felt after his hockey team won a Gold Medal in the 1980 Olympics. He stated that it meant a big wheel or big shot.
8. What author coined the phrase "the Jazz Age" in reference to the Roaring Twenties?
9. Who coined the slang term "copasetic," meaning everything's agreeable?
10. What term did Winston Churchill introduce in a speech at Westminster College on March 5, 1946?

3. *Public Enemy*
4. Petrol
5. *The Flim Flam Man*
6. Lift and lorry, respectively
7. *Casino Royale* by Ian Fleming
8. Torch
9. *Jim Thorpe, All-American*
10. *Abbott and Costello Meet the Ghosts*

Coined Words and Expressions (Answers)
1. G-Men (meaning government men)
2. "Hands Up"
3. John Galbraith
4. Walter Winchell
5. Aquacade
6. Author Jack Kerouac
7. Doolie
8. F. Scott Fitzgerald
9. Dancer Bill "Bojangles" Robinson
10. Iron Curtain

11. What columnist coined the phrase "making whoopie" in his column?
12. What Texas legislator with the first name of Samuel lent his last name for the name of unbranded cattle?
13. What word did author Norman Mailer coin to be used for another swear word in his 1947 novel *The Naked and the Dead*?
14. What word was coined by two little old ladies in the 1936 movie *Mr. Deeds Goes to Town* to describe the mental condition of Longfellow Deeds?
15. In the 1940 film *Meet John Doe* what word did Walter Brennan use to describe the average person of the world?
16. What U.S. president is credited with coining the word "normalcy"?
17. What U.S. president is credited with coining the word "chiseler"?
18. Who named Hollywood "Tinsel Town" in his expression "Strip the phony tinsel off Hollywood and you'll find the real tinsel underneath"?
19. What San Franciso columnist is credited with coining the word "beatnik"?
20. What architect introduced the word "carport"?

Definitions

1. What is the name given to the ends of a shoelace?
2. What is the part of the anchor chain that is attached to the ship?
3. A sailor who has not yet crossed the equator is referred to by what name?
4. What is a citizen of the British city of Liverpool called?
5. What is a citizen of the West Coast city of Los Angeles called?
6. What is made up of the pile, shaft, fletching, and nock?
7. What character in Richard Sheridan's 1775 comedy *The Rivals* lent her name to the word used to describe her misapplication of words?
8. What are the four dimensions?
9. What is one followed by 100 zeros called?
10. On radio and TV game shows subjects to be guessed correctly have commonly been broken down into what three categories?

11. Walter Winchell
12. Samuel Maverick
13. Fug
14. Pixilated
15. Helot
16. Warren G. Harding
17. President Franklin D. Roosevelt
18. Oscar Levant
19. Herb Caen
20. Frank Lloyd Wright

Definitions (Answers)

1. Aglets
2. Bitter end
3. Pollywog
4. Liverpudlian
5. Angelino
6. An arrow
7. Mrs. Malaprop
8. Length, width, depth, and time
9. Googol
10. Animal, vegetable, or mineral

FAA Airport Designators

Give the airport that is identified by the following three-letter designators:

1. LAX
2. MIA
3. JFK
4. DFW
5. SEA
6. STL
7. ORD
8. PHX
9. PHI
10. ATL

Famous Quotes

1. Whose 1928 screen test was evaluated as "can't act, can't sing, balding, can dance a little"?
2. Sports announcer Howard Cosell referred to Alvin Garrett, the Washington Redskin's black wide receiver, by what two words in the opening game of the 1983 season?
3. Who said, "If people don't want to see a picture, there's no way you can stop them"?
4. Who, on November 10, 1933, stated, "I am insulted by the persistent assertion that I want war. Am I a fool? War! It would settle nothing."
5. What stock reply did comedian W. C. Fields give as an answer when asked if he liked children?
6. Aside from Samuel Goldwyn, only one other person could have said the following—name him. "You've got to be very careful if you don't know where you are going, because you might not get there."
7. Aside from Yogi Berra, only one other person could have said, "You've got to take the bull between your teeth." Who was it?
8. Who said this classic line to her maid and in what movie? "Beulah, peel me a grape."

FAA Airport Designators (Answers)

1. Los Angeles (California)
2. Miami (Florida)
3. New York City (John F. Kennedy)
4. Dallas—Fort Worth (Texas)
5. Seattle (Washington)
6. St. Louis (Missouri)
7. Chicago—O'Hare (Illinois)
8. Phoenix (Arizona)
9. Philadelphia (Pennsylvania)
10. Atlanta (Georgia)

Famous Quotes (Answers)

1. Fred Astaire
2. "Little Monkey"
3. Samuel Goldwyn
4. Adolf Hitler
5. "Yes, if they're properly cooked."
6. Yogi Bera
7. Samuel Goldwyn
8. Mae West in *I'm No Angel* (1933)

9. Who is credited with coining the phrase "You can fool all of the people some of the time, some of the people all of the time, but you can't fool all of the people all of the time"?
10. Which comedian once noted, "Military intelligence is a contradiction in terms"?

Favorite Expressions

1. What southern belle was always saying "Fiddle-dee-dee"?
2. "Gloryosky!" was the favorite expression of what little comic strip girl?
3. When poor old Charlie Brown has been victimized again he uses what expression (two words)?
4. Clark Kent and Lois Lane's editor Perry White often yelled what expression when he was upset, which was often?
5. What comic strip hero used "leapin' lizards" as her favorite expression?
6. What orchestra leader used the words "Wunderful, Wunderful"?
7. What cartoon character often said, "Gladly pay you Tuesday for a hamburger today"?
8. Although hard to believe, what little fairy's favorite expression was "Silly Little Ass"?
9. "Be careful Matt" was said almost every week by whom and on what TV series?
10. "Here's looking at you, kid" was whose favorite line?

First Words

1. What is the first word of the U.S. Constitution?
2. What were Woody Woodpecker's first two words when he made his 1950 cartoon debut, titled *Knock, Knock?*
3. What were the first three words spoken by Suzanne Sommers in her 1973 movie debut, *American Graffiti?*
4. What were the first words spoken over the telephone on March 10, 1876?
5. What were the exact first words spoken by Al Jolson in the 1927 Warner Bros. talkie *The Jazz Singer?*

9. Abraham Lincoln
10. Groucho Marx

Favorite Expressions (Answers)

1. Scarlett O'Hara
2. Little Annie Rooney
3. "Good grief"
4. "Great Caesar's Ghost"
5. Little Orphan Annie
6. Lawrence Welk
7. Wimpy
8. Tinker Bell (in the original J.M. Barrie novel/play)
9. Kitty on "Gunsmoke"
10. Rick Blaine (Humphrey Bogart) in the 1942 movie *Casablanca*

First Words (Answers)

1. "We"
2. "Guess who?"
3. "I love you" (said to Richard Dreyfuss).
4. "Mr. Watson, come here, I need you," said by Alexander Graham Bell to his assistant Thomas A. Watson.
5. "Wait a minute, you ain't heard nothing yet."

6. What is the first word in the text of the Declaration of Independence?
7. Who said these famous first words and to whom were they said? "I perceive you have been in Afghanistan."
8. In the Bible, what were the first words spoken by God to man?
9. What classic novel began with the words "Call me Ishmael"?
10. What actress's first words in her first talkie were "Gif me a viskey, ginger ale on the side, an' don't be stingy, baby!"?

Gangster Nicknames

Give the real names of the following gangsters/mobsters:
1. Scarface
2. Dutch
3. Legs
4. Pretty Boy
5. Baby Face
6. Mad Dog
7. The Enforcer
8. Lucky
9. Old Creepy
10. Machine Gun

Initials

1. What does the *B* in movie producer/director Cecil B. DeMille stand for?
2. Academy Award-winning actor George C. Scott's middle name is what?
3. What do the initials stand for in O. J. Simpson's name?
4. Edgar Lawrence is the first and middle name of what U. S. novelist responsible for such works as *Welcome To Hard Times* and *Ragtime?*
5. What do the initials J.C. stand for in the J. C. Penny chain store name?
6. What syndicated columnist was known by his initials F.P.A.?
7. What does the *L* stand for in author L. Frank Baum's (creator of *The Wizard of Oz*) name?

6.   "When"
7.   Sherlock Holmes to Dr. Watson when they first met.
8.   "Be fruitful and multiply."
9.   Herman Melville's *Moby Dick*
10. Greta Garbo (in the 1930 movie *Anna Christie*)

Gangster Nicknames (Answers)

1.   Al Capone
2.   Arthur Schultz (born Arthur Flegenheimer)
3.   John Diamond (John T. Nolan)
4.   Charles Floyd
5.   George Nelson (Lester Gillis)
6.   Vincent Coll
7.   Frank Nitti
8.   Charles Luciano
9.   Alvin Karpis (Abin Karpowicz)
10. George Kelly

Initials (Answers)

1.   Blount
2.   Campbell
3.   Orenthal James
4.   E. L. Doctorow
5.   James Cash
6.   Franklin P. Adams
7.   Lymon

8. The first two names of this science fiction writer are Howard Phillips, but he only uses the initials. Name him.
9. What does the *A.J.* in race driver A. J. Foyt's name stand for?
10. What were the first two initials of the San Francisco 49ers quarterback with the last name of Tittle?

Introductions

1. This radio commentator began each of his news shows with "Ah, there's good news tonight." Who was he?
2. How does James Bond introduce himself upon meeting someone for the first time?
3. Who said, "Heigh-ho, everybody!"?

Name the people who gave the following opening statements:
4. "My fellow Americans"
5. "Howdy, bub"
6. "Hey kids, what time is it?"
7. This belle of prohibition met her customers with the line, "Hello suckers!"
8. What country comedian always greeted her audiences with a very friendly "Howddddddy!"
9. Who introduced himself with the words "Nanu Nanu"?
10. What famous radio newscaster greeted his audience with "Good evening, Mr. and Mrs. North and South America and all the ships at sea. Let's go to press"?

Languages

1. What is the official language of Brazil?
2. What are the two official languages of Canada?
3. In air traffic control what is the international language spoken, other than the language of the countries involved?
4. What is known as the "dead language"?
5. In 1961 John D. Loudermilk recorded what song with the word *language* in the title?
6. What six official languages are spoken at the United Nations?
7. What is the only state that has two official languages?

8. H.P. Lovecraft
9. Anthony Joseph
10. Y.A.

Introductions (Answers)

1. Gabriel Heater
2. "My name is Bond, James Bond."
3. Singer Rudy Vallee
4. Lyndon B. Johnson
5. Titus Moody (Parker Fennelly) of "Allen's Alley," Fred Allen's radio program
6. Buffalo Bob Smith (on TV's Howdy Doody")
7. Texas Guinan
8. Minnie Pearl
9. Mork (Robin Williams) of the TV series "Mork and Mindy"
10. Walter Winchell

Languages (Answers)

1. Portuguese
2. English and French
3. English
4. Latin
5. "Language of Love"
6. English, Russian, Spanish, French, Chinese, and Arabic
7. New Mexico (English and Spanish)

8. What is Etoanir Shdlu?
9. What language is spoken by more people in the world than any other?
10. What one man created the Cherokee alphabet?

Last Words

1. Actor Dustin Hoffman once dared Paul McCartney to compose a song based on the last words of artist Pablo Picasso. McCartney took up the challenge and with his group, Wings, recorded what song?
2. What were the last two words spoken by Paul Muni in the 1932 movie *I Am A Fugitive From A Chain Gang?*
3. Honolulu police detective Steve McGarrett, played by Jack Lord, makes what two-word statement each week in the closing scene of each "Hawaii Five-O" episode?
4. On the last episode of the TV series "Howdy Doody," telecast on September 30, 1960, Clarabelle the Clown, who never spoke in the 2,343 previous episodes, spoke for the first and last time when he looked at the camera and said what?
5. "It is a far, far better thing that I do, than I have ever done, it is a far, far better rest that I go to, than I have ever known" is the final line that appears in what classic 1859 novel?
6. When the announcer spoke these five words over the P.A. system at an Elvis Presley concert, the audience then knew that the concert was over. What were they?
7. What classic last line did General Douglas McArthur utter to the cadets at West Point in his last speech before his forced retirement?
8. What was the single word that the lost colony of Roanoke Island left carved on a door post?
9. What was Rhett Butler's classic last line to his wife, Scarlett, in the 1939 movie *Gone With the Wind?*
10. The last words said by Herman Melville's Billy Budd before he was hanged were ironically the last words of Melville on his death bed in 1891. What were the four words?
11. What great world ruler's last dying word was his wife's name, Josephine?
12. "That was the best ice cream soda I ever tasted" were the last words ever spoken by what film comedian (he died on March 3, 1959)?

8. The most used letters in the English language in order of usage
9. Chinese
10. Sequoya

Last Words (Answers)

1. "Drink to Me . . ."
2. "I steal."
3. "Book 'em."
4. "Good-bye, kids."
5. *A Tale of Two Cities* by Charles Dickens
6. "Elvis has left the building."
7. "Old soldiers never die, they just fade away."
8. "Croatoan"
9. "Frankly, my dear, I don't give a damn."
10. "God Bless Captain Vere."
11. Napoleon
12. Lou Costello

13. What were the final dying words of Charles Foster Kane?
14. What gangster yelled, "The bullet hasn't been made that can kill me," before he died in 1931?
15. Name the Ernest Hemingway novel that was titled with General Stonewall Jackson's last words?
16. What number, in journalism, means that the article is finished?
17. On January 3, 1970, "I, Me, Mine" became the last song for whom?
18. Civil War general John Sedgwick's last words were one of history's greatest misjudgments. What were they?
19. Hard-drinking Civil War general Ulysses S. Grant's single last word was out of character for him. What was it?
20. Whose last words were, "Thomas Jefferson still survives"?

Letters

1. What two letters are not found on a telephone dial?
2. Hester Prynne wore what letter on her dress in Nathaniel Hawthorne's classic novel *The Scarlet Letter?*
3. How many letters can be found in the Hawaiian alphabet?
4. How is the last letter in the English alphabet pronounced in Britain?
5. What are the first and last letters of the Greek alphabet?
6. What letter is the designator for aircraft registration in the United States?
7. What did the letters *A*, *B*, and *C* that could be found on automobile windshields during World War II refer to?
8. Which four cities beginning with the letter *M* have been the host for a summer Olympics between 1968 and 1980?
9. The 1943 movie *Sahara* starred three actors whose last names begin with the letter *B*. Name them?
10. The best-selling book *The Sensuous Woman* was credited to an author with what single-letter pseudonym?
11. What do the three *M*s stand for in the 3M Company?
12. What is so unusual about the word "uncopyrightable"?
13. What is the only word in the English language that both begins and ends with *und?*
14. What fourteen-letter word beginning with the letter *A* uses all five vowels without repeating letters?

13. "Rosebud" *(Citizen Kane* [1941])
14. "Legs" Diamond
15. *Across the River and Into the Trees*
16. 30
17. The last song that the Beatles recorded together
18. "They couldn't hit an elephant at this dist——"
19. "Water"
20. Former president John Adams

Letters (Answers)

1. *Q* and *Z*
2. *A* for adultress
3. 12
4. "Zed"
5. Alpha and omega
6. *N*
7. Gas rationing
8. Mexico City (1968), Munich (1972), Montreal (1976), and Moscow (1980)
9. Humphrey Bogart, Bruce Bennett, and Lloyd Bridges
10. *J*
11. Minnesota Mining and Manufacturing
12. All vowels are present and no letters are repeated
13. Underground
14. Ambidextrously

15.   Name the only four words in the English language that end in the letters *dous?*

16.   What is the only letter not present in the spellings of the names of the fifty states?

17.   What are the first two letters for boat registration in California?

18.   The book *The Sensuous Man* was credited to an author with what single-letter pseudonym?

19.   In 1939, Ernest Vincent wrote a 50,000-word novel titled *Gadsby,* without once including what letter of the alphabet?

20.   No street in Washington, DC, begins with what letter?

Lines Never Said

1.   What line that has been said over and over again by Basil Rathbone in Sherlock Holmes films, was never spoken in Arthur Conan Doyle's novels?

2.   What actor never said, "Judy, Judy, Judy," in any of his films, though he is credited as such?

3.   After the Japanese attacked Pearl Harbor, President Roosevelt, in his speech to congress, never said, "A day that will live in infamy." What did he say?

4.   Who is credited with, but never actually offered, the classic phrase "you dirty rat" in films?

5.   Who never said the line "Drop the gun, Louie" in any of his films? (The closest he came was in saying, "Not so fast, Louie," to Claude Rains in a 1942 film.)

6.   "Come with me to the Casbah" was a line erroneously credited to Charles Boyer from what 1938 motion picture?

7.   Although she's been credited with saying the classic line "I want to be alone" in the 1932 film *Grand Hotel,* she never said it. Who is she?

8.   In "The Mourning Bride," by William Congreve, what classic line is often misquoted, "Music has charms that will soothe a _____"

9.   If Johnny Weismueller did not say, "Me Tarzan, you Jane," what did he actually say?

10.   What does 1 Timothy 6:10 of the Bible state is the root of all evil?

15. Hazardous, horendous, stupendous, and tremendous
16. *Q*
17. *CF*
18. *M*
19. *E*
20. *J* because it closely resembles an *I*

Lines Never Said (Answers)

1. "Elementary, my dear Watson."
2. Cary Grant
3. "A date that will live in infamy"
4. James Cagney
5. Humphrey Bogart *(Casablanca)*
6. *Algiers*
7. Greta Garbo
8. Savage breast (not beast)
9. "Tarzan—Jane, Tarzan—Jane" (for a total of 17 times, pointing back and forth)
10. The love of money (not money itself)

Logos

1. What logo does Lacoste Straits of Switzerland sew onto their products?
2. On many of Pink Floyd's albums what animal is present?
3. Television producer Bill Bohnert posed for the trademark of this young boy logo for what paint company?
4. The rock group, Fleetwood Mac, uses what animal logo?
5. What tire company uses Mercury's winged shoe as its logo?
6. Maisey and Daisy are the cute little twin girls who grace the cover of what toilet tissue?
7. What television network uses a logo of a Peacock?
8. Pegasus, the winged-horse of Greek mythology, is the logo (or colophon) for what major magazine?
9. Which product uses a little girl carrying an umbrella?
10. What insurance company uses an elk as its logo?

Middle Initials

1. What popular science fiction writer's middle initial stands for the name Anson?
2. John is the middle name of what industrialist whose middle initial is prominent in his name as well as the name of the automobile he manufactured?
3. Taliaferro is the middle name of what black educator?
4. What does the *V* stand for in Eugene V. Deb's name?
5. What does the *D* in John D. Rockefeller's name stand for?
6. What does the *G* stand for in author H. G. Wells's middle name? Also what does the *H* stand for?
7. What is the middle name of blues composer William C. Handy?
8. What does the *F* in William F. Cody ("Buffalo Bill") stand for?
9. What was the middle name of Hollywood producer Darryl F. Zanuck?
10. Blount is the middle name of what Hollywood producer responsible for both versions of the film *The Ten Commandments?*

Logos (Answers)

1. An alligator
2. Pig
3. Dutch Boy Paint
4. Penquin
5. Goodyear tires
6. MD Tissues
7. NBC
8. *Reader's Digest*
9. Morton Salt
10. Hartford

Middle Initials (Answers)

1. Robert A. Heinlein
2. Henry J. Kaiser
3. Booker T. Washington
4. Victor
5. Davison
6. George and Herbert, respectively
7. Christopher
8. Frederick
9. Francis
10. Cecil B. DeMille

Military Abbreviations

What do the following abbreviations stand for?
1. SAM
2. SAC
3. AWOL
4. NATO
5. WAVES
6. LST
7. CINCPAC
8. AWACS
9. POW
10. D-day (June 6, 1944)

Mnemonics

1. "Kings playing chess on fine grain sand" is the mnemonic for what biological classifications?
2. What name will help to recall the colors, in order of the spectrum?
3. What sentence helps in memorizing the five lines of a treble staff?
4. "Homes" is a mnemonic used to recall what geographical location?
5. "When all judge many methods and jeer valuable historical truisms, picture the future pessimistically. Berate life's justice, gripe, hiss, howl, abstain!" If you take the first letter what order will it provide?
6. What saying helped young children to spell the word "arithmetic" correctly?
7. What three entertainment industry awards are represented by the initials *TOE* which only a handful have won more than one?
8. "Fat boys eat apple dumpling gradually" is used to remember what?
9. Likewise "Good deeds are ever bearing fruit" is used to locate what?
10. What four-letter word is used to identify the spaces on a staff?

Military Abbreviations (Answers)

1. Surface to Air Missile
2. Strategic Air Command
3. Absent Without Leave
4. North Atlantic Treaty Organization
5. Women Accepted for Volunteer Emergency Service
6. Landing Ship, Tank
7. Commander in Chief (U.S. Forces), Pacific
8. Airborne Warning and Control Systems
9. Prisoner of War
10. Departure Day

Mnemonics (Answers)

1. Kindom, phylum, class, order, family, genus, species
2. Roy G. Biv (Red, orange, yellow, green, blue, indigo, violet)
3. Every good boy does fine (EGBDF).
4. The Great Lakes (Huron, Ontario, Michigan, Erie, and Superior)
5. The last names of the first 21 U.S. presidents
6. A rat in the house might eat the ice cream
7. Tony, Oscar, and Emmy
8. Key signatures in ascending order of flats
9. Key signatures in ascending order of sharps
10. Face

Monetary Units

Give the monetary unit for the following countries:
1. Canada
2. Soviet Union
3. Japan
4. Poland
5. Italy
6. Spain
7. Britain
8. France
9. Mexico
10. Germany (West and East)

Mottoes

1. What was the motto of Korea's 4077th MASH unit in the TV series "M*A*S*H"?
2. "Weaving spiders come not here" is the motto of what prestigious San Francisco private club?
3. This Walt Disney hero of the 1950s TV used the motto "Be sure you're right, then go ahead."
4. Which one of the 50 U.S. states does *not* have a motto?
5. What is the motto of *Rolling Stone* magazine?
6. *Semper paratus* (Always prepared) is the motto of what military service?
7. "Death to the Fascist insect that preys upon the life of the people" was the motto of what radical group?
8. What movie studio uses the motto *Ars gratia artis* (Art for art's sake)?
9. What became the national motto of the United States as of July 30, 1956?
10. "Certainly, security, and celerity" is the motto of what government agency?
11. "He best serves himself who serves others" is the motto of what guild?
12. What is the motto of the Boy Scouts of America?

Monetary Units (Answers)

1. Dollar
2. Ruble
3. Yen
4. Zolts
5. Lira
6. Pesetas
7. Pound
8. Franc
9. Peso
10. Mark

Mottoes (Answers)

1. "Best care anywhere"
2. Bohemian Club
3. Davy Crockett, as portrayed by Fess Parker
4. Alaska
5. "All the news that fits"
6. U.S. Coast Guard
7. SLA (Symbionese Liberation Army)
8. MGM
9. "In God we trust"
10. U.S. Post Office
11. Screen Actors Guild
12. "Be prepared"

13. What charitable organization uses the motto or the emblem of "Blood and Fire"?
14. "Building boys is better than mending men" is the motto of what organization?
15. What is the two-word motto of the United States Navy Seabees?
16. "Duty—Honor—Country" is the motto of what school?
17. When translated, this motto, which is found on the Great Seal of the United States, means "Out of many, one." Name the motto?
18. What organization uses the motto *Non silba sed anthar*, which translated means "Not for self but for others"?
19. Who uses the motto "One on all, all on one"?
20. What was the motto of Alexander Dumas's Three Musketeers?

Names

1. What is the most common name signed by discreet unmarried couples staying at a hotel or motel?
2. 85,000,000 people have what last name, the most popular one in the world?
3. What leader of the radical group the Black Panthers first began referring to the police as pigs?
4. What is the last name of Queen Elizabeth II of Great Britain?
5. What is pro football quarterback Sonny Jurgenson's Christian name?
6. The U.S. Weather Service gave what the name of Bud on June 19, 1978? It was the first time a male name was used.
7. Old-timer western cowboy Gabby Hayes called his young fans by what name?
8. What is so unusual about the name of major league players Ed and Jose Figueroa?
9. What did Adolf Hitler plan on renaming Berlin after the war was over?
10. What is the most popular name for a street in the United States?
11. What popular name did servicemen give to their life preservers during World War II?
12. Who coined the name United States of America?
13. What did Alfalfa, of the "Our Gang"/"Little Rascals" fame call his cowlick?
14. What is an Arkansas Toothpick?

13. Salvation Army
14. Boys Club of America
15. "Can do"
16. West Point
17. *E pluribus unum*
18. Ku Klux Klan
19. Hell's Angels motorcycle club
20. "All for one—one for all"

Names (Answers)

1. Smith
2. Chang
3. Huey Newton
4. Montbatten-Windsor
5. Christian
6. Tropical storm
7. Buckeroos
8. Their last name contains all five English vowels
9. Germanis
10. Park Street
11. Mae Wests
12. Thomas Paine
13. My personality
14. Bowie knife

15. What is the name of golfer Bobby Jones's favorite putter?
16. What was the name given to the 10,000-pound atomic bomb dropped on Hiroshima on August 6, 1945?
17. What is known as the Senior Service?
18. What was Seward's Folly?
19. By what more popular names do we know the constellations Ursa Minor and Ursa Major?
20. After whom was the dance the lindy hop named?

Nicknames Conferred By

1. To what popular romantic author did *People* magazine give the nickname of "The First Lady of Lust"?
2. Author Ernest Hemingway affectionately called what actress "The Kraut"?
3. Who gave Bobby Vinton his nickname of the "Polish Prince"?
4. Name the close actor-friend of actress Elizabeth Taylor who conferred the nickname "Bessie Mae" on her.
5. President Richard M. Nixon called what songstress an "Ambassador of Love"?
6. By what nickname did actor Ronald Reagan refer to his actress-wife Jane Wyman?
7. It was TV host Garry Moore who gave singer Georgia Gibbs her nickname. What was it?
8. It was actress Brooke Shields who conferred the nickname of "Peter Pan" upon whom?
9. What popular nickname did columnist Walter Winchell give to actress Lauren Bacall?
10. Who nicknamed gangster Arnold Rothstein "The Brain" because he caused the 1919 Black Sox Scandal by rigging the 1919 World Series?

Numbers

1. By law only 400 of which vehicles are allowed to operate at one time in the Italian city of Venice?
2. Within ten, how many holes are there in a Chinese checkerboard?
3. There are 3,070 of what land groups in the United States?

15. Calamity Jane
16. Little Boy
17. British Royal Navy
18. The purchase of Alaska by the United States from Russia (1867)
19. Big and Little Dippers
20. Aviator Charles Lindbergh

Nicknames Conferred By (Answers)

1. Rosemary Rogers
2. Marlene Dietrich (she called him "Papa")
3. Chicago Mayor Richard Daley
4. Montgomery Cliff
5. Pearl Bailey
6. Button Nose
7. Her Nibs
8. Michael Jackson
9. The Look
10. Damon Runyon

Numbers (Answers)

1. Gondolas
2. 121
3. Counties

4. What word is given to the number one, followed by 303 zeros in American math and 600 zeros in British math?
5. How is the year 1888 written in Roman numerals?
6. How many times does the number one and the word *one* appear on both sides of the dollar bill (not counting serial numbers)?
7. How many sheets of paper to a ream?
8. How many zeros are there in a trillion?
9. What number follows a trillion?
10. What are the five numbers 6, 28, 496, 8,128, and 33,550,336 called?

Phobias

Give the layman's definition of the following fears:
1. Ergophobia
2. Agoraphobia
3. Claustrophobia
4. Phobiaphobia
5. Acrophobia
6. Hydrophobia
7. Arachnophobia
8. Triskaidekaphobia
9. Demophobia
10. Nyctaphobia

Roman Numerals

Give the following single Roman Numerals:
1. 5
2. 10
3. 50
4. 100
5. 500
6. 1,000
7. 5,000
8. 10,000
9. 100,000
10. 1,000,000

4. Centillion
5. MDCCCLXXXVIII (M = 1,000, DCCC = 800,
LXXX = 80, and VIII = 8)
6. Sixteen times (eight on each side)
7. 500
8. 12
9. Quadrillion
10. Perfect numbers (positive integer that is equal to the sum of its
factors)

Phobias (Answers)

1. Word
2. Open spaces
3. Enclosed spaces
4. Fear of fears
5. Heights
6. Water
7. Spiders
8. Number 13
9. Crowds
10. Darkness

Roman Numerals (Answers)

1. V
2. X
3. L
4. C
5. D
6. M
7. V̄
8. X̄
9. C̄
10. M̄

Sentences

1. What single sentence did Jack Torrence (played by Jack Nicholson) type over and over again in various designs in the 1980 movie *The Shining?*
2. The single sentence "In 1600 an Englishman named Will Adams went to Japan and became a Samurai" read in a history text book inspired James Clavell to write what novel?
3. "In the beginning God created the heaven and the earth" is the first sentence found where?
4. What sentence can be found on matchbook covers?
5. What was the sign on President Harry S. Truman's oval office desk?
6. What famous sentence did Charles E. Weller create as a typing exercise?
7. What was the sentence that Samuel F. B. Morse sent on May 24, 1844, as the first message ever sent via telegraph?
8. In the 1968 film *Charly,* Charley Gordon (Cliff Robertson) asked Alice Kinian (Claire Bloom) to punctuate the word grouping "That that is is that that is not is not is that it it is." Can you punctuate it?
9. A good reporter should ask questions that begin with what six words?
10. What statement on tags attached to pillows have become the butt of many jokes?

Speeches

1. Who gave the famous "Cross of Gold" speech in 1896?
2. What famous speech given on November 19, 1863, begins with "Four score and seven years ago"?
3. What U.S. President, who died just 32 days after his inauguration, gave the longest inauguration address, which lasted nearly two hours?
4. What portion of Martin Luther King's famous March 1963, Washington, DC, address, appears on his tombstone?

Sentences (Answers)

1. All work and no play makes Jack a dull boy.
2. *Shōgun*
3. In the Bible (Genesis 1:1)
4. Close cover before striking.
5. The Buck Stops Here
6. "Now is the time for all good men to come to the aid of their party."
7. "What hath God wrought?"
8. That that is, is. That that is not, is not. Is that it? It is!
9. Who, what, when, where, why, and how
10. Do not remove under penalty of law (which was meant for the sellar, not the buyer).

Speeches (Answers)

1. William Jennings Bryan
2. Abraham Lincoln's Gettysburg Address
3. William Henry Harrison
4. "Free at last, free at last, thank God almighty, I'm free at last."

5. In a speech given by President John F. Kennedy, given after the Bay of Pigs fiasco, what saying did he borrow from Benito Mussolini's foreign minister Count Galeazzo Ciamo?
6. Where was Nikita Khruschev when he banged his shoe and threatened the American people with "We will bury you"?
7. What U.S. President established a record of speaking in public at a rate of 327 words per minute? The fastest of any public official.
8. Speaking only 134 words, what U.S. President gave the shortest inaugural speech?
9. Who made a speech to the U.S. Senate on June 1, 1950, that was called the Declaration of Conscience Speech?
10. Which famous Winston Churchill speech was actually delivered by British actor Norman Shelley on June 4, 1940, because Churchill was not available to give it?

Spelling

1. Country singer Tammy Wynette had a hit record in 1968 with a song in which the title is spelled out. What was the title of the song?
2. What bottled food can be spelled two different ways and yet pronounced only one way?
3. Although it can be stated correctly, what sentence cannot be written correctly?
4. What extra letter do the British add to many words that Americans omit?
5. Railroad crossing, look out for the cars—can you spell it without any *r*'s?
6. What U.S. city, for a short time, dropped the last letter of its name?
7. What singer/actress dropped the letter *a* from her first name?
8. What word is misspelled on the Liberty Bell?
9. In television advertisements, how do you spell relief?
10. In what song, by Bobby Goldsboro, did the little boy spell Mom and Dad "PRLFQ"?

5. "Victory has a hundred fathers, and defeat is an orphan."
6. United Nations
7. President John F. Kennedy
8. George Washington (in his second inauguration)
9. Senator Margaret Chase Smith
10. The British defeat at Dunkirk—"We shall fight on the beaches . . ."

Spelling (Answers)

1. "D-I-V-O-R-C-E"
2. Ketchup or catsup
3. There are three ways to write the word two. (Several other homynyms can be used in lieu of "two/to/too.")
4. *U*, as in colour, honour, favour, etc.
5. I-T
6. Pittsburgh, Pennsylvania
7. Barbra Streisand
8. Pen(n)sylvania
9. R-O-L-A-I-D-S
10. "Watching Scotty Grow"

State Mottoes

1. What state uses the single word *Eureka*, meaning "I have found it"?
2. What state uses the motto "In God We Trust," which is also found on U.S. coins?
3. "Crossroads of America" is the motto of the Hoosier State. Name it.
4. What phrase is now the motto of Kentucky?
5. Whose state motto mentions both sexes in it?
6. What state uses the single word *Excelsior*, meaning "upward"?
7. Rhode Island, the smallest state, also has one of the two smallest mottoes. What is the four-letter word?
8. Virginia's state motto is also the statement that John Wilkes Booth yelled after assassinating President Abraham Lincoln. What is it?
9. Only four states—Arizona, Florida, Ohio, and South Dakota—use a reference to what being in their mottos?
10. What state motto includes the first name of a former Vice President of the United States?

Subjects

Name the disciplines that study the following subjects:
1. Animals
2. Birds
3. Religion
4. Life
5. Fish
6. Rocks and minerals
7. Human behavior
8. Weather
9. Crime
10. Books

QUESTIONS

State Mottoes (Answers)

1. California
2. Florida
3. Indiana
4. "United we stand"
5. Maryland (*Fati maschii, parole femine*, "Manly deeds, womanly words")
6. New York
7. Hope (Washington state uses *Alki*)
8. *Sic semper tyrannis* (Thus ever to tyrants)
9. God (only Arizona mentions God in a language other than English)
10. South Carolina *Dum spiro, spero* (While I breathe I hope)

Subjects (Answers)

1. Zoology
2. Ornithology
3. Theology
4. Biology
5. Ichthyology
6. Geology
7. Psychology
8. Meteorology
9. Criminology
10. Bibliology

Words

1. Henry C. Traute coined this famous saying in 1896, which appears on all matchbook and matchbox covers. What is it?

2. In a 1983 edition of what magazine was the word "control" (in Arms Control) misspelled as Cohtol on the cover? (The issue was immediately re-called, delaying publication by two days.)

3. What dancer coined the word "copasetic"?

4. What San Francisco columnist coined the word "beatnik"?

5. What is the shortest word in the English language that contains the first six letters of the alphabet?

6. Name the only three words in the English language that end in *gry*.

7. What famous architect coined the word "carport"?

8. What are the only two words in the English language that have all the vowels in the proper order?

9. In one of Shakespeare's plays what character gave a soliloquy consisting of 262 words?

10. The last name of this Erne, Ireland, land agent against whom the farmers formed a sit-down strike in 1880 was incorporated into the English language. What was it?

11. What American Civil War general lent his name to a style of facial hair?

12. Inventor Thomas Edison introduced the word "hello" as a greeting for people when they answered the newly invented telephone. What expression had been used up to that time?

13. One of the popular songs sung by the cowboys out West was "Green Grow the Lilacs." Because the cowboys sang the song so often the Mexicans began calling them by what name?

14. Wit Dorothy Parker was once challenged to create a saying using the word horticulture. What did she come up with?

15. Gertrude Hurlbutt won $100 from the *National Sportsman* magazine, when she coined what word for the sport of trap shooting?

16. What was the two-letter word that teacher Annie Sullivan first taught Hellen Keller to articulate?

17. Name the only three words in the English language that end with *ceed?*

Words (Answers)

1. Close cover before striking.
2. *Time* magazine (Lee Iacocca was on the cover.)
3. Bill "Bojangles" Robinson
4. Herb Caen
5. Feedback
6. Angry, hungry, and pugry
7. Frank Lloyd Wright
8. Abstemiously and facetiously
9. Hamlet
10. Boycott (Charles Boycott)
11. General Ambrose Burnside (His name was the source of the word "sideburn.")
12. "Ahoy"
13. Gringos
14. "You can lead a horticulture, but you can't make her think."
15. Skeet
16. It
17. Exceed, proceed, and succeed

18. Name three words that are colors that do not rhyme with any other words?

19. What three British counties was Eliza Doolittle taught to pronounce properly by Professor Henry Higgins?

20. What is the only word with three consecutive double letters?

18. Orange, silver, purple
19. Hartford, Hereford, and Hampshire
20. Bookkeeping

Odds and Ends

Ages

1. In Barbara Cartland's romantic novels, all her heroines are what age?
2. Among other stipulations, a person must be at least what age to become President of the United States?
3. What two ages are mentioned in the lyric of the popular song "Have Yourself a Merry Little Christmas"?
4. Rock 'n' rollers, Jim Morrison, Jimi Hendrix, and Janis Joplin all died at what (same) age?
5. What is the perpetual age of Little Orphan Annie?
6. At what age does a filly become a mare and a colt become a horse?
7. What is Popeye the sailor's perpetual age?
8. At age 18 years, 10 months, which New York Giant became the youngest player to play a World Series game when he played in the 1924 World Series?
9. What was Baby Snooks's perpetual age on radio's "Baby Snooks"?
10. What is the minimum age for a boy scout to become an explorer scout?
11. Who died at the age of 969?
12. According to Shakespeare's *As You Like It,* what are the seven ages of man?
13. How old is a Chinese baby the day it is born?
14. What sportscaster was one of the youngest majors in the U.S. Army during World War II?
15. How old must a horse be to run in the Kentucky Derby?
16. At what age does a Jewish boy celebrate his bar mitzvah?
17. A person under 18 cannot join the French Foreign Legion. What is the other age limit?
18. How old was actor Cary Grant when his wife Dyan Cannon gave birth, on February 26, 1966, to their daughter Jennifer?

Ages (Answers)

1. 19 years old
2. 35 years old
3. 1 to 92
4. 27 years old
5. 11 years old
6. 5 years
7. 34 years old
8. Freddie Lindstrom
9. 4 years old
10. 14 years old
11. Methuselah
12. Infant, schoolboy, lover, soldier, justice, pantaloon, (retirement), and second childhood
13. 1 year old
14. Howard Cosell
15. 3 years old
16. 13 years old
17. Over 40 years old
18. 62 years old

19. At what age was country singer Louis Jones first referred to by his stage name of Grampa Jones?
20. What perpetual age did comedian Jack Benny always claim to be?

Assumed Names

1. Which Nazi leader was living in Argentina under the name of Klement Ricardo when he was discovered and captured by the Israelis in 1960?
2. What late great country artist sometimes traveled under the name of Herman P. Willis when he didn't want to be recognized?
3. What Academy Award-winning actor often signs the name of Lord Greystoke on hotel registers?
4. Elton Thomas was a name used by what Hollywood actor in order to write movie scripts?
5. When this young couple went on their honeymoon in 1946 they signed hotel registers under the name of Emil and Emma Glutz. Who were they?
6. When they were secretly married in Tonapah, Nevada, on March 13, 1957, they gave their names as G. A. Johnson and Mary Ann Evans. Who were they?
7. G. C. Luther was an assumed name used by what major league ballplayer whenever he went on one of his many fishing trips?
8. What name did the hijacker of Northwest Flight 305 give as his name before he bailed out with $200,000 on November 24, 1971?
9. What name did Patty Hearst adopt when she finally decided to join the SLA?
10. John Burrows was the assumed name used by which entertainer to answer the telephone when he was at home?

Battleships

1. What was the name of the U.S. battleship blown up in Havana Harbor on November 18, 1890?
2. What was the name of the largest Japanese battleship of World War II, which was sunk on April 7, 1945?
3. On what U.S. battleship did Japan sign the surrender papers on September 2, 1945, ending World War II?

19. 23 years old
20. 39 years old

Assumed Names (Answers)

1. Adolph Eichmann
2. Hank Williams
3. Marlon Brando
4. Douglas Fairbanks
5. John Agar and Shirley Temple
6. Howard Hughes and actress Jean Peters
7. Ted Williams
8. Dan Cooper (D. B. Cooper or Daniel B. Cooper)
9. Tanya
10. Elvis Presley

Battleships (Answers)

1. U.S.S. *Maine*
2. *Yamamoto*
3. U.S.S. *Missouri*

4. All U.S. battleships were named for states with the exception of one, which was named for another vessel lost in the West Indies in 1894. Name it.

5. What is the only U.S. battleship to be present at both Pearl Harbor on December 7, 1941 and at Normandy on D-day June 6, 1944?

6. What was the name of the captured German battleship that General Billy Mitchell sank by aerial bombing on July 21, 1921, in order to prove the importance of aircraft?

7. When he was in the Navy, gangster John Dillinger served on what U.S. battleship that was later sunk at Pearl Harbor?

8. What was the name of the largest German battleship, which was finally sunk in Brest, France on May 27, 1941?

9. What battleship sits on the bottom of Pearl Harbor and today is part of a national monument?

10. What was the name of the German pocket battleship that was scuttled by its crew off Montevideo harbor in December 1939?

Birds

1. The Valley Quail is the official state bird for the state of California. What is the official state bird of Utah?

2. What bird is the official state bird of Arkansas, Florida, Mississippi, North Carolina, Ohio, Tennessee, Texas, Virginia, and West Virginia?

3. On approximately March 19, every year, the town of Hinckley, Ohio, turns out to watch the return of what birds?

4. What is the only bird that swims but does not fly?

5. What two birds are mentioned in the lyric of Debbie Reynolds's 1957 hit ballad "Tammy"?

6. How many eggs do humming birds lay during their lifetime?

7. Name the major league baseball teams named for birds.

8. The DC-3 transport aircraft has been nicknamed after what extinct bird?

9. What has been the official state bird of the state of Maryland since 1947?

10. Because of his love for birds, as well as the fact that he authored several books about them, what man was nicknamed "The Birdman of Alcatraz"?

4. U.S.S. *Kearsarge*
5. U.S.S. *Nevada*
6. *Ostfriesland*
7. U.S.S. *Utah*
8. *Bismarck*
9. U.S.S. *Arizona*
10. *Graf Spee*

Birds (Answers)

1. Seagull
2. Mockingbird
3. Turkey buzzards
4. Penguin
5. Owl and Dove
6. Two
7. Baltimore Orioles, St. Louis Cardinals, and Toronto Bluejays
8. Gooney Bird
9. Baltimore oriole
10. Robert Stroud

Cards

1. What fictional detective owns a houseboat called the *Busted Flush?*
2. Television game show host Wink Martindale recorded a song in 1959 about a soldier using playing cards as a prayer book. Name the hit song.
3. "Shoot the Moon" is a term used in what card game?
4. The only film that actor Marlon Brando directed had the title of what two playing cards?
5. They are named Alexander, Caesar, Charles, and David. What are they?
6. Excluding nines, how many cards are in a double deck of pinochle cards?
7. Harold S. Vanderbilt created what style of bridge in 1925?
8. What two cards constitute a pinochle?
9. In the card game of casino, what cards are known as the big casino and the little casino?
10. What queen's face was used as the model of the four queens in a standard deck of playing cards?

Cats

1. How many lives is a cat supposed to have?
2. In 1982, seven books about what cat were on *The New York Times* best-sellers list at the same time?
3. In the comic strip "Gordo," by Gus Arriola, what is the name of Gordo's mischievous cat?
4. What was the name of Gepetto's cat in Pinocchio?
5. What is the normal body temperature of a cat?
6. In a story, and later a movie, written by H. Allen Smith, what lucky cat inherits a major league baseball team?
7. What cartoon cat holds the unique distinction of being the first image transmitted on experimental TV in the 1920s?
8. Who has become the most popular cat to appear on TV commercials?
9. In aviation language, what does C.A.T. mean?

Cards (Answers)

1. Travis McGee
2. "Deck of Cards"
3. Hearts
4. *One-Eyed Jacks* (1961)
5. The kings in a deck of cards
6. 80 cards
7. Contract bridge
8. Queen of spades and jack of diamonds
9. Ten of diamonds and deuce of spades, respectively
10. Elizabeth of York

Cats (Answers)

1. Nine
2. Garfield (books by Jim Davis)
3. Pussy Gato
4. Figaro
5. 101.5 degrees
6. Rhubarb
7. Felix the Cat
8. Morris the Cat (9-Lives cat food)
9. Clear Air Turbulence

10. A cat's name appeared in the title of a film, along with that of a character played by an actor who won the Academy Award for Best Actor for the role. Name the film.

Churches

1. In 1956, in the basement of New Haven, Connecticut, East Haven Catholic Church, a group called the Five Satins recorded what do-wop classic song?
2. On St. Joseph's day each year, where do the swallows return to?
3. San Antonio de Valero, a mission founded in 1718, served as a fortress on February 23, 1836 during a siege that lasted two weeks. By what other name is this small church known?
4. Quasimodo was the bell-ringer for what Paris church?
5. What is the name of the cathedral in London that is the burial place for all the kings of England?
6. What is the largest Christian church in the world?
7. In what London cathedral were Prince Charles and Lady Diana Spencer married, on July 29, 1981?
8. What large church features 375 members in its choir?
9. From what church tower did Paul Revere receive his signal to make his famous ride on the night of April 18, 1775?
10. George M. Cohan's "Over There" was played at his funeral, becoming the first nonreligious song to be heard in what New York City cathedral?

Codes

1. AF was the Japanese code for what U.S.-held island during World War II?
2. In CB lingo, what does the number 10-20 mean?
3. What popular comic strip by George McManus was nicknamed the Wall Street comic strip, when it was discovered in 1948 to be using a coded message to alert stock market investors to sell or buy certain stocks?
4. When this beautiful Swedish-born actress telephoned Elvis Presley at his Memphis home of Graceland, she used the code name of "Bunny." Name her.

10. *Harry and Tonto* (Tonto was the cat; Harry was played by Art Carney.)

Churches (Answers)

1. "In the Still of the Night"
2. San Juan Capistrano
3. The Alamo
4. Notre Dame
5. Westminster Abbey
6. St. Peter's in the Vatican
7. St. Paul's Cathedral
8. Mormon Tabernacle
9. Old North Church
10. St. Patrick's

Codes (Answers)

1. Midway
2. Location
3. "Bringing up Father"
4. Ann-Margret

5. In 1966, while being interviewed by the North Vietnamese for a confession, on a film which was shown throughout the world, American Prisoner Jeremiah Denton blinked what word in Morse code for the cameras?

6. During World War II the Japanese used what code that had been broken by the United States prior to Pearl Harbor?

7. What is the international distress telegraph signal?

8. What was the password of the D-day invasion of June 6, 1944?

9. How did the U.S. Army disguise its messages over radios or walkie-talkies during World War II?

10. What poem by Verlaine was broadcast by the BBC in 1945 in order to inform the French underground that the D-day invasion was to commence?

Colors

1. Whenever Gary Player plays his favorite sport, golf, he wears what color shoes?

2. The majority of the candies in a package of M & M's are what color?

3. What country singer is known as the man in black?

4. What was actress Jayne Mansfield's favorite color? (Her house as well as her automobile were this color.)

5. Name the four seas named for colors.

6. Can you name the color of Spock's blood on TV's "Star Trek"?

7. What is the traditional color of a bullfighter's cape, although bulls are color-blind?

8. What color shoes does Jack Nicklaus always wear when he golfs?

9. What color are Smurfs?

10. What are the colors of the horses ridden by the four horsemen of the Apocolypse?

11. What is the color of the #1 ball in pool?

12. Which one of the Beatles' movies had a color in the title?

13. What is the name given to two colors that produce a neutral color when mixed together?

14. What are the three primary colors of light?

15. Two #1 hit songs had three-word titles that featured one color that includes all the different colors and another that contains no colors. Name them and the artists that performed them.

5. Torture
6. Purple code
7. S.O.S.
8. Mickey Mouse
9. They used Navajo Indians, who talked to one another in their native tongue.
10. "Ode to Autumn" (It was the second line of the poem that gave the message.)

Colors (Answers)

1. Black
2. Brown
3. Johnny Cash
4. Pink
5. Black, red, yellow, and white
6. Green (because of its copper base)
7. Red
8. White
9. Blue (their clothing is white)
10. White, War; black, Famine; red, Pestilence; and pale green, Death
11. Yellow
12. *Yellow Submarine* (animated film)
13. Complementary colors
14. Red, green and blue
15. "Black and White" by Three Dog Night/"Ebony and Ivory" by Paul McCartney and Stevie Wonder

16. Prior to 1943, the National Broadcasting Company had two radio networks named after colors. What were they?
17. What color is Pennsylvania Avenue on a Monopoly board?
18. What is the color of a bride's wedding gown in China?
19. What color is spelled differently in Great Britain?
20. What is the royal color?

Days

1. What is the first day of Lent called?
2. Thanksgiving Day always falls on what day of the week?
3. On what day in what month does the Supreme Court begin each term?
4. Columbus Day is always celebrated on what day?
5. When is Mothers' Day celebrated?
6. On what day of the week is Mardi Gras celebrated?
7. What happened on Red Sunday, June 25, 1876?
8. What two days of the week do not appear in any title of *Billboard*'s Top 40 hit records?
9. If Monday's child is fair of face, what is Tuesday's child?
10. When is national Election Day?

Distances

1. This cute alien was a mere 3,000,000 miles away from home when he landed on the planet earth. Who was he?
2. What nautical term is used for the distance of three miles?
3. What is the closest distance that Cuba is from the United States?
4. What is the distance between the pitcher's rubber and the home plate in major league baseball?
5. What two cities were at the terminals of the Pony Express route?
6. How far from the coast line do the territorial waters of the United States extend, and how was this determined?
7. Furlongs are used to measure distances in horse racing. How long is a furlong?
8. What is the distance between the stakes in the game of horseshoes?

16. Red and blue
17. Green
18. Red
19. Gray (spelled grey)
20. Purple

Days (Answers)

1. Ash Wednesday
2. Thursday
3. The first Monday in October
4. Monday (the second one in October)
5. The second Sunday in May
6. Tuesday
7. General Custer and his soldiers were defeated at the Battle of the Little Big Horn
8. Wednesday and Thursday
9. Full of grace
10. First Tuesday after the first Monday in November

Distances (Answers)

1. E.T.
2. League
3. 90 miles
4. 60 feet 6 inches
5. St. Joseph, Missouri, and Sacramento, California
6. 3 miles. It was the distance that a coastal cannon could fire a shot.
7. 220 yards
8. 40 feet

9. His home run (which he hit in an exhibition game at Tampa, Florida) on April 4, 1919, was estimated at 579 feet, the longest ever recorded in baseball. Who hit it?

10. What is the length of an Olympic rowing course?

11. What British captain drifted in an open boat with 18 other sailors for nearly 4,000 miles in the South Pacific after his crew mutined in 1789?

12. What is the distance of the Olympic marathon race?

13. What was the distance of the Wright Brothers' first successful flight, which occurred on December 17, 1903?

14. What is the most frequently run distance in sports?

15. Approximately what is the distance of the earth from the sun?

16. Approximately how far is the moon from the earth?

17. How high above the earth would you have to fly to be one mile high?

18. Jules Verne authored a novel about a submarine called the *Nautilus*. What was the title and how many feet underwater did his title represent?

19. What was the very first race run in the modern Olympics?

20. What are the two distances of men's and women's Olympic rowing events?

Dolls

1. Jack Ryan, the sixth husband of actress Zsa Zsa Gabor, created what 11½-inch-tall doll in 1958?

2. What is Barbie's last name?

3. What was the name of the doll that Billy Joe McAllister (Robby Benson) accidently dropped off the Tallahatchee Bridge in the 1976 movie *Ode To Billy Joe?*

4. What was the name of Katharine Hepburn's sailor doll in the 1981 movie *On Golden Pond?*

5. What is the name of the first homosexual doll (which was first marketed in 1978)?

6. What company produced the first Shirley Temple dolls in 1934?

7. What doll with a pointed curl on its head was originated in drawings by Rose O'Neill in 1909? (For years the doll was a prize giveaway at festivals.)

8. What was the name of Buffy's (Anissa Jones) favorite doll on the TV series "Family Affair"?

9. Babe Ruth
10. 1 mile, 427 yards
11. Captain William Bligh
12. 26 miles, 385 yards
13. 120 feet
14. 90 feet (baseball—distance to first base)
15. 93,000,000 miles
16. 238,857 miles (mean distance)
17. 5,280 feet
18. *20,000 Leagues under the Sea* (60,000 miles—league = 3 miles)
19. 100 meters
20. 2,000 meters for men, 1,000 meters for women

Dolls (Answers)

1. Barbie
2. Roberts
3. Benjamin
4. Elmer
5. Gay Bob
6. Ideal (Novelty and Toy Company)
7. Kewpie Doll
8. Mrs. Beasley

9. What is the name of the male doll for boys that has been on the market since the 1960s?
10. In his stories what two very popular rag dolls did Johnny Gruelle create?

Dubious Awards

List the source of the following tongue-in-cheek awards:
1. Dubious Achievement Awards
2. Red Suspenders Awards
3. J. Fred Muggs Awards
4. Fickle Finger of Fate Awards
5. Golden Fleece Awards
6. Plastic Pig Awards (for TV and commercial ads)
7. Sour Apple Award
8. National Lampoon Awards
9. What humorous awards were given on the "Steve Allen Show" on TV?
10. To whom does the *Harvard Lampoon* annually present its Arrested-Development Obligation?

Estates

1. What novelist wrote his exciting stories at his Jamaican retreat called Goldeneye?
2. On November 22, 1916, what American novelist died at his Glen Ellen, California, ranch named Beauty Ranch?
3. What is the name of the country home estate of the British queen or king?
4. What is the name of the Memphis home of the late singer Elvis Presley?
5. Abbotsford is the name of what Scottish novelist (who is called the father of the historical novel)?
6. Falcon's Lair was the exotic Hollywood home of what silent actor?
7. Beatrice Potter created her Peter Rabbit stories at Britain's 400-acre Garfield Place. What other famous female author makes it her home today?

9. G.I. Joe
10. Raggedy Ann and Andy

Dubious Awards (Answers)

1. *Esquire* Magazine
2. *Rolling Stone* Magazine
3. *TV Guide* Magazine
4. TV's "Laugh In"
5. Senator William Proxmire
6. Women Against Pornography (Manhattan group)
7. Hollywood Women's Press Club
8. Harvard University
9. Lousy Awards
10. Jerry Lewis

Estates (Answers)

1. Ian Fleming
2. Jack London
3. Windsor Castle
4. Graceland
5. Sir Walter Scott
6. Rudolph Valentino
7. Barbara Cartland

8. Rolling Stones guitarist Brian Jones lived at this Sussex, England, estate (named Cotchford Farms) until his death in 1969. What famous author of children's stories once lived there?

9. What is the name of the castle of King Arthur, the leader of the Knights of the Round Table?

10. What is the London residence of British royalty (since 1837) called?

Fakes

What schemes are the following two people responsible for?

1. Janet Cooke

2. Clifford Irving

3. This civil war hero, using the name of Frank Thompson, fought at Bull Run in 1861 and Fredericksburg in 1862, also spying behind Confederate lines dressed as a female. What was so unusual about Thompson?

4. What religious name did George Baker use when he founded the Peace Mission Movement?

5. George Hull pulled off what hoax in 1869 when he claimed to have found a 2,990-pound giant near Cooperstown, New York?

6. Who was known as the Great Imposter?

7. What snake pretends it is a cobra when it is in danger?

8. What animal, when it is in danger, pretends it is dead?

9. What 17th-century poet faked the Rowley manuscripts?

10. What Austrian-U.S. violinist created musical pieces that he deceptively attributed to the masters such as Boccherini and Paganini?

Fast Food

1. In 1909, Roy Allen and Fred Wright opened their first root beer stand in Lodi, California. What was its name?

2. Shakey Johnson opened his first store in Sacramento, California, in 1956. What food did he specialize in?

3. William James Harlin founded a stand to sell his unique orange drink, which he decided to name after one of his employees, Julius Freed. What was the drink's name?

8. A. A. Milne
9. Camelot
10. Buckingham Palace

Fakes (Answers)

1. She was the *Washington Post* reporter who won the Pulitzer Prize in 1981 for a story she fabricated.
2. He faked an interview with recluse billionaire Howard Hughes.
3. He was really Sarah Edmonds, who disguised herself as a man.
4. Father Divine
5. Cardiff Giant
6. Ferdinand Waldo Demara
7. Hognose snake
8. Opossum
9. Thomas Chatterton
10. Fritz Kreisler

Fast Food (Answers)

1. A & W Root Beer
2. Pizza (Shakey's Pizza)
3. Orange Julius

4. How many herbs and spices are in Kentucky Fried Chicken?
5. Ray Kroc founded, in 1955, what fast food hamburger chain and became the owner, in 1974, of what major league baseball team?
6. McDonald Hamburgers' training school is located at Elk Grove Village, Illinois. What is its name?
7. The McDonald family did an advertisement on television for what hamburger outlet?
8. In 1984, what fast food chain introduced the cute "Where's the Beef" TV commercial?
9. What type of food do White Castle restaurants feature?
10. Who opened a chain of popcorn stores in Los Angeles in 1983 called Jack's Corn Crib?

Food

1. George Crum is credited with introducing what new food, which he first served to Commodore Cornelius Vanderbilt in 1853?
2. What is Jiggs's favorite food in the comic strip "Bringing Up Father"?
3. In the 1970 movie *Five Easy Pieces*, what did Jack Nicholson order with his chicken salad sandwich?
4. During a space flight on March 23, 1965, astronaut John Young snuck what sandwich on board, for which he was later reprimanded because the crumbs got into the equipment?
5. What special flavor of ice cream did Baskin-Robbins create to celebrate the Beatles' arrival in the United States in February 1964?
6. At his lunch counter in New Haven, Connecticut, in 1900, Louis Lassen invented one of America's favorite meals. What was it?
7. What naturalist is credited with inventing raisin bread?
8. What product calls itself the Butter of Margarine?
9. In 1981, actor Paul Newman began making a product named Newman's Own. What is it?
10. What is the favorite food of J. R. Tolkien's Hobbits?
11. What manufacturer began an annual bake-off in 1949?
12. Housewife Mrs. Ralph E. Smafield became the first winner, with her water-rising twists, of what annual contest?
13. Terlingua, Texas is the annual site of what cook-off?
14. The U.S. Army is the second-biggest supplier of food each day. Who is the first?

4. Eleven
5. McDonalds and the San Diego Padres
6. Hamburger U
7. Burger King
8. Wendy's
9. Hamburgers
10. Jack Klugman

Food (Answers)

1. Potato chips
2. Corned beef and cabbage
3. Sliced tomatoes
4. Corned beef
5. Beatle Nut
6. The hamburger sandwich
7. Henry David Thoreau
8. Imperial margarine
9. Olive oil and vinegar dressing
10. Mushrooms
11. Pillsbury
12. Pillsbury Bake-off
13. International Chili Society
14. McDonald's Hamburgers

15. In 1930, Ruth G. Wakefield introduced what new cookie delight?
16. What traditional dessert food is served at Wimbledon each year?
17. What is the only soup served each and every day in the Congressional cafeteria since 1904, by law?
18. What breakfast cereal was originally called Elijah's Manna?
19. Peter Cooper invented what colorful dessert in 1845?
20. Both Dolly Madison and the wife of a U.S. Navy officer, Nancy Johnson, have been credited with inventing what dessert?

Funerals

1. Who sang "The Battle Hymn of the Republic" at Robert Kennedy's funeral?
2. What two U.S. Presidents are buried at Arlington National Cemetery, the same place that heavyweight boxing champion Joe Louis rests?
3. Who gave the eulogy at the funeral of Stan Laurel in February 1965?
4. Crooner Rudy Vallee sang "Empty Saddles" at what movie cowboy's funeral in October 1940?
5. What was the name of the riderless horse that marched in the funeral of President John F. Kennedy?
6. What New York City mortuary, located on Madison Avenue, handled the funerals of such noted personalities as Rudolph Valentino, in 1928; Judy Garland, in 1969; and John Lennon in 1980?
7. Normally, what is the maximum number of gunshots that can be fired to salute a commonor at a British funeral (royalty gets 20)?
8. Red Foley sang "Peace in the Valley," Ernest Tubb sang "Beyond the Sunset," and Roy Acuff sang "I Saw the Light" at the January 4, 1952 funeral of what singer?
9. When Speaker of the House Sam Rayburn died in 1961, what four U.S. Presidents attended his funeral?
10. As an inside joke, the closest friend of what late comedian played the Ventures instrumental "The 2,000 Pound Bee" at his 1982 funeral?

15. Chocolate chip cookies
16. Strawberries and cream
17. Yankee soup
18. Post Toasties
19. Jell-O (gelatin)
20. Ice cream

Funerals (Answers)

1. Andy Williams
2. William Howard Taft (1932) and John F. Kennedy (1963)
3. Dick Van Dyke
4. Tom Mix's
5. Black Jack
6. Frank E. Cambell
7. 17
8. Hank Williams
9. Harry Truman (past), Dwight D. Eisenhower (past), John F. Kennedy (present) and Lyndon B. Johnson (future)
10. John Belushi (set up by Dan Aykroyd)

Heights

1. What monument stands exactly 555 feet 5½ inches tall?
2. At 6 feet 1 inch tall, what Kansas City Kings player became the shortest player ever to win an NBA scoring title (1972–1973)?
3. How tall is actress Margaux Hemingway?
4. Actors James Dean and Paul Newman were not only rivals for each other's roles in the 1950s, but they were the same height. How tall were they?
5. How tall is the world's highest mountain?
6. This author of horror novels peaks at 6 feet 3 inches. Who is he?
7. Who, in 1956, became the first athlete to high-jump over 7 feet?
8. What is the name of the American who won a Gold Medal when he jumped backward in the high jump?
9. At 6 feet 6¼ inches, who was the tallest heavyweight boxing champion?
10. At 5 feet 4 inches, who was the shortest U.S. President?

Holidays

1. When is Bastille Day?
2. What was the previous name for Veterans Day, which occurs every November 11? The name was changed in 1954.
3. When is Labor Day celebrated in both the United States and Canada?
4. When is Boxing Day?
5. On what day is Thanksgiving celebrated?
6. What was the first national holiday in the United States, occurring on April 30, 1889?
7. What British holiday is named for an unsuccessful assassin of King James I, who was executed for the attempt?
8. Many southern states celebrate whose birthday on January 19?
9. What Presidents' birthdays are national holidays?
10. What religious holiday immediately follows Halloween?

Heights (Answers)

1. The Washington Monument
2. Nate "Tiny" Archibald
3. 6 feet tall
4. 5 feet 9 inches
5. 29,028 feet (Mt. Everest)
6. Stephen King
7. Charlie Dums
8. Dick Fosbury
9. Jess Willard
10. James Madison

Holidays (Answers)

1. July 14
2. Armistice Day
3. First Monday in September
4. December 26
5. Fourth Thursday in November
6. George Washington's inauguration (It did not become an annual event.)
7. Guy Fawkes Day (November 5)
8. Robert E. Lee's
9. George Washington's (only one)
10. All Saints Day

Hospitals

1. What movie, and later television, physician worked at Blair General Hospital?
2. On July 1, 1955, when Eugene Schneider was treated at New York City's Polyclinic Hospital, he was the first patient on what insurance?
3. In what Dallas hospital did President John F. Kennedy die on November 22, 1963?
4. What Washington, DC, hospital is named for an Army physician who went to Cuba to study yellow fever?
5. On May 11, 1751, in what city was the first hospital founded in the United States?
6. In what New York city hospital did composer Stephen Foster die in the charity ward on January 13, 1864?
7. What is the name of the United States' first hospital ship?
8. What is the name of the U.S. hospital ship launched on September 22, 1960, and established by the Health Opportunity for People Everywhere?
9. What entertainer is responsible for the founding of Saint Jude's hospital in Memphis, Tennessee?
10. In what state is Johns Hopkins Hospital located?

Idiosyncrasies

1. Opera singer Luciano Pavarotti keeps what object in his pocket for good luck whenever he sings?
2. Carol Burnette did something each week as a message to her grandmother to signal that everything was all right. What was it?
3. Singer Michael Jackson wears a fresh piece of clothing whenever he performs. What is it?
4. Basketball great Wilt Chamberland always wears what item on his wrist?
5. Actress Claudette Colbert would never allow the camera to film which side of her face?
6. Johnny Cash will only perform wearing what color clothing?

Hospitals (Answers)

1. Dr. Kildare (and his boss Dr. Gillespie)
2. Medicare
3. Parkland Hospital
4. Walter Reed
5. Pennsylvania Hospital in Philadelphia
6. Bellevue
7. U.S.S. *Red Rover*
8. *Hope*
9. Danny Thomas
10. Maryland

Idiosyncrasies (Answers)

1. A bent nail
2. She would tug slightly on her left earlobe
3. A glove on his right hand
4. A rubber band
5. Right side
6. Black

7. What heavyweight boxer always put on his left glove first?
8. For luck, what did Peter Maravich do in his four years of college basketball playing?
9. Who considers it unlucky if you say "good luck"?
10. What TV series comedienne always wore a scarf as part of her dress?

Jewels

1. The Blue Water was a sapphire stolen in what classic 1924 novel by Percival Christopher Wren?
2. What was the name given to the 69.42-carat white diamond that Richard Burton bought for his wife Elizabeth Taylor in March of 1969?
3. What series of films as well as a cartoon character is named for a stolen jewel?
4. The sapphire is the birthstone for what month?
5. The topaz is the birthstone for what month?
6. What seller of railroad equipment had such a love for certain jewels that he nicknamed himself after one?
7. What was the name given to the 45.5-carat diamond that is believed by some to have a curse on it?
8. What is the slogan of Beers diamonds, which Ian Fleming used as a title of one of his novels?
9. What is the name of the world's largest diamond at 530 carats, which is kept in the Tower of London?
10. The Star of Delhi is the world's largest what?

Last Names

1. In 1948, two fellows named Burton and Irving founded an ice cream store chain. What are their last names?
2. On April 7, 1818, brothers Henry and Daniel opened a men's clothing store in Manhattan. What were their last names?
3. A manufacturer with the first name of Walter began producing what automobile in 1924 that is still being produced today?
4. In 1796, a surveyor with the first name of Moses founded what Ohio settlement, which he named in his own honor?

7. Joe Louis
8. He wore the same pair of socks
9. Actors when going on stage
10. Beatrice Arthur (on "Maude")

Jewels (Answers)

1. Beau Geste
2. Cartier—Burton Diamond
3. The Pink Panther, which was a diamond
4. September
5. November
6. Diamond Jim Brady
7. The Hope Diamond
8. "Diamonds are forever"
9. Star of Africa
10. Emerald

Last Names (Answers)

1. Baskin and Robbins, respectively
2. Brooks (Brooks Brothers)
3. Chrysler
4. Cleveland

5. What young doctor by the name of George became a well-known poll taker?

6. Baseball great Hank Greenberg's father-in-law, Bernard, founded a New York City department store in Herald Square, which rivals Macy's and bears his last name. Name it.

7. A man named Milton introduced this milk chocolate bar in 1895, naming it after himself. What was his famous last name?

8. John founded an automobile rental company in 1923 which he originally named The Drive-Ur-Self System. Give John's famous last name?

9. This turn-of-the-century piano salesman, Matt Honk, lent his name to what style of piano music?

10. In 1950, a man named Arthur established the television rating system. What was Arthur's last name?

11. In 1904, two British gentlemen by the names of Charles and Frederick founded an automobile manufacturing company that is still working today. Name the car they created?

12. Henry and William founded a stagecoach line, which today has evolved into a huge banking firm west of the Mississippi. Name it.

13. Henry and Richard decided to establish a company in 1956 to help people with their income taxes. What company did they found?

14. What are the last names of 1950s rock singers Fabian and Dion?

15. What is the last name of actress Ann-Margret?

16. What two candy makers are represented by one of their candies— M & M's?

17. What First Lady did not have to change her last name when she married her future-President husband?

18. There have been four sets of Presidents that have had the same last names. Name them.

19. What is British folk singer Donovan's last name?

20. What is American soul singer Little Richard's last name?

Lasts

1. The last movie that Babe Ruth attended took place on July 26, 1948; it was also his last public appearance. What was the film's title?

5. Dr. George Gallup
6. Gimbels
7. Hershey
8. Hertz
9. Honky Tonk
10. Neilsen
11. Rolls-Royce (Charles Rolls and Frederick Royce)
12. Wells Fargo (Henry Wells and William Fargo)
13. H & R Block
14. Forte and DiMucci, respectively
15. Olsson
16. Mars and Murray
17. Eleanor Roosevelt
18. John Adams and John Quincy Adams, Andrew Johnson and Lyndon Johnson, William Henry Harrison and Benjamin Harrison, and Theodore Roosevelt and Franklin Roosevelt
19. Leitch
20. Penniman

Lasts (Answers)

1. *The Babe Ruth Story* starring William Bendix

2. Heisman trophy-winner John Cappeletti, in 1977, caught the very last pass thrown in a game by what quarterback?

3. On December 21, 1941, Chicago Bear's Ray "Scooter" McLean performed the last one of these in a NFL game. What was it?

4. What was the title of the last episode of the TV series "M*A*S*H"? This special episode ran 2½ hours in 1983.

5. In 1920, pitcher Burleigh Grimes became the last major league player to do what?

6. Who was the lone survivor of the Yana Indian tribe that made contact with white people for the first time in Oroville, California, in 1911?

7. Who appeared on the cover of the last issue of *Collier*'s magazine on January 4, 1957?

8. In March 1952, John Thomas Moore, aged 65, committed suicide. He had been the last surviving witness of what historical event of December 17, 1903?

9. What was both Marilyn Monroe's and Clark Gable's last completed film (which was released on Gable's 60th birthday on February 1, 1961)?

10. What was the name of the U.S. Coast Guard cutter that, on July 3, 1937, made the last communication with aviator Amelia Earhart before her disappearance?

Medals

1. What is the Soviet Union's highest military honor?

2. What American Medal of Honor winner was decorated with the service cross of the German Eagle in 1938 by Herman Goering?

3. What is the highest military medal given in the United Kingdom?

4. President George Washington authorized the first U.S. medal. What was it?

5. On June 12, 1965, Queen Elizabeth II conferred what medal on the rock band the Beatles?

6. What medal is presented as the highest award a civilian can receive in the United States?

7. What medal was originally called the "Badge of Military Merit"?

8. What U.S. military medal can only be awarded to enlisted men?

9. In a ceremony in March 1984, Private Adam Paczkowski was awarded a Purple Heart for injuries he received in battle. In what war was he injured?

2. Joe Namath
3. Drop-kick
4. "Good-bye, Farewell, and Amen"
5. Be authorized to throw a spitball (until he retired in 1934)
6. Ishi
7. Grace Kelly
8. The Wright Brothers's first flight near Kitty Hawk
9. *The Misfits*
10. U.S.S. *Itasca*

Medals (Answers)

1. Order of Lenin
2. Charles Lindbergh
3. Victoria Cross
4. Purple Heart
5. MBE (Members of the Order of the British Empire)
6. President's Medal
7. Purple Heart
8. Good Conduct Medal
9. World War I

10. Who was the only U.S. President to have received the highest award given by the United States?

Money

1. A check was drawn in August 1983 for the amount of $813,487,500. What was the significance of the check?
2. Although she made as much as $300,000 per film, what young actress received a weekly allowance of just $4.25?
3. How much did the room to let cost in the lyric of Roger Miller's 1965 hit record "King of the Road"?
4. Lucy Holcombe Pickens's likeness appeared on the $1 and on the $100 note of what country in 1862?
5. In 1983, the wife of what entertainer asked the courts for monthly alimony payments of $220,000?
6. What sports philosopher once noted, "A nickle ain't worth a dime anymore"?
7. By law one need not accept any payment in pennies over how much money?
8. What unit of measure is the equivalent of one-tenth of a penny?
9. What gimmick did Melville E. Stone introduce in 1875 with respect to the pricing of merchandise?
10. Whose portrait is on the U.S. $2.00 bill?

Monuments

1. What U.S. President's 555-foot-tall monument in Washington, DC, was designed by Robert Mills in 1836?
2. Although it was presented to the United States in 1884, it wasn't until 1924 that what became a national monument?
3. Industrialist William Henry Vanderbilt contributed $100,000 for the erection of what monument in New York City's Central Park?
4. There is a duplicate of this monument in Niles, Illinois, but the original can still be found in Pisa, Italy. Name it.
5. What is the only mobile national monument in the United States?
6. In what state is Craters of the Moon monument located? (It was established there in 1924.)

10. George Washington (he was presented the Congressional Medal in 1776, which at the time was the country's highest award)

Money (Answers)

1. It was Chrysler president Lee Iaccoca's final loan payment to the U.S. government (seven years ahead of schedule).
2. Shirley Temple
3. 50¢
4. The Confederate States of America
5. Johnny Carson. The request was made by his wife, Joanna.
6. Yogi Berra
7. 25¢
8. A mill.
9. He subtracted a penny from the price, making it appear to be cheaper, i.e., $1.99, $3.99, etc.
10. Thomas Jefferson

Monuments (Answers)

1. George Washington's (Washington Monument)
2. The Statue of Liberty
3. Cleopatra's Needle
4. The Leaning Tower of Pisa
5. San Francisco's cable cars
6. Idaho

7. What U.S. vessel, permanently moved to Houston, became the first battleship to become a state shrine?
8. What memorial dedicated on November 13, 1982, has 57,939 names on it?
9. In what city is Grant's Tomb located?
10. In Nashville, Tennessee, there is a memorial to what public enemy?

Mysteries

1. What nickname was given to the mysterious woman who would place 13 roses on the grave of film star Rudolph Valentino?
2. Whom did Martin Luther King's assassin, James Earl Ray, claim was his contact?
3. An unknown mysterious creature called Yeti has been seen in the Himalayas. How is his cousin who has been spotted in Northern California referred to?
4. Who is the Swedish businessman who saved over 30,000 lives during World War II only to be arrested by the Russians in 1945? (His fate remains unknown today.)
5. What mysterious underwater creature is named for the Scottish lake in which it resides?
6. At what incident did a mysterious man with an umbrella appear who was later identified but not before he caused much speculation?
7. According to Plato, what island nation once existed in the Atlantic Ocean?
8. What mysterious Canadian island is the location of a treasure that has yet to be dug up?
9. On what South Pacific Island are located huge mysterious rock statues that were carved by a people long extinct?
10. What mystery writer disappeared for a period of 11 days in 1926? (An event that she never explained.)

7. U.S.S. *Texas*
8. Vietnam Veterans Memorial in Washington, DC
9. New York City
10. John Dillinger

Mysteries (Answers)

1. The Lady in Black
2. Raoul
3. Big Foot
4. Raoul Wallenberg
5. Loch Ness Monster ("Nessie")
6. President John F. Kennedy's assassination
7. Atlantis
8. Oak Island
9. Easter Island
10. Agatha Christie

Nemeses

1. Black Pete was the nemesis of what early cartoon rodent?
2. Six-feet 8-inch, 372-pound Bluto is the nemesis of what mild-mannered sailor?
3. Who is the archenemy of Woody Woodpecker?
4. Captain Cold is chief nemesis of what comic book hero?
5. Lex Luthor is whose chief nemesis?
6. Although his sole purpose for living is trying to capture the Road Runner, he has yet to trap the speedy bird. Name him.
7. The Dragon Lady was the oriental enemy of what all-American hero?
8. What Emperor of the planet Mongo did Flash Gordon constantly battle?
9. Ernest Stavro Blofeld is one of whose nemeses?
10. The Riddler and the Catwoman were only two of a number of evil villains battled by whom?

Onlys

1. This actress won an Oscar nomination for Best Supporting Actress for the 1966 film *Hawaii*, which would be her *only* movie appearance. Name her.
2. *The Cardinal's Mistress* is the title of the *only* novel ever written by what World War II axis leader?
3. *Discourse on the Aborigines Of the Valley Of Ohio*, written in 1839, is the title of the *only* book ever written by what American President?
4. Ludwig Beethoven *only* wrote one opera, which was originally titled *Lenore*. What is its title today?
5. Who is the *only* football player to have won the Heisman Trophy twice (1974–1975)?
6. Lionel, Ethel, and John Barrymore *only* appeared together once in motion pictures. What is the name of the 1932 film?
7. Who was the *only* American athlete to win a Gold Medal at the 1964 Winter Olympics at Innsbruck, Austria?

Nemeses (Answers)

1. Mickey Mouse
2. Popeye
3. Buzz Buzzard
4. The Flash
5. Superman's
6. Wile E. Coyote
7. Terry (Terry and the Pirates)
8. Ming
9. James Bond's
10. Batman and Robin

Onlys (Answers)

1. Jocelyne Lagarde
2. Benito Mussolini
3. William Henry Harrison
4. *Fidelio*
5. Archie Griffin
6. *Rasputin and the Empress*
7. Terry McDermott (500-meter speed skating race)

8. Who was the *only* boxer to have met both Rocky Marciano (in 1955) and Muhammad Ali (in 1962) in the ring?

9. Who is the only person to have scaled Mt. Everest and to have undergone a sex change?

10. The Rose Bowl game was not played in Pasadena, California, *only* once, in 1942. Where was it played that year?

Pairs

1. What two animals' names describe the action of the stock market?

2. What pair of guitarists recorded a country album in 1977 under the title of Chester and Lester?

3. The only time that this brother and sister dance team appeared together on film was recorded in the 1931 short subject *Funny Face*. Who were they?

4. With his partner, Mark Goodson, he created such TV game shows as "What's My Line?," "I've Got A Secret," and "Password." Who is he?

5. What did New York Yankee players Mike Kokich and Fritz Peterson give one another in 1973?

6. What unusual duo recorded the 1982 British hit song "Peace On Earth"?

7. What singing and acting couple were named "America's Sweethearts"?

8. Moss Hart collaborated with what other playwright to write *You Can't Take It with You* and *The Man Who Came to Dinner?*

9. Who were the two drifters who were the heroes of John Steinbeck's novel *Of Mice and Men?*

10. The 1940 film *My Little Chickadee* saw the only movie pairing of what comedians?

Prisons

1. Name the Federal prison that sat on an island in the San Francisco Bay from 1933 until 1963.

2. What film director spent a four-month sentence at the Wayside Honor Farm in Castaic, California, in 1952 for the shooting of agent Jennings Lang?

8. Archie Moore
9. James (now Jan) Morris
10. Durham, North Carolina

Pairs (Answers)

1. Bull and bear
2. Chet Atkins and Les Paul
3. Fred Astaire and Adele Astaire
4. Bill Todman
5. They swapped wives
6. Bing Crosby and David Bowie
7. Nelson Eddy and Jeanette McDonald
8. George S. Kaufman
9. Lennie and George
10. Mae West and W. C. Fields

Prisons (Answers)

1. Alcatraz
2. Walter Wanger

3. Herbert Youngblood was the black man who accompanied what public enemy #1 when he broke out of Indiana's Crown Point Prison on March 3, 1934?

4. What was the main cell block corridor at Alcatraz prison called?

5. In 1971, a riot at what prison caused more casualties in any single engagement between Americans since the Civil War?

6. In 1924, he wrote his autobiography (the title of which translates as "My Struggle") in cell 7 in Landsberg Prison near Munich. Name him.

7. In what two California prisons has Johnny Cash recorded live albums?

8. What was the name of the French Island prison colony off the French Guiana?

9. What French writer spent 27 years of his life in prison for sexual offenses?

10. Lewis E. Lawes, author of several books, such as *Invisible Stripes* (1940) and *Castle on the Hudson* (1940), as well as host of a TV series, was the warden of what prison?

11. What country singer had a hit with the song "11 months and 29 days," the length of time that he once spent in prison?

12. What Detroit Tigers baseball player spent time in prison for theft before he played major league baseball?

13. John Dillinger once served in a state prison in 1917 that had the same name as the battleship he was once stationed on in the Navy. Name the prison.

14. By what name is Sing Sing prison known today?

15. Name the six federal penitentiary locations?

16. What short story writer, who created *The Cisco Kid*, was sent to a federal penitentiary in Columbus, Ohio, for band fund embezzlement?

17. Who is the only inmate of Spandau Prison in West Berlin?

18. Billy Hayes authored what book later made into a movie that told about his experiences in a Turkish prison?

19. What was the name of the largest Confederate prison camp (located at Americus, Georgia)?

20. What was the name of the largest concentration camp established by the Germans during World War II?

3. John Dillinger
4. Broadway
5. Attica Prison in New York State
6. Adolf Hitler
7. Folsom Prison and San Quentin
8. Devil's Island
9. Marquis de Sade
10. Sing Sing
11. Johnny Paycheck
12. Ron LeFlore
13. Utah State Prison (U.S.S. *Utah*)
14. Ossining
15. Atlanta, GA; Leavenworth, KS; Lewisburg, PA; McNeil Island, WA; Marion, IL; and Terre Haute, IN
16. O. Henry (William Porter)
17. Rudolph Hess
18. *Midnight Express*
19. Andersonville
20. Auschwitz

Ranches

1. What was the name of the house of prostitution in the country in the 1982 movie *The Best Little Whorehouse in Texas?*
2. What is the biggest ranch in Hawaii?
3. Radio's Bobby Benson owned what Texas big band country ranch on radio?
4. On what Texas ranch did the owner half bury a certain make of automobile? (It inspired a song by Bruce Springsteen.)
5. What is the name of the rock group Chicago's Boulder, Colorado recording studio?
6. What 1965–1969 TV series took place on the 30,000-acre Barkley Ranch?
7. Hop-a-Long Cassidy, played by William Boyd, lived on what ranch?
8. What huge, 500,000-acre Texas ranch near Corpus Christi is the size of the state of Delaware?
9. In what classic western novel, which has been filmed a number of times, would one find the Box H Ranch?
10. What is the name of movie producer George Lucas's $50-million, 1,735-acre Marin County California studio ranch?

Restaurants

1. In what Times Square restaurant in New York City did Gene MacKran once work as a doorman, Tony Franciosa as a waiter, and both Sandy Duncan and Lily Tomlin as waitresses?
2. What humorous columnist and book author always sits at table 12 in the Sans Souci Restaurant in Washington, DC?
3. What Hollywood restaurant on Wilshire Blvd., designed by Cecil B. DeMille, was a favorite hangout for columnists Louella O. Parsons and Hedda Hopper?
4. What Stockbridge, Massachusetts, cafe, owned by Alice May Brock, became the subject of both a 1969 hit song and a movie?
5. What New York City restaurant is alluded to in many stories by Damon Runyon?

Ranches (Answers)

1. Chicken Ranch
2. Parker Ranch
3. B Bar B Ranch
4. Cadillac Ranch
5. Caribou Ranch
6. The Big Valley
7. Bar-20 Ranch
8. King Ranch
9. *The Virginian*
10. Sky Walker Ranch

Restaurants (Answers)

1. Howard Johnson's
2. Art Buchwald
3. The Brown Derby
4. Alice's Restaurant (which inspired Arlo Guthrie's "Alice's Rock & Roll Restaurant")
5. Lindy's

6. What famous New York City restaurant became the first to offer printed menus in 1836?
7. What world-famous Hollywood landmark drug store and restaurant closed forever in December 1983?
8. Where do the casts of a new Broadway play traditionally go to celebrate opening night?
9. Who was the Hollywood restaurant owner who proclaimed that he was a Russian prince?
10. What is the famous New York City restaurant and nightclub that is named for its address?

Safe Places

1. Where is the Declaration of Independence kept?
2. Where is the gold supply of the United States located?
3. Where are the British royal crowns safely kept?
4. Where is one of the world's most popular paintings, the *Mona Lisa,* kept?
5. Where can one find the world's largest emerald, the Star of Deli?
6. Coded 7X, the secret ingredients of this product are kept in a safe in Atlanta, Georgia. Name the product.
7. What is the most common method of creating a combination for one's own safe?
8. Where is the Wright brothers' first airplane kept?
9. In 1870, prospector Jacob Walz discovered what famous gold mine in the Superstition Mountains, the location of which remains a mystery today?
10. The forty thieves kept all their treasures safely in a cave until Ali Baba learned the magic words to open the cave door. What were the secret words?

Sevens

1. What are the seven deadly sins?
2. Name the seven dwarfs.
3. What are traditionally known as the seven seas?
4. What are the seven virtues?
5. Name the seven wonders of the classical world.

6. Delmonico's Restaurant
7. Schwab's
8. Sardi's
9. Mike Romanoff
10. "21"

Safe Places (Answers)

1. National Archives
2. Fort Knox
3. The Tower of London
4. The Louvre
5. Tower of London
6. Coca-Cola
7. Using one's birthdate (e.g., 9-22-43)
8. Smithsonian Institute
9. Lost Dutchman
10. "Open Sesame"

Sevens (Answers)

1. Pride, Avarice, Wrath, Envy, Gluttony, Sloth, and Lust
2. Bashful, Doc, Dopey, Grumpy, Happy, Sleepy, and Sneezy
3. Indian, North Pacific, South Pacific, Antarctic, Arctic, North Atlantic, and the South Atlantic
4. Faith, Hope, Charity (Love), Fortitude, Justice, Prudence, and Temperance
5. Colossus of Rhodes, Egyptian Pyramids, Hanging Gardens of Babylon, lighthouse at Alexandria, mausoleum at Halicarnassus, statue of Zeus at Olympia, Temple of Diana at Ephesus

6. What are the seven works of mercy?
7. Dasher was the first of Santa's reindeer. Name the other seven.
8. In what constellation would one find the seven sisters?
9. The seven blocks of granite was the nickname of the line of what college football team in the 1930s?
10. What grouping do the following seven men belong to: Bias, Chilon, Cleobulus, Periander, Pittacus, Solon, and Thales?

Signs

1. What did the HOLLYWOOD sign on Mt. Lee overlooking Hollywood, California, originally read before it was changed?
2. On the TV show "The Partridge Family" what sign was printed on the back of the family bus?
3. What does the world-famous neon cigarette billboard in Times Square advertise?
4. What square in London is the site of many colorful neon signs?
5. Where can be found the most expensive billboards advertising artist's latest movie and record releases?
6. What aftershave company gave little witty sayings on their roadside signs from the 1930s to the 1950s?
7. What popular Australian rock group took their name from a road sign?
8. On what European structure was the largest sign ever created, to advertise the movie *The Longest Day?*
9. P. T. Barnum created what sign in his New York City museum in order to keep crowds moving?
10. At the Scopes Monkey trial in 1925, what was the sign on the wall behind what was supposed to be an impartial judge, John T. Raulston?

Stamps

1. Who was the first comic strip character to appear on a postage stamp (issued in Turkey in 1952)?
2. What was the first country to use an adhesive postage stamp?
3. What is the only nation that is not required to include its name on its stamp?

6. Bury the dead, clothe the naked, feed the hungry, give drink to the thirsty, house the homeless, tend the sick, and visit the fatherless and afflicted.
7. Dancer, Prancer, Vixon, Comet, Cupid, Donner, and Blitzen
8. Pleiades
9. Fordham University
10. The Seven Sages of Greece (or Seven Wise Men)

Signs (Answers)

1. HOLLYWOODLAND
2. Slow, Nervous mother driving
3. Camel cigarettes
4. Picadilly Circus
5. Sunset Blvd. in Hollywood
6. Burma Shave
7. Men At Work
8. Eiffel Tower
9. TO THE EGRESS (which was really the exit)
10. READ YOUR BIBLE

Stamps (Answers)

1. Henry
2. Iraq
3. Britain

4. In 1956, actress Grace Kelly became the first American actress to have her portrait on a stamp. What country issued it?

5. What was the first U.S. postage stamp to be pulled off the market since the Civil War?

6. In what years did the U.S. government issue its first stamp?

7. What is the name of the U.S. 24¢ airmail stamp that showed the airplane on it, upside down? (A single stamp today is worth $36,000.)

8. What is the name of the extremely rare postage stamp that was the first to bear a portrait of Queen Victoria?

9. Scotsman James Chalmers introduced what postal innovation?

10. Who was the first living American to be depicted on a postage stamp?

Symbols

1. The Rock of Gibraltar is the symbol of what life insurance company?

2. The Blue Eagle was the symbol of what New Deal administration?

3. What profession uses the Caduceus as its symbol?

4. What is the name of the lion that is both the symbol and the trademark of MGM pictures in Hollywood?

5. What is the chemical symbol for ice?

6. What is the name for the character "&" ?

7. What bird did Benjamin Franklin want as the national symbol of the United States?

8. What gasoline company once used the symbol of a flying red horse?

9. Artist Frank Liberman named his Kangaroo trademark symbol of Pocket Books after his mother-in-law. Name her.

10. Sixteen-year-old Jane Chester posed for what company's logo (called the Proud Lady)?

4. Monaco
5. Olympics 1980 (15¢)
6. 1847
7. Inverted Jenny
8. Penny Black
9. Adhesive postage stamp
10. Charles Lindbergh

Symbols (Answers)

1. Prudential
2. NRA (National Recovery Administration)
3. Medical
4. Leo
5. H_2O
6. Ampersand
7. Turkey
8. Mobil Oil
9. Gertrude
10. Columbia Pictures

Time

1. In what year was standard time adopted throughout the United States?
2. How many minutes does it take for light to travel from the sun to the earth?
3. In the nursery rhyme at what time did Wee Willie Winkle run through town?
4. How long is a time-out in the NFL (National Football League)?
5. How long, in playing time, is an average professional basketball game?
6. What first occurred on April 24, 1932?
7. What is a period of play called in a polo game?
8. When Anthony Quinn won an Academy Award for Best Supporting Actor, for the 1956 movie *Lust For Life,* he spent the shortest time on film of any actor to win an Oscar. How long was he on screen?
9. The Steeple Clock of Miss Havisham's house was intentionally stopped at 8:40 and left at that time in Charles Dickens's novel *Great Expectations.* Why did Miss Havisham stop the clock?
10. What time is shown on a bar of Dial soap?

Trees

1. From what tree was the killer Tom Dooley hung in the 1958 hit song "Tom Dooley," by the Kingston Trio?
2. How many yellow ribbons were tied around the old oak tree in the 1972 hit song "Tie A Yellow Ribbon 'Round the Ole Oak Tree" by Tony Orlando and Dawn?
3. Standing 272 feet, 4 inches tall, this giant sequoia, located at the Sequoia National Park, is considered the largest tree in the world. What is its name?
4. A koala bear's only food is the leaves from what kind of a tree?
5. Thor Heyerdahl's 1947 raft *Kon-Tiki* was made out of wood of what tree?
6. What is the nickname of John Chapman, who, during the years 1774 to 1845, planted thousands of trees throughout the Allegheny and Ohio valleys?

Time (Answers)

1. 1884
2. 8 minutes
3. 8:00
4. 2 minutes
5. 48 minutes
6. Daylight savings time
7. A chucker
8. 8 minutes
9. It was the exact time that her wedding had been called off.
10. 8:00

Trees (Answers)

1. Oak tree
2. 100
3. General Sherman
4. Eucalyptus tree
5. Balsa tree
6. Johnny Appleseed

7. Scottish botanist David Douglas had a tree named for him that can be found in the western United States. Name it.
8. What was the cargo of the H.M.S. *Bounty* at the time of the famous mutiny in 1789?
9. President William Taft's wife, First Lady Helen Taft, requested that what trees should be planted throughout Washington, DC, after she visited Japan?
10. What tree has the most leaves?

Trick Questions

1. How many months have 28 days in them?
2. What king lived in, and had the leadership of, the United States?
3. What is the answer to this riddle: Brothers and sisters, I have none, but this man's father is my father's son?
4. How many grooves are on one side of a 33⅓ rpm record that runs exactly 3 minutes long, with a lead-in of 30 seconds and a overrun of 30 more seconds?
5. Does the widow of the Unknown Soldier receive a government pension and does his son win an automatic admission into West Point?
6. Is it legal for a man to marry his widow's sister?
7. Who all is buried in Grant's Tomb?
8. What creature goes on four feet in the morning, on two at noon, and on three in the evening?
9. What was the President's name exactly 20 years ago?
10. How much dirt is in a hole 2½ feet by 2½ feet by 2 feet?

Trophies

Name the trophy awarded to the winners of the following contests:
1. The annual football game between Michigan State and Indiana.
2. The Academy of Motion Pictures Arts and Sciences Awards.
3. The annual football games between Pittsburgh, Penn State, and West Virginia University.
4. The annual football game between Brigham Young and Utah State.
5. The annual football game between Northwest Louisiana and Louisiana Tech.

7. Douglas fir (or spruce)
8. Breadfruit trees
9. Cherry trees
10. Cypress

Trick Questions (Answers)

1. 12
2. Leslie King (Gerald Ford's born name)
3. My son
4. 1 groove
5. No—the Unknown Soldier is unknown.
6. No, but since he's dead it's really academic.
7. Ulysses S. Grant and his wife, Julie Denton Grant (Since the question asked for *all*, both names must be answered)
8. Man (crawls as a baby, walks as a man, and uses a cane as an elderly person)
9. The same as it is today
10. None—there is no dirt in a hole.

Trophies (Answers)

1. Old Brass Spittoon
2. The Oscar
3. Old Ironsides
4. Old Wagon Wheel
5. Rag

6. The annual football game between Lamar Tech and Southwest Louisiana.

7. The annual Notre Dame-Southern California and Notre Dame-Purdue football games.

8. The annual football game between Virginia Military Institute and the Citadel.

9. In 1949, Roy Conacher became the first recipient of the Art Ross Trophy. For what sport is it awarded?

10. Prior to being given rings, what trophy was the winning team of the World Series presented with?

11. The Avco World Trophy is awarded to the winner of what association?

12. The Bermuda Bowl is presented to the winner in what game?

13. Hockey's Golden Memorial Trophy is presented to what player each year?

14. Football's Super Bowl trophy is named in whose honor?

15. Who is the only woman to have her name inscribed on the Stanley Cup?

16. The Walker Cup is given in what sport?

17. The Art Ross Trophy is annually awarded to the top scorer in what league?

18. The Bendix Trophy is a coveted award in what field?

19. What magazine gives out the Grecian Urn to the sportsman of the year?

20. To what amateur team is the Eisenhower Trophy presented?

Voices

1. Who provides the "rap" narration on Michael Jackson's 1983 hit song "Thriller"?

2. This voice of dozens of Warner Bros. cartoon characters was provided by the "Man of a Thousand Voices." Name him.

3. Who was the uncredited voice of the devil in the 1973 movie *The Exorcist?*

4. Who is the voice of Charlie the Tuna in TV commercials?

5. What well-known television actor was once the public address announcer at Ebbets Field in Flatbush, New York?

6. During World War II, by what popular name was Iva Toguri d'Aquino better known?

6. Sabine Shoe
7. Shillelagh
8. Silver Shako
9. Hockey
10. Watches
11. World Hockey
12. Bridge (cards)
13. NHL's Rookie of the Year
14. Vince Lombardi
15. Marguerite Norris Riker (president of Detroit Red Wings)
16. Amateur golf
17. NHL (National Hockey League)
18. Aviation
19. *Sports Illustrated*
20. Golf

Voices (Answers)

1. Vincent Price
2. Mel Blanc
3. Mercedes McCambridge
4. Herschel Bernardi
5. John Forsythe
6. Tokyo Rose

7.   Who provided the singing voice of Prince Charming in the 1950 Walt Disney animated film *Cinderella?*
8.   John "Shorty" Powers was one of the voices of what?
9.   Who is the voice of the Mermaid on Chicken of the Sea TV commercials?
10. What soprano dubbed the singing voice for Audrey Hepburn in the 1964 film *My Fair Lady* and for Natalie Wood in the 1961 film *West Side Story?*

Weight

1.   350 pounds is the minimum weight to become what kind of wrestler?
2.   How many pounds are in a ton?
3.   How much did Charles Atlas weigh before he began his body-building program?
4.   What famous rock weighs 7 tons?
5.   What fraction of the earth's surface is the moon's?
6.   What cwazzy Warner Bros. cartoon wabbit weighs in at 6⅞ pounds?
7.   What weight must all horses carry in the Triple Crown?
8.   Who is the only heavyweight boxer who was outweighed in all of his 13 heavyweight championship bouts?
9.   What weighs more, a pound of feathers or a pound of gold?
10. Whose hamburger patties weigh exactly 1.6 ounces?

7. Mike Douglas
8. Mission Control at Cape Canaveral
9. Darla Hood
10. Marni Nixon

Weight (Answers)

1. Sumo wrestlers
2. 2,000
3. 97 pounds
4. Plymouth Rock
5. ⅙
6. Bugs Bunny
7. 126 pounds
8. Floyd Patterson
9. Feathers (Feathers are weighed in avoirdupois at 16 ounces per pound, while gold is weighed in tons at 12 ounces per pound.)
10. McDonald's

The Entertainment

World

Academy Awards

1. Who was the only person to present himself with an Academy Award, when he announced his own name after opening the envelope for Best Song of 1942?
2. In 1928, Joseph Farnham won three Academy Awards for a category in which no one else has ever been nominated. Name the category.
3. What was the first color film to win the Oscar for Best Picture?
4. What fashion designer is the winner of 11 Academy Awards?
5. In 1981, who won an Oscar for Best Director in his debut as a director?
6. Who won an Academy Award for Best Actor, portraying a military Medal of Honor winner?
7. Who is the only actor to win an Academy Award for Best Actor for playing two different people?
8. What 1958 film received 9 Oscars out of its 9 nominations?
9. What was the only western to win Best Film, in 1930/1931?
10. What two films have won the top 5 Oscars: Best Picture, Best Actor, Best Actress, Best Director, and Best Screenplay?

Actresses-Autobiographies

1. *Change Lobsters and Dance* is the 1975 autobiography of what Austrian-born actress?
2. *Changing* is the title of the 1977 autobiography of what Norwegian actress?
3. Who is the "I" in the 1983 autobiography *Charles Laughton and I?*
4. Two of her autobiographies are titled *Don't Fall Off the Mountain* and *You Can Get There from Here*. Who is she?

Academy Awards (Answers)

1. Irving Berlin
2. Writing the titles for slient films
3. *Gone with the Wind* (1939)
4. Edith Head
5. Robert Redford for *Ordinary People* (1980)
6. Gary Cooper, who portrayed Sgt. Alvin York in the 1941 *Sergeant York*
7. Lee Marvin in *Cat Ballou* (1971) (Fredric March won for *Dr. Jekyl and Mr. Hyde*, but that was playing one person with two personalities.)
8. *Gigi*
9. *Cimarron*
10. *It Happened One Night* (1934) and *One Flew Over the Cuckoo's Nest* (1975)

Actresses-Autobiographies (Answers)

1. Lilli Palmer
2. Liv Ullmann
3. Elsa Lanchester
4. Shirley MacLaine

5. What actress had two autobiographies, the first about her early life, titled *Early Havoc*, and the sequel about her later life, *Cry Havoc?*

6. What Austrian-born actress wrote her autobiography in 1966 under the title of *Ecstasy and Me?*

7. Who wrote her memoirs in 1949, titling the book *A Feather on My Nose?*

8. *Goodness Had Nothing to Do with It* was the 1959 autobiography of what sexy actress?

9. The title of actress Rosalind Russell's 1977 autobiography was taken from a line she said in the play *Auntie Mame*. Name it.

10. *The Lonely Life* and *Mother Goddam* are two autobiographies of what actress?

11. *My Heart Belongs* is the title of the 1976 autobiography of actor Larry Hagman's mother. Who is she?

12. Garson Kanin's actress wife has written two books of memoirs—*My Side* and *An Open Book*. Name her.

13. *My Story* is the 1980 title of the huge volume of memoirs from what Swedish-born actress?

14. *My Young Life* is the title of what child actresses's autobiography?

15. Olivia DeHaviland's sister wrote the autobiography *No Bed of Roses* in 1978. Give her name.

16. One of three sisters, this actress named her kiss-and-tell book *Orchids and Salami*. Who is she?

17. *The Quality of Mercy* is the title of the 1981 autobiography of whom?

18. Whose autobiography is titled *Scarlett O'Hara's Younger Sister?*

19. *Shelley, Also Known as Shirley* is the first autobiography of which actress named Shelley?

20. *Sunshine and Shadow* is the 1955 life story of what actress of the silent screen?

Banned

1. While Queen Elizabeth II toured Canada in 1960, what popular song, by Johnny Horton, was banned on that country's radios?

2. Who does a comedy skit about the seven words that are banned on television?

 5. June Havoc
 6. Hedy Lamarr
 7. Billie Burke
 8. Mae West
 9. *Life is a Banquet*
10. Bette Davis
11. Mary Martin
12. Ruth Gordon
13. Ingrid Bergman
14. Shirley Temple's
15. Joan Fontaine
16. Eva Gabor
17. Mercedes McCambridge
18. Evelyn Keyes
19. Shelley Winters
20. Mary Pickford

Banned (Answers)

 1. "Battle of New Orleans"
 2. George Carlin

3. When the Everly Brothers' 1957 hit song "Wake Up, Little Susie" was released, what U.S. city actually banned the record?

4. What Marlon Brando film was banned in Great Britain for eleven years?

5. What movie was banned in Egypt for 20 years because the female star had converted to Judaism?

6. What song would CBS not allow Bob Dylan to sing on the "Ed Sullivan Show" in 1963? (Dylan refused to appear.)

7. What name was given to the men who appeared before the House Committee on Unamerican Activities Hearings in 1947? (Because they decided to take the 5th Amendment, they were banned from their industry.)

8. What is the name of Boston's organization that does the banning of all types of items?

9. Donald Duck's comic strip was banned in Finland in 1978 for what ridiculous reason?

10. During World War II, Benito Mussolini banned all American comic strip characters but one. Who was he?

Cartoonists

1. What *Playboy* cartoonist composed the Grammy Award-winning song "A Boy Named Sue," which was recorded by Johnny Cash?

2. What award-winning cartoonist is nicknamed "Sparky"?

3. What underground cartoonist is known for his *Keep on Trucking* designs?

4. Born in 1907, what cartoonist created such comic strips as *Terry and the Pirates* and *Steve Canyon*?

5. What cartoonist played a bit role in the 1951 movie *The Red Badge of Courage*?

6. What cartoonist drew the people of Dogpatch for many years?

7. What cartoonist's illustrations of facts (first published in 1918) took the world by storm?

8. This *Harper's* weekly cartoonist created the donkey and elephant symbols for the Democratic and Republican parties, as well as the popular picture of Santa Claus, as we now picture him. Name him.

9. What early cartoonist drew the comic strip "Gertie," about a 13-million-year-old dinosaur?

3. Boston
4. *The Wild One*
5. *Cleopatra* (1963), starring Elizabeth Taylor
6. "Talking John Birch Society Blues"
7. Hollywood Ten
8. Watch and Wand Society
9. Because he and Daisy Duck had never been married
10. Mickey Mouse

Cartoonists (Answers)

1. Shel Silverstein
2. Charles Schulz
3. Robert Crumb
4. Milton Caniff
5. Bill Mauldin
6. Al Capp (he created *Li'l Abner*)
7. Robert L. Ripley ("Believe It or Not")
8. Thomas Nast
9. Winsor McCay

10. Cartoonist Al Hirschfield always hid the name of his daughter at least once in his drawings. What was her name?

Catch Lines

1. What is Bugs Bunny's favorite line?
2. When Charlie Chan's chauffeur Brimingham Brown, played by Mantan Moreland, wanted to get away from the scene as fast as possible, he would say what?
3. "Can we talk here?" is a question often asked by what female comedienne?
4. What was radio comedian Joe Penner's favorite question?
5. One of her characters used the line "Is this the party to whom I am speaking"? Name her.
6. "Would you believe?" belongs to what TV comedian?
7. "Well ex-cuussse me" is the arrogant apology put forth by whom?
8. What comedian is famous for his discouraging words "I don't get no respect"?
9. His character, Geraldine, often states, "What you see is what you get!" Who is he?
10. Who often said, "What a revoltin' development this is"?

Characters

1. Tyrone Green is one of this comedian's radical-poet characters. Name him.
2. What is the name of the dandy who wears both a monocle and a top hat associated with the *New Yorker* magazine?
3. Who played the nutty Hollywood producer Montaigne Fink on radio?
4. Some of her roles are Baba WaWa, Rhoda Weiss, and Roseanna Roseannadanna. Who is she?
5. Some of her characters are Ernestine, Agnest Angst, and Purvis Hawkins. Who is she?
6. Percy Dovetonsils, Matzoh Hepplewhite, and Eugene Wee are three characters of what late TV comedian?
7. Freddie Johnson, Reverend Leroy, and Danny Danger are three of whose characters?

10. Nina

Catch Lines (Answers)
1. "What's up, Doc?"
2. "Feets, do your stuff!"
3. Joan Rivers
4. "Wanna buy a duck?"
5. Lily Tomlin
6. Don Adams (as Maxwell Smart)
7. Steve Martin
8. Rodney Dangerfield
9. Flip Wilson
10. Radio/TV character Chester A. Riley

Characters (Answers)
1. Eddie Murphy
2. Eustice Tilly
3. Fred Allen
4. Gilda Radner
5. Lily Tomlin
6. Ernie Kovacs
7. Flip Wilson's

8. Winslow G. Flydipper, Lance Loveguard, and Lamar Gene Gumbody are three of what comedian's looney characters?
9. San Fernando Red, Cauliflower McPugg, and Junior are just three of whose characters?
10. Her characters are Nora Rosmond, Mrs. Wiggins, and Eunice Higgins. Who is she?

Clowns

1. Who was nicknamed the Clown Prince of Baseball?
2. What comedian's paintings of clowns sell for thousands of dollars and have now become world-famous?
3. Give the name of the silent clown on the "Howdy Doody Show"?
4. What is the name of Emmett Kelly's sad-faced clown, whom he introduced in 1931?
5. Larry Harmon introduced this clown in the early 1950s. Today he is part of the expression "Don't be a _____."
6. Who played Buttons the Clown in the 1950 movie *The Greatest Show on Earth*?
7. What is the first name of the adult who played the big clown on Circus Day (every Thursday) on TV's "Mickey Mouse Club"?
8. In 1960, the Everly Brothers had a song with the word "clown" in the title that went to #1 on the charts. Ten years later, Smokey Robinson and The Miracles did the same thing. Name both songs.
9. Who played the role of Joey, the clown on the 1956–1958 TV series "Circus Boy"?
10. Who was known as the Clown Prince of Basketball?

Dancers

1. *The Two of Us* is the 1976 autobiography of dancer Cyd Charisse, but who else is she referring to in the title?
2. *Miller's High Life* is the 1974 life story of what dancer/singer?
3. What dancer's 1959 autobiography is titled *Steps in Time?*
4. What popular dancer once set a world's record by running backward?

8. Jonathan Winters's
9. Red Skelton's
10. Carol Burnett

Clowns (Answers)

1. Al Schacht
2. Red Skelton's
3. Clarabelle
4. Willie the Tramp
5. Bozo
6. James Stewart
7. Roy Williams
8. "Cathy's Clown" and "Tears of a Clown"
9. Noah Beery, Jr.
10. Meadowlark Lemon

Dancers (Answers)

1. Her husband Tony Martin
2. Ann Miller
3. Fred Astaire's
4. Bill "Bojangles" Robinson

5. What actress, dancer, and choreographer had a #1 hit record in 1982 with "Mickey"?
6. *Go into Your Dance* was the only film in which dancer Ruby Keeler appeared with her husband. Name him.
7. What famous dance instructor not only had his own TV series, but owned a chain of 450 dancing schools?
8. What was the name of the dance troupe of 32 females who appeared on the TV series *The Jackie Gleason Show?*
9. Who performed the dance of the seven veils?
10. Who did the dancing for Jennifer Beals in *Flashdance?*

Dummies

1. Which one of Edgar Bergen's dummies claims Snerdsville, Iowa, as his hometown?
2. What is the name of Paul Winchell's precocious 25-pound boy dummy?
3. Which of Edgar Bergen's dummies wears size 2AAA shoe?
4. What comedian and TV talk show host used a ventriloquist's dummy named Eddie early in his career?
5. What was the name of Max Terhune's dummy in western films?
6. What is the name of comedian Rod Hulls's crazy Australian bird?
7. What is the name of ventriloquist Jimmy Nelson's wise-cracking boy dummy?
8. What is the name of Danny O'Day's dog dummy that sings the commercials for Nestles Chocolate?
9. What was the name of the evil dummy that appeared in the 1978 movie *Magic?*
10. What was the name of ventriloquist Chuck Cambell's (Jay Johnson) dummy in the TV series "Soap"?

Fictional Locations

1. The Admiral Benbow Inn can be found in what 1883 novel?
2. What is the name of the Scottish town that appears for a single day every 100 years?
3. Where does the great Wizard live in L. Frank Baum's 1900 story *The Wizard of Oz?*

5.   Toni Basil
6.   Al Jolson
7.   Arthur Murray
8.   The June Taylor Dancers
9.   Salome
10. Maren Jahan

Dummies (Answers)
1.   Mortimer Snerd
2.   Jerry Mahoney
3.   Charlie McCarthy
4.   Johnny Carson
5.   Elmer Sneezeweed
6.   Emu
7.   Danny O'Day
8.   Farfel
9.   Fats
10. Bob

Fictional Locations (Answers)
1.   *Treasure Island* by Robert Louis Stevenson
2.   Brigadoon
3.   Emerald City

4. What is the land of giants called in Jonathan Swift's 1726 novel *Gulliver's Travels?*

5. Where were Captain Dan Reid, John Reid, and several other Texas Rangers ambushed by Butch Cavendish and the Hole in the Wall gang? (John Reid later became the Lone Ranger.)

6. In Andy Hardy films, starring Mickey Rooney, what was Andy's hometown?

7. What musical (later made into a film) is set in Charleston, South Carolina's, Catfish Row?

8. Sweet Apple, Ohio, is the small town setting of what 1963 movie?

9. What two cartoon characters live in Frostbite Falls, Minnesota?

10. What is the land of the little people called in Jonathan Swift's *Gulliver's Travels?*

Game Shows

1. On what TV game show did Tom Selleck appear twice, each time losing out to another contestant?

2. Singer Patsy Cline and General Omar Bradley were both contestants on what TV game show hosted by a veteran of vaudeville?

3. On the TV game show "PDQ," what did the title stand for?

4. Both James Dean and Nick Adams were employed by what early TV game show as stunt testers?

5. Kathy Godfrey, the younger sister of Arthur Godfrey, hosted what 1953–1954 television game show?

6. Who hosted 2,858 consecutive episodes of the TV game show "Jeopardy" without ever missing a single show?

7. Who hosted the TV game show "Who Do You Trust," later titled "Do You Trust Your Wife?"

8. What two brothers have both hosted TV game shows?

9. What well-known female novelist has hosted the TV game show "Your Surprise Store"?

10. John Daly and Quincy Howe hosted a game show called "It's News to Me." Who was the third host?

4. Brobdingnag
5. Bryant's Gap
6. Carvel
7. *Porgy and Bess*
8. *Bye-Bye Birdie*
9. Rocky and Bullwinkle
10. Lilliput

Game Shows (Answers)

1. "The Dating Game"
2. "You Bet Your Life" (Groucho Marx)
3. Please Do Quickly
4. "Beat the Clock"
5. "On Your Way"
6. Art Fleming
7. Johnny Carson
8. Jack Narz and Tom Kennedy
9. Jacqueline Susann
10. Walter Cronkite

Illustrators

1. What illustrator's drawings of women were so popular in the early 1900s that they were named in his honor?
2. British illustrator Joseph Cundall introduced what seasonal art form in 1846?
3. It was British artist Sir Edwin Landseer who first began showing what type of dog with small brandy casks around their necks, even though the dogs never really wore them?
4. Dan Beard, who illustrated the first editon of Mark Twain's *A Connecticut Yankee at King Arthur's Court* in 1889, was the founder of what group in 1910?
5. Maude Humphrey Bogart, the mother of actor Humphrey Bogart, created the baby portrait for what baby food company?
6. When he designed the famous poster of Uncle Sam pointing his finger and stating, "I want you," this artist used himself as the model for Uncle Sam. Name the artist.
7. When Art Linkletter's book *Kids Say the Darndest Things* was published in 1957, what cartoonist illustrated the book?
8. John R. Neil signed the name Jno to the illustrations used in what series of juvenile books?
9. Whose drawings made their printed debut in the 1929 book *Is Sex Necessary?* written with E. B. White?
10. What is the name of the illustrator who originally drew Mickey Mouse?

Last Lines—Movies

1. Silent actress Norma Desmond (Gloria Swanson) had what last line in the 1950 motion picture *Sunset Boulevard?*
2. Doorman Jean Hersholt gave the last line from the 1933 movie *Grand Hotel.* What was it?
3. In what film did comedian Joe E. Brown give the hilarious last line "Well, nobody's perfect" when Jack Lemmon revealed to him that he was not a female?
4. "Hello, everybody, this is Mrs. Norman Maine" closed what 181-minute-long 1954 movie classic? Who said the line?

Illustrators (Answers)

1. Charles Dana Gibson, the creator of the "Gibson Girl"
2. Christmas cards
3. St. Bernards
4. Boy Scouts of America
5. Mellins Baby Food (not Gerber Baby Foods)
6. James Montgomery Flagg
7. Charles Schulz
8. L. Frank Baum's *Wizard of Oz* series
9. James Thurber's
10. Ub Iwerks

Last Lines—Movies (Answers)

1. "All right, Mr. DeMille, I'm ready for a close-up now."
2. "Always the same, people come, people go, nothing ever happens."
3. *Some Like It Hot* (1959)
4. *A Star Is Born,* said by Judy Garland

5. Burt Lancaster gave the last line "It's good to be home" in what 1952 movie?

6. "Shut up and deal," said by Shirley MacLaine to Jack Lemmon, was the last line of what 1960 Academy Award-winning film?

7. What was Edward G. Robinson's last line before he died in the 1930 movie *Little Caesar?*

8. What was the final line of the 1939 movie *Gone with the Wind,* and who said it?

9. Dorothy McGuire's only line—"189, Doctor Perry! Come! It's I, Helen"—was also the last line of what 1946 movie?

10. Before he was killed, Captain America said, "We blew it," to his sidekick Billy. What 1969 motion picture ended with this scene?

Movies Based on Novels

1. Irving Shulman's novel *Children of the Dark* was the basis for what 1955 movie?

2. John Klempner's novel *A Letter to Five Wives* was the basis for what 1949 motion picture?

3. Pierre Boulle's novel *Monkey Planet* was the basis for what 1968 movie?

4. Edison Marshall's novel *The Viking* was the basis for what 1958 Kirk Douglas/Tony Curtis movie?

5. *Anna and the King of Siam,* a novel written by Margaret Landon, was the basis for two movies, each with a different title. Name them.

6. H. G. Wells's 1905 book *Kipps* was the basis for what 1969 movie musical?

7. What 1902 novel was the basis for the 1979 Francis Ford Coppola film *Apocalypse Now?*

8. The 1965 Robert Redford film *Situation Hopeless, but Not Serious* was based on the novel *The Hiding Place.* Who authored the book?

9. What 1973 Bob Hope comedy was based on western writer Louis L'Amour's novel *Broken Gun?*

10. What 1958 book by T. H. White was the basis for the 1967 motion picture *Camelot?*

11. Kathryn Forbes's novel *Mama's Bank Account* was the basis for what play and 1948 movie?

5. *Come Back Little Sheba*
6. *The Apartment*
7. "Mother of Mercy, is this the end of Rico?"
8. "After all, tomorrow is another day," said by Scarlett (Vivian Leigh).
9. *The Spiral Staircase*
10. *Easy Rider*

Movies Based on Novels (Answers)

1. *Rebel Without a Cause*
2. *A Letter to Three Wives*
3. *Planet of the Apes*
4. *The Vikings* (note the plural title)
5. *Anna and the King of Siam* (1946) and *The King and I* (1956)
6. *Half a Sixpence*
7. *Heart of Darkness* by Joseph Conrad
8. Actor Robert Shaw
9. *Cancel My Reservation*
10. *The Once and Future King*
11. *I Remember Mama*

12. On what story by Arthur C. Clarke is the 1968 movie *2001: A Space Odyssey* based?

13. Harold Robbins's novel *A Stone for Danny Fisher* became the basis for what 1958 Elvis Presley motion picture?

14. In the April 10, 1937, issue of *Collier's* magazine, two stories appeared—"Bringing up Baby" by Hagar Wilde, which was the basis for the 1938 movie of the same title, and Ernest Haycox's "Stage to Lordsbury," which was the basis for what 1938 film?

15. Nik Cohn's article "Tribal Rites of the New Saturday Night" published in *New York* magazine became the source for what 1977 movie?

16. Robert Redford's 1975 film *Three Days of the Condor* was based on what novel by James Grody?

17. Damon Runyon's short story "The Idyll of Miss Sarah Brown" was later retitled when it was made into both a musical play and a movie. Name it.

18. What is the exact title of Pierre Boulle's novel upon which the 1957 motion picture *The Bridge On the River Kwai* is based?

19. Charles Brackett and Billy Wilder's story "A Can of Beans" was the basis for what classic 1950 motion picture?

20. Christopher Isherwood's 1939 book *Good-bye to Berlin* was the basis for what musical play and later motion picture?

Movie Publicity Advertising

1. What film gave the following hype: Brando Sings!

2. What 1948 Clark Gable-Lana Turner film featured the ad hype line "The team that generates STEAM"?

3. "Who will survive . . . And what will be left of them?" was a publicity line for what 1974 horror film?

4. What 1980 John Travolta film was hyped as "Hard Hat Days and Honky Tonk Nights"?

5. What 1932 Clark Gable-Jean Harlow film used the tag line "He treated her rough—and she loved it" (a line that couldn't be used today)?

6. "How'd you like to tussle with Russell" was used to stir up the male theater-goers for what Howard Hughes classic?

7. What movie used the advertisement "Just when you thought it was safe to go back in the water"?

12. *The Sentinel*
13. *King Creole*
14. *Stagecoach*
15. *Saturday Night Fever*
16. *Six Days of the Condor*
17. *Guys and Dolls*
18. *The Bridge Over the River Kwai*
19. *Sunset Boulevard*
20. *Cabaret*

Movie Publicity Advertising (Answers)

1. *Guys and Dolls* (1955)
2. *Homecoming*
3. *The Texas Chainsaw Massacre*
4. *Urban Cowboy*
5. *Red Dust*
6. *The Outlaw* (Jane Russell's film debut)
7. *Jaws 2*

8. What 1929 musical film received the impressive billing of "100% All talking, 100% All singing, 100% All dancing"?
9. What 1967 film used the line "They're Young—They're in Love—and They Kill People"?
10. "A Thousand Thrills and Hayley Mills" was the ad line for what 1962 film?

Newscasters

1. Who was teamed with Chet Huntley on NBC TV news until Huntley's retirement in 1970?
2. What NBC newscaster was the director of the Voice of America from 1966 until 1967?
3. Who, in 1976, became the first woman to anchor a network TV news program, when she joined ABC Evening News?
4. Cathy, the daughter of what newscaster, made her film debut in the 1974 movie *Billy Jack?*
5. Name the WLS radio news reporter who broke down in tears as he was describing the destruction of the *Hindenburg* when it exploded on the night of May 6, 1937?
6. Cartoonist Gary Trudeau married what newscaster?
7. What newscaster was beaten up on the floor of the 1968 Democratic National Convention?
8. What network anchorman moderated the first Richard Nixon-John F. Kennedy Presidential debates?
9. Who was the first black network anchorman?
10. What female newscaster, called NBC's golden girl, was killed when her automobile fell into a canal in 1983?

Nicknames of Actresses

Identify the following actresses from their nicknames:
1. The Champagne Blonde
2. Steel Butterfly
3. America's Sweetie
4. Blonde Bombshell/Platinum Bombshell
5. Cinderella Girl
6. America's Sweetheart

8. *Broadway Melody*
9. *Bonnie and Clyde*
10. *In Search of the Castaways*

Newscasters (Answers)

1. David Brinkley
2. John Chancellor
3. Barbara Walters
4. Walter Cronkite
5. Herb Morrison
6. Jane Pauley
7. Dan Rather
8. Howard K. Smith
9. Max Robinson
10. Jessica Savitch

Nicknames of Actresses (Answers)

1. Adele Jergens
2. Loretta Young
3. Nancy Carrol
4. Jean Harlow
5. Linda Darnell
6. Mary Pickford

7. The Body
8. The Face
9. Incendiary Blonde
10. Queen of the Creepies
11. Ice Cream Blonde
12. Iron Butterfly
13. The It Girl
14. Palomino Blonde
15. Legs
16. Queen of the Swashbucklers
17. Sex Kitten
18. Statue of Libido
19. Sweater Girl
20. Oomph Girl

Nightclubs/Pubs/Bars

1. What popular singer began as the piano man at the Executive Lounge in Los Angeles in the 1970s?
2. Cowboy actor Buck Jones was killed in November 28, 1942, when this Boston nightclub caught on fire. Name the club.
3. Sybil Burton opened a Manhattan nightclub, which she named after Ringo Starr's hair, as he referred to it in the 1964 Beatles movie *A Hard Day's Night.* Name the club.
4. At which Munich beer hall did Adolf Hitler, on November 9, 1923, declare himself chancellor of all Germany?
5. What two well-known fictional characters met for the first time in the London pub The Criterion Bar, in 1881?
6. What Los Angeles nightclub was John Lennon thrown out of, one night in March of 1969, after consuming too many Brandy Alexanders?
7. What Pasadena, Texas, nightclub is featured in the 1980 movie *Urban Cowboy?*
8. What is the name of the Berlin cabaret where Lola Lola sang?
9. In what Liverpool club did Brian Epstein discover the Beatles, in 1961?
10. What is the name of the Hamburg, Germany, nightclub where the Beatles performed and where a tape was made of their singing that was released on a 1977 album?

7. Marie MacDonald
8. Anita Colby
9. Betty Hutton
10. Jamie Lee Curtis
11. Thelma Todd
12. Jeanette MacDonald
13. Clara Bow
14. Anne Francis
15. Betty Grable
16. Maureen O'Hara
17. Brigitte Bardot
18. Mae West
19. Lana Turner
20. Ann Sheridan

Nightclubs/Pubs/Bars (Answers)
1. Billy Joel, whose hit "Piano Man" tells of those days
2. Coconut Grove
3. Arthur
4. Bügerbrau Keller
5. Sherlock Holmes and Dr. Watson
6. Troubadour
7. Gilley's
8. The Blue Angel
9. The Cavern
10. Star Club

Original Titles

1. What was to have been the title of George Lucas's 1983 movie *Return of the Jedi*, before he changed it?
2. Gary B. Trudeau originally drew his comic strip *Doonesbury* while at Yale University, but under what other name?
3. What was the previous name of the Department of Defense?
4. *Shirley* was the original title of what 1982 Dustin Hoffman box-office blockbuster?
5. First published in the San Francisco *Examiner* on June 3, 1888, the original title of what poem was "A Ballad of the Republic, Sung in the Year 1888"?
6. *Bogart Slept Here* was the original title for what Neil Simon play that was brought to the silver screen in 1977, starring his then-wife Marsha Mason?
7. Who originally titled his 1981 album *Dead Giveaway*, then, upon the death of his friend John Lennon, changed it to *Can't Fight Lightnin'*?
8. *Facts* was the original title considered for what magazine?
9. *Welcome to Berlin* was the original title of what musical play?
10. *Away We Go* was the original title of what musical adapted from Lynn Riggs's book *Green Grow the Lilacs?*

Panelists

1. TV's "What's My Line" panelist Bennett Cerf was the founder, in 1927, of what major publishing firm?
2. Who was once a contestant on the $64,000 Question and later a panelist on "The Gong Show"?
3. Miss America (1945) and newspaper columnist, Bess Myerson, was a member of the panel for what CBS TV quiz show?
4. What NBC-TV news anchorman and spokesman for Timex watches served as a panelist on the radio show "Who Said That"?
5. Who was the only panelist to appear on both the first and last shows of the TV game show "Hollywood Squares"?
6. What panelist was fired on radio's "Information Please" after he hit M. C. Dan Golenpaul in the nose?

Original Titles (Answers)

1. *Revenge of the Jedi*
2. *Bull Tales*
3. War Department
4. *Tootsie*
5. "Casey at the Bat"
6. *The Goodbye Girl*
7. Ringo Starr
8. *Time* magazine
9. *Cabaret*
10. *Oklahoma!*

Panelists (Answers)

1. Random House
2. Dr. Joyce Brothers
3. "I've Got a Secret"
4. John Cameron Swayze
5. Rose Marie
6. Oscar Levant

7. Who usually sat in the center square of the TV game show "Hollywood Squares"?

8. Columnist Rex Reed, singer Jaye P. Morgan, and Jamie Farr have been regular panelists for what show?

9. Vincent Price, Jackie Coogan, Rocky Graziano, Carol Burnett, and Dick Van Dyke have been regular panelists on what 1950–1963 TV Game show?

10. Who were the two Allens who appeared as panelists on TV's "What's My Line"?

Pornography

1. Who is the publisher of *Hustler* magazine?

2. What is the name of the porno film star who dated Prince Andrew?

3. Lena Nyran starred in both the 1969 Swedish X-rated film *I Am Curious* (Yellow) and its 1970 sequel. Name the sequel's title?

4. What is the annual trophy given to the best porno film of the year?

5. Chuck Traynor has been married to what two porno queens?

6. What is the significance of the 1915 American film, *A Grass Sandwich?*

7. Prior to his 1971 movie debut in *Bananas*, Sylvester Stallone appeared in a porno film. What was its re-release title (taking advantage of Stallone's popularity)?

8. The title of what porno film was later borrowed as the cover for an unidentified Watergate informer?

9. What award from the Hollywood Women's Press Club was addressed to "Pornographic Movie Makers" in 1976?

10. Who appeared nude in a sequence of the 1933 Czech film *Ecstasy?*

Sequels

1. What was the sequel to the movie *King Kong*, (both films were released in the same year, 1933)?

2. *Of Time and the River* by Thomas Wolfe was his 1935 sequel to what 1929 novel?

7. Paul Lynde
8. "The Gong Show"
9. "Pantomine Quiz"
10. Fred Allen and Steve Allen

Pornography (Answers)

1. Larry Flynt
2. Koo Stark
3. *I Am Curious (Blue)*
4. Erotica Award
5. Marilyn Chambers and Linda Lovelace
6. It is considered to be the first American pornographic film
7. *The Italian Stallion* (it was originally titled *Party at Kitty's*)
8. *Deep Throat*
9. Sour Apple Award (least cooperative)
10. Hedy Lamarr

Sequels (Answers)

1. *Son of Kong*
2. *Look Homeward Angel*

3. What was Louisa May Alcott's 1871 sequel novel to her successful 1868 novel *Little Women?*

4. What was the 1952 sequel to the 1951 Ronald Reagan movie *Bedtime for Bonzo?*

5. In 1973, Richard Lester set a precedent when he filmed the sequel movie simultaneously with the original. Name both films?

6. Name Erich Segal's 1977 novel, which was the sequel to his 1970 novel *Love Story?*

7. What is the full title of the 1977 sequel of the 1973 horror film *The Exorcist?*

8. Give the title of the sequel poem, written by Grantland Rice, as an answer to Ernest L. Thayer's "Casey at the Bat" poem?

9. What was Arthur C. Clarke's sequel to his story that was filmed in 1968 as *2001: A Space Odyssey?*

10. What was the only film that Barbra Streisand appeared in that was a sequel to another film (which she also starred in)?

Sign-Offs

1. Who signs off each week with "Keep your feet on the ground and keep reaching for the stars"?

2. What television comic always closed his show with "Good night and God bless thank you"?

3. Who said, "Take it easy, but take it"?

4. What late television commentator closed with "Good night and good luck"?

5. Each week he closed his hour-long show with "We're in touch, so you be in touch." Name this newsman.

6. "And that's the way it is" (date) was the sign-off of what CBS evening news anchorman?

7. Who will always be remembered for his mysterious last line, "Good night Mrs. Calabash, wherever you are"?

8. "Don't you cry I'll be back again, someday" is the annual farewell address said by whom?

9. "So long until tomorrow" was the sign-off of what radio newscaster for 49 years?

10. "Th-that's all folks!" is the sign-off for Warner Bros. cartoons. What character utters (or stutters) these words?

3. *Little Men*
4. *Bonzo Goes to College* (Reagan did not appear in it.)
5. *The Three Musketeers* and *The Four Musketeers*
6. *Oliver's Story*
7. *Exorcist II: The Heretic*
8. "Casey's Revenge"
9. *2010: Odyssey Two*
10. *Funny Lady* (1975) (sequel to *Funny Girl* [1968])

Sign-Offs (Answers)

1. Casey Kasem
2. Red Skelton
3. Studs Terkel
4. Edward R. Murrow
5. Hugh Downs
6. Walter Cronkite
7. Jimmy Durante
8. Frosty the Snowman
9. Lowell Thomas
10. Porky Pig

Stage Names

Give the stage names of the following individuals:
1.   Carol Jane Peters
2.   James Bumgarner
3.   Joseph Levitch
4.   Joe Yule, Jr.
5.   Natasha Gurdin
6.   Peter Arness
7.   James Stewart
8.   Betty Joan Perske
9.   Dino Crocetti
10. Julie Peck

Television Commercials

1.   The last one of these occurred on December 31, 1970?
2.   Flushing, New York, was the location where what product's commercials were first taped?
3.   What is the name of the statuette awarded annually to the best television commercial?
4.   Who produced and directed the 1975–1976 Dodge Aspen TV commercials, which showed Rex Harrison in the setting of *My Fair Lady?*
5.   What popular 1972 hit song by the Hillside Singers began as a television Coca-Cola commercial?
6.   What actress plays Madge the manicurist for Palmolive dishwashing liquid?
7.   Name the actress who played Josephine the plumber in Comet cleanser TV commercials?
8.   Before her death in 1979, what character actress played the role of Maxine the Maxwell House instant coffee caterer on TV?
9.   In the 1950s who appeared in TV commercials as Happy Hotpoint, a happy little pixie?
10. Who played Folger Coffee's Mrs. Olson?

Stage Names (Answers)

1. Carole Lombard
2. James Garner
3. Jerry Lewis
4. Mickey Rooney
5. Natalie Wood
6. Peter Graves
7. Stewart Granger
8. Lauren Bacall
9. Dean Martin
10. Julie London

Television Commercials (Answers)

1. Cigarette commercials on TV
2. Charmin
3. Clio
4. Mervyn LeRoy
5. "I'd Like to Teach the World to Sing"
6. Jan Miner
7. Jane Withers
8. Vivian Vance
9. Mary Tyler Moore
10. Virginia Christine

Television Pitchmen

1. Dustin Hoffman once appeared on television in 1964 for an advertisement for what German automobile?
2. What aftershave did Tom Selleck advertise before he became well-known?
3. What pro basketball player was nicknamed Dr. Chapstick on Chapstick TV commercials?
4. In the 1970s an elaborate commercial for the Great American Soup was staged with a chorus line of dancers featuring what female dancer?
5. In the 1950s a very young Grace Kelly pitched what toothpaste to the American public?
6. What was the name of the 6-inch-high butler played by Dick Cutting on TV's Kleenex Napkins commercials?
7. Who played the character Marathon John in the Marathon Candy Bar TV commercial?
8. Who is the Tidy Bowl Man?
9. For what foreign automobile company did Susan Ford, the daughter of Gerald Ford, appear on TV in 1979?
10. One-time film character actor Dick Wilson became better known as what grocery clerk?

Television (Syndication) Re-run Titles

Listed are the syndicated rerun titles. Name the original network titles:
1. "Brave Stallion"
2. "Badge 714"
3. "Matt Dillon"
4. "Jeff's Collie"
5. "The Bounty Hunter"
6. "Ponderosa"
7. "San Francisco Beat"
8. "Major Adams—Trailmaster"
9. "Carol Burnett and Company"
10. "Call of the West"

Television Pitchmen (Answers)

1. Volkswagen
2. Chaz
3. Julius Irving
4. Ann Miller
5. Ipana
6. Manners
7. Patrick Wayne
8. Bob Caliban
9. Subaru
10. Mr. Whipple (Charmin toilet paper)

Television (Syndication) Re-run Titles (Answers)

1. "Fury"
2. "Dragnet"
3. "Gunsmoke"
4. "Lassie"
5. "Wanted—Dead or Alive"
6. "Bonanza"
7. "Line Up"
8. "Wagon Train"
9. "Carol Burnett Show"
10. "Death Valley Days"

Theaters

1. On August 16, 1957, Buddy Holly and the Crickets became the first white act to play this famous Harlem theater?
2. The Grand Ole Opry was broadcast from what Nashville Theater from 1942 until 1974?
3. Public enemy number one, John Dillinger, was gunned down outside of what Chicago theater on July 22, 1934, by federal agents led by Melvin G. Purvis?
4. This is the most popular movie theater in Hollywood and is the site of numerous film premieres. Name it.
5. The Los Angeles porno theatre, the Pussycat Theatre, ran what X-rated film for ten years, from 1971 until 1981?
6. What theater, located in Rockefeller Center, is the home of the Rockettes?
7. What motion picture made its premiere at Loew's Grant Theater in Atlanta, Georgia, on December 15, 1939?
8. Douglas Fairbanks's 1922 classic *Robin Hood* became the first motion picture to make its premiere at what Hollywood theater?
9. Named for Samuel Rothafel, what theater opened in New York City in 1927 and closed its doors in 1960?
10. What New York City theater presented Frank Sinatra in the 1940's, Alan Freed's rock 'n' roll shows, and the premiere of Elvis Presley's *Love Me Tender?*

Tourist Attractions

1. In what country is the Blue Grotto located?
2. Where can tourists kiss the Blarney Stone?
3. In order to visit the original Madame Tussaud's Wax Museum one would have to go to what European city?
4. In what California city can the rambling mystery Winchester House be found?
5. In what U.S. city is the Space Needle located?
6. In what city would one find the Watts Towers?
7. In what city would one throw one or more coins into the Trevi Fountain?

Theaters (Answers)

1. Apollo
2. Ryman Auditorium
3. Biograph Theatre
4. Grauman's Chinese Theatre (AKA Mann's Chinese Theatre)
5. *Deep Throat*
6. Radio City Music Hall
7. *Gone with the Wind*
8. Grauman's Egyptian Theatre
9. The Roxy
10. Paramount Theatre

Tourist Attractions (Answers)

1. Capri, Italy
2. Cork, Ireland
3. London
4. San Jose
5. Seattle
6. Los Angeles
7. Rome

8. A tall statue of Christ with outstretched arms overlooks what beautiful South American city?

9. Beautiful Lake Lucerne can be visited in what European country?

10. What state would you travel to in order to visit the site of the Civil War battle of Gettysburg?

8. Rio De Janeiro
9. Switzerland
10. Pennsylvania

History

Airplane Crashes

1. What former world heavyweight boxing champion was killed in an airplane crash on August 31, 1969, one day prior to his birthday?
2. What World War II hero was killed in an aircraft on May, 28, 1971?
3. On March 31, 1931, what football coach was killed in a crash of the airliner in which he was a passenger?
4. What two beloved Americans were killed when their private plane crashed at Pt. Barrow, Alaska, on August 15, 1935?
5. What Baseball Hall-Of-Famer died in a plane crash in 1972, after he made his 3,000th career hit?
6. What British 14-time Grand Prix winner was killed in an airplane crash on November 29, 1975?
7. What New York Yankee catcher was killed when his Lear Jet crashed in 1976?
8. What was the name of Clark Gable's actress wife who died when the airliner which she was in crashed near Las Vegas, Nevada, on January 16, 1942?
9. What famous big band leader was reported missing in action after the small aircraft he was riding in disappeared during World War II?
10. The greatest one-day tragedy to ever hit rock 'n' roll music occurred on February 3, 1959 when three rock singers died in the same plane crash. Name them.

Aviation

1. Who was the first person to fly across the English Channel?
2. Where did the Wright brothers really fly their airplane the first time?

Airplane Crashes (Answers)

1. Rocky Marciano
2. Audie Murphy
3. Knute Rockne
4. Humorist Will Rogers and his pilot Wiley Post
5. Roberto Clemente
6. Graham Hill
7. Thurman Munson
8. Carole Lombard
9. Glenn Miller
10. Buddy Holly, Ritchie Valens, and the "Big Bopper" (Jiles Perry Richardson)

Aviation (Answers)

1. Louis Bleriot
2. Kill Devil Hill

3. Where was the Spirit of St. Louis built?
4. Name Wiley Post's famous airplane, in which he flew around the world?
5. Who was the first woman to fly the Atlantic?
6. What was the prize Charles Lindbergh received for flying solo across the Atlantic?
7. Name the Wright brothers' first aircraft.
8. What was the first plane built for transport?
9. Name the trophy given for speed of a seaplane in the early days of aviation?
10. What Russian emigre to the United States is credited with inventing the helicopter?
11. Who pulled the chocks from the wheels of the Spirit of St. Louis when it made the historic crossing of the Atlantic?
12. What was the name for British military aviation in World War I?
13. Who was the first person to take off and land an airplane strictly by instruments?
14. What American aircraft designer and builder pioneered float-plane construction?
15. Name the Canadian family who built the DM-4 bomber and the DH-9 fighter for the British?
16. Who was the first woman to fly faster than the speed of sound?
17. Which of the Wright brothers actually made the first flight?
18. What is the largest airplane flying operationally today?
19. Name the largest aircraft manufacturer in the world?
20. What famous American aviation pioneer flew combat missions in the Pacific as a civilian during World War II?

Battles

1. What was the first modern naval engagement in which surface ships did not exchange a single shot or sight each other? It occurred on May 7–8, 1942.
2. What famous battle occurred two weeks after the end of the War of 1812, (because of slow communications, the participants were unaware of the war's end)?
3. In what battle that occurred on October 21, 1805, was Lord Nelson killed?
4. What were the three American aircraft carriers involved in the battle of Midway?

3. Ryan aircraft plant, San Diego, California
4. *Winnie May*
5. Amelia Earhardt
6. $25,000
7. *Wright Flyer I*
8. Douglas DC-3
9. Schneider Trophy
10. Igor Sikorsky
11. Douglas "Wrong Way" Corrigan
12. Royal Flying Corps
13. James Doolittle
14. Glenn Curtis
15. DeHavilland
16. Jaqueline Cochrane
17. Orville
18. C-5A Galaxy (U.S. Air Force)
19. Boeing (Seattle)
20. Charles Lindbergh

Battles (Answers)

1. Battle of the Coral Sea
2. Battle of New Orleans
3. Trafalgar
4. *Enterprise*, *Hornet*, and *Yorktown*

5. During the American Civil War, how did the North and the South name the same battles (each giving a different name for the same battle)?

6. What is the famous date of the battle of Hastings between the Normans and the Saxons?

7. What two commanding generals were killed at the Plains of Abraham in Quebec in 1759?

8. What war saw the first confrontation between jet aircraft?

9. British general Lord Chelmsford led 800 British soldiers to their death in a battle in 1879 against whom?

10. Where, on June 4–6, 1942, did the first defeat since the 16th century of the Japanese Navy occur?

Black Firsts

1. When he was elected mayor of Cleveland in 1967, he became the first black mayor of a large American city. Name him.

2. Who, on June 30, 1967, became the first black astronaut?

3. In 1960, who became the first black entertainer to win an Emmy for his December 10, 1959, television special?

4. "Musical Chairs" in 1975 became the first TV game show to be hosted by a black. Who was the show's M.C.?

5. In 1927 4-feet 10-inch tall harmonica player DeFord Bailey became the first black artist to appear on what program broadcast over WSM radio?

6. On June 15, 1877, Henry Flipper became the first black graduate of what school?

7. Who, on November 1, 1961, became the first black to attend the University of Mississippi?

8. *Raisin In the Sun* was the first Broadway play written by a black playwright. Name her.

9. Who became the first black mayor of the city of Los Angeles?

10. Who was the first black to win an Academy Award for acting?

5. The North named them for the nearest river, while the South named them for the nearest town.
6. October 4, 1066
7. Louis Montcalm and James Wolfe
8. Korean War
9. Zulu tribe warriors in Africa
10. Midway Island

Black Firsts (Answers)

1. Carl B. Stokes
2. Robert H. Lawrence
3. Harry Belafonte
4. Singer Adam Wade
5. *Grand Ole Opry*
6. West Point
7. James Meredith
8. Lorraine Hansberry
9. Thomas Bradley
10. Hattie McDaniel for *Gone with the Wind* (Best Supporting Actress)

Campaigns

1. What famous composer wrote the 1952 campaign song "I Like Ike"?
2. Whose election campaign slogan was AuH20?
3. What noted personality composed the Republican campaign song "Harding, you're the man for us," for Warren G. Harding?
4. This Presidential candidate leased a Boeing 727 nicknamed *Leadership 80*. Who was it?
5. What Pulitzer Prize-winning author ran for governor of California in 1934 on a platform based on the initials EPIC? Also what did the initials stand for?
6. Who was the first dark horse candidate to be elected President of the United States?
7. What was John F. Kennedy's campaign song?
8. What Presidential candidate used the slogan "Tippicanoe and Tyler too"?
9. What President used the song "A Hot Time in the Old Town" as his campaign theme song?
10. What President used the campaign slogan "Two chickens in every pot"?

Civil War

1. At 21, who was the youngest general of the Civil War?
2. What Massachusetts arsenal was one of the most important suppliers of arms to the Union forces?
3. What famous figure from Cooperstown, New York, is alleged to have fired the first shot of the Civil War for the Union?
4. The *Monitor* and the *Merrimack* fought the first battle of iron-clads. Which was the Confederate Navy ship?
5. What was Robert E. Lee's profession prior to commanding troops for the Confederacy?
6. Where in Virginia was the little red school house that was the site of the signing of the armistice ending the Civil War?
7. Civil War veterans later adopted the letters *GAR* as their official emblem. What did they stand for?

Campaigns (Answers)

1. Irving Berlin
2. Barry Goldwater, Sr.'s
3. Al Jolson
4. Ronald Reagan
5. Upton Sinclair—End Poverty in California
6. James K. Polk
7. "High Hopes"
8. William H. Harrison
9. Theodore Roosevelt
10. Herbert Hoover

Civil War (Answers)

1. George Armstrong Custer
2. Springfield Arsenal
3. Abner Doubleday
4. *Merrimack*
5. He was an engineer officer in the Union Army
6. Appomatox
7. Grand Army of the Republic

8. What Confederate general was accidentally shot and killed by one of his own men?

9. Stephen Crane wrote a very famous story about a young soldier taking part in his first battle. Name the story.

10. The Confederate Navy had a ship specially constructed in England to run the Union Blockade. What was its name?

11. What Union general was reputed to be a drunkard, yet Lincoln maintained the Union needed more like him?

12. What was the title of the band of Confederate cavalry that terrorized the border states and were called criminals by the U.S. government?

13. What was the capital of the Confederacy?

14. Name the states of the Confederacy.

15. What slaves were freed by the Emancipation Proclamation of 1863?

16. The forerunner of the machine gun was invented during the Civil War and was named after its inventor. Name it.

17. What was the name of the most notorious Confederate prisoner of war camp?

18. The Union Army was more widely known as the Army of the _____?

19. The Battle of Bull Run had another, less famous name. What was it?

20. What cavalry officer was known as the Grey Ghost of the Confederacy?

Coincidences

1. Name the Cincinnati Reds player and the Los Angeles Dodgers player who hit their 2,000th career hits on the same day, June 19, 1973?

2. Who was in the audience as a prisoner the first time that Johnny Cash gave a free concert at San Quentin Prison in California on January 1, 1960?

3. What is the middle name of George Grinnel, who in 1886 founded the Audubon Society, which he named for naturalist and artist John James Audubon?

4. On May 2, 1939, the day that New York Yankee Lou Gehrig benched himself, what occurred at Flushing Meadows, Long Island?

8. Stonewall Jackson
9. *The Red Badge of Courage*
10. *Alabama*
11. U.S. Grant
12. Quantrill's Raiders
13. Montgomery, Alabama
14. North Carolina, South Carolina, Virginia, Georgia, Florida, Alabama, Mississippi, Texas, and Tennessee
15. Only those in the non-Confederate states
16. The Gatling gun
17. Andersonville (The commander was executed after the war.)
18. Potomac
19. First Battle of Manassas
20. John Mosby, leader of Mosby's Raiders

Coincidences (Answers)

1. Pete Rose and Willie Davis, respectively
2. Merle Haggard
3. Bird
4. The New York World's Fair opened

5. What two firsts occurred in the fifth World Series game of 1920, played on October 10, between the Cleveland Indians and the Brooklyn Dodgers?

6. During the Boer War what future prime minister of the Union of South Africa, as a soldier, captured what future prime minister of Britain, as a journalist?

7. On August 6, 1890 William Kemater became the first person to be executed in the electric chair. What baseball great made his debut in his first major league game that same day?

8. What was the result of the first bomb dropped on the Russian city of Leningrad by the German Luftwaffe during World War II?

9. On the afternoon of September 22, 1927, when Lou Gehrig broke Babe Ruth's record of 170 RBI's, what historic event occurred in the world of boxing?

10. What happened in Chicago on February 14, 1929, the day that the Brown Derby Restaurant opened in Hollywood?

Dates

1. May 3 is the date on which one of Bram Stoker's 1896 novels begins. Name it.

2. What English author/poet and what Spanish author/poet died on the same day in 1616?

3. Name the three outfielders that played for the San Francisco Giants in their game against the Mets at the Polo Grounds on September 15, 1963?

4. What event always falls on the 14th?

5. According to Archbishop James Ussher of Armagh, Ireland, what occurred on Sunday, October 23, 4004 B.C. at exactly 9:30 A.M.?

6. What is the universally accepted birthday of every race horse?

7. In a non-leap year, what date is the exact middle of the year (182 days before it and 182 days to go)?

8. When is the "Twelfth Night"?

9. On what date does the fiscal year begin?

10. On what date are taxes due each year?

11. Playwright William Shakespeare was born (1564) and died (1616) on what same date?

12. What will be the first date of the 21st century?

5. Elmer Smith hit the first grand slam in World Series play and William Wambsganss executed the first (and only) unassisted triple play in the history of World Series play.

6. Louis Botha captured Winston Churchill.

7. Cy Young

8. It killed the only elephant in the city's zoo.

9. Jack Dempsey fought Gene Tunney for the heavyweight championship in a fight that became known as the Long Count.

10. The St. Valentine's Day Massacre

Dates (Answers)

1. *Dracula*
2. William Shakespeare and Miguel de Cervantes
3. Brothers Felipe Alou, Matty Alou, and Jesus Alou
4. Valentines Day
5. The world was created by God.
6. January 1 (those born after January 1 will have their birthdays on the next January 1)
7. June 2
8. January 6 (the Feast of the Epiphany or the Twelfth Night of Christmas)
9. July 1
10. April 15
11. April 23
12. January 1, 2001 (not the year 2,000, which is the last year of the 20th century)

13. What British politician father and son both died on January 24, the father in 1895 and his son in 1965?

14. In what same month did the following begin: American Revolution (1775), American Civil War (1861), Spanish American War (1898), and the U.S. declaration of war on Germany (1917)?

15. What religion begins its calendar on September 13, 622?

16. What was the date of the assassination of President John F. Kennedy?

17. What was the exact date that Neil Armstrong became the first man to walk on the moon's surface?

18. When are the Ides of March?

19. What occurred in New York City between September 3 and 13, 1752?

20. What was born on July 16, 1945, at 5:30 A.M.?

Deaths

1. How many years after a person's disappearance can he or she be declared legally dead?

2. What world figure was reading the book *The Imitation of Christ* by Thomas a Kempis when he died on September 29, 1978?

3. His suicide note read "To my friends, my work is done, why wait?" when he shot himself in 1932. Name this inventor.

4. On his body were found 38¢ and a scrap of paper that read "Dear friends and gentle hearts," when he died in the charity ward of Bellevue Hospital on January 13, 1864. Who was he?

5. What English poet fell from his boat *Ariel* and drowned in the Bay of Lerici during a storm on July 8, 1822?

6. What two American Presidents both died on July 4, 1826?

7. January 14, 1914, was a double-tragedy day for Theodore Roosevelt. What two people died?

8. What world-famous novelist was born in the year 1835 when Halley's Comet could be seen from the earth, and died 76 years later when the comet again appeared?

9. Who is the only baseball player to have been killed in a major league game?

10. Death is one of the inevitables, what is the other?

13. Lord Randloph Churchill and his son Sir Winston Churchill
14. April
15. Islam (date on which Mohammed traveled from Mecca to Medina)
16. November 22, 1963
17. July 20, 1969
18. March 15
19. Nothing—those dates never existed. When the Gregorian calender changed to the Julian calender, September 2 was followed by the 14th.
20. The Atomic Age (The first atomic bomb was tested at Alamogordo, New Mexico.)

Deaths (Answers)

1. Seven
2. Pope John Paul I
3. George Eastman (he developed the Kodak camera)
4. Composer Stephen Foster
5. Percy Bysshe Shelley
6. Thomas Jefferson and John Adams
7. His wife (in childbirth) and his mother (of typhoid)
8. Mark Twain (Samuel Clemens)
9. Raymond Chapman (August 16, 1920, hit by a pitch)
10. Taxes

Decades—1920s

1. What married couple lived at the Hollywood estate called Pick-fair?
2. In 1921, Margaret Gorman became the first winnner of what contest?
3. What famous evangelist disappeared for 37 days, in 1926, later claiming that she had been kidnapped?
4. In what city did the famous Scopes Monkey Trial take place in July 1925?
5. Nicknamed the "Happy Warrior," who was the 1928 Democratic candidate for President?
6. What famous race horse of the 1920s was nicknamed Big Red?
7. Who was known as the "It Girl"?
8. For a short time, who was known as the "It Boy"?
9. Whose New York funeral in 1926 attracted over 100,000 mourners over the two days that his body was displayed at Campbell's Funeral Parlor?
10. Who was Illinois's Galloping Ghost?

Decades—1930s

1. What modern passenger train of the 1930s was built of stainless steel?
2. What do the initials WPA stand for?
3. At the 1939 New York World's Fair, how was the daily attendance shown to the public?
4. Who was radio's "All-American Boy"?
5. What famous couple went on a bank-robbing rampage in the early 1930s?
6. What hero of the future was introduced in 1934?
7. The year that saw such classic's as *Gone with the Wind, Wuthering Heights, Gunga Din, Beau Geste, Good-bye Mr. Chips, The Wizard of Oz*, and others has been considered by many movie buffs to be the single greatest year ever for films. Name the year.
8. When did Hitler become chancellor of Germany?

Decades—1920s (Answers)

1. Douglas Fairbanks, Sr., and Mary Pickford
2. Miss America
3. Aimee Semple McPhearson
4. Dayton, Tennessee
5. Alfred E. Smith
6. Man of War
7. Clara Bow
8. Gary Cooper
9. Rudolph Valentino
10. Red Grange

Decades—1930s (Answers)

1. Burlington Zephyr
2. Works Progress Administration
3. On a huge red cash register which was part of the National Cash Register Building
4. Jack Armstrong
5. Clyde Barrow and Bonnie Parker
6. Flash Gordon
7. 1939
8. January 1933

9. Name the family featured in John Steinbeck's classic novel *The Grapes of Wrath*?
10. Who became the youngest person to be listed in *Who's Who*?

Decades—1940s

1. Artist Norman Rockwell painted the covers for what popular magazine?
2. What was CD?
3. Who were the two most popular pin-up girls of World War II?
4. What crooner of the 1940s was nicknamed the Voice?
5. During World War II what innocent group of people was incarcerated within the United States?
6. What Broadway musical closed in 1948 after 2,248 performances?
7. What was the year in which the United States entered World War II, and in what year did it end?
8. Who served as secretary of state from 1933 until 1944 and in 1945 was awarded the Nobel Peace Prize?
9. What baseball player was shot in his Chicago hotel room on June 15, 1949, by 19-year-old Ann Ruth Steinhagen?
10. What 1948 Pulitzer Prize-winning novel later inspired an immortal Rogers and Hammerstein musical?

Decades—1950s

1. What two automobile companies merged on May 1, 1954?
2. What rock 'n' roll singer had the best-selling non-fiction book for 1959?
3. From what city was the daily Dick Clark TV program "American Bandstand" televised?
4. What was the name of the production company that produced the TV series "Dragnet"?
5. From what state was Joseph McCarthy a senator?
6. Who authored the beat novel *On the Road*?
7. What gimmick did writer Roger Price introduce on television in 1953?

9. Joads
10. Shirley Temple

Decades—1940s (Answers)

1. *Saturday Evening Post*
2. Civil Defense
3. Betty Grable and Rita Hayworth
4. Frank Sinatra
5. Japanese Americans
6. *Oklahoma!*
7. 1941–1945
8. Cordell Hull
9. Eddie Waitkus
10. *Tales of the South Pacific* by James Michener

Decades—1950s (Answers)

1. Hudson Motor Car Company and Nash-Kelvinator Motor Car Company
2. Pat Boone *(Twixt Twelve and Twenty)*
3. Philadelphia
4. Mark VII
5. Wisconsin
6. Jack Kerouac
7. Droodles (symbolic, humorous drawings)

8. On June 30, 1956, the first midair collision between two passenger aircrft occurred when a TWA Super Constellation and a United DC-7 hit in the air. Where was the collision?

9. What popular comic strip still running today made its debut on October 2, 1950?

10. Topps produced their first one in 1951 and is today the largest manufacturer of what product?

Decades—1960s

1. What was the name of the prank pig that ran for President in 1968?

2. What political figure enjoyed showing off his gallbladder scar after his operation?

3. Deoxyribonucleic acid, which was discovered by three scientists in the 1960s, is more popularly known as what?

4. Who coined the phrase "Effete snobs for peace"?

5. Whom did singer Frank Sinatra marry at the Sands Casino in Las Vegas on July 19, 1966?

6. What was dairy farmer Max Yasgur's contribution to rock music?

7. In 1969, who was the recipient of the first *Rolling Stone Man of the Year* award?

8. On May 25, 1963, what became the only Japanese song to go to #1 on the U.S. record charts?

9. In what comic strip of the 1960s could a radical group called "Students Wildly Indignant about Nearly Everything (S.W.I.N.E.)" be found?

10. Name the subject of a 1978 TV movie who became the first female to be named UPI Athlete of the Year.

Decades—1970s

1. Four college students were shot and killed by the National Guard at what college on May 4, 1970?

2. Where were the 1972 Summer Olympics held?

3. Who directed the 28-minute film titled *Independence*, made in 1975 and shown 32 times a day, 7 days a week, at Independence Hall in Philadelphia?

8. Over Grand Canyon
9. *Peanuts* by Charles Schulz
10. Baseball cards

Decades—1960s (Answers)

1. Pigasus
2. President Lyndon Johnson
3. DNA
4. Vice-President Spiro T. Agnew
5. Mia Farrow
6. It was his 600-acre farm that was the site of the Woodstock Festival (August 15–17, 1969)
7. John Lennon
8. "Sukiyaki" (by Kyu Sakamoto)
9. Al Capp's "Li'l Abner"
10. Wilma Rudolph

Decades—1970s (Answers)

1. Kent State
2. Munich
3. John Huston

4. What television program were Patty Hearst and Steven Weed watching on February 4, 1974, when the SLA kidnapped Patty Hearst?

5. Who won the Vardon Trophy with the lowest average in the PGA in 1970, 1971, and 1972?

6. What royal couple was divorced in 53 seconds in May 1978?

7. Who produced the 1979 TV movie *Elvis*?

8. What occurred at San Francisco's Candlestick Park on May 6, 1975, when Houston Astro Bob Watson crossed home plate?

9. Who claimed to have erased 18½ minutes of a taped conversation between President Nixon and H. R. Haldeman on June 20, 1972?

10. What name was given to the landing site of Viking I on the planet Mars on July 20, 1976?

Female Achievements

1. In 1970, this beautiful actress played a disfigured woman in the John Wayne movie *Rio Lobo*. Ten years later she became the president of production of 20th Century-Fox. Name her.

2. What is the name of the New York City hotel that opened in 1903 as the first hotel exclusively for women?

3. What is the name of the Hollywood stunt woman and racing car driver, born deaf, who has set 22 records in various racing sports?

4. In 1869, what was the first state to give the women the right to vote?

5. What woman became an American Revolutionary hero during a battle at Fort Washington when she took over a cannon after her husband had been killed?

6. In 1865, Mary Edwards Walker was the only female to have won what medal, although it was revoked in 1917 and given back to her in 1960?

7. On September 12, 1910, Alice Wells was sworn in as the first what in Los Angeles?

8. On May 15, 1930, Miss Ellen Church became the very first person to serve in what new occupation?

9. Who was the first real woman to appear on a U.S. coin?

10. Who was the first woman to be elected to the Aviation Hall of Fame?

4. "The Magician"
5. Lee Trevino
6. Princess Margaret and Lord Snowdon
7. Dick Clark
8. The 1,000,000th run in major league history was scored
9. Rose Mary Wood (President Nixon's secretary)
10. Bradbury (in honor of author Ray Bradbury)

Female Achievements (Answers)

1. Sherry Lansing
2. Martha Washington Hotel
3. Kitty O'Neil
4. Wyoming
5. Margaret Corbin
6. Congressional Medal of Honor
7. Policewoman
8. Airline hostess
9. Susan B. Anthony (Silver dollar)
10. Jacqueline Cochran

Female Firsts

1. Who was the first woman to guest-host Johnny Carson's "The Tonight Show"?
2. In 1980, Kathleen Conley became the first female graduate of what Colorado school?
3. On July 30, 1923, Italian stage actress Elenora Duse, Sarah Bernhardt's rival at the time, became the first female to have her photographs on the cover of what magazine?
4. What famous political first did viscountess Nancy Astor establish in Great Britain?
5. Arabella Mansfield became the first woman to be admitted to what profession in the United States in 1869?
6. Who, in September 1979, became the first woman to sign a contract in the NBA, with the Indiana Pacers?
7. Who was the first female golfer to earn over $100,000 in one season (1976)?
8. On February 22, 1969, who became the first female jockey to win a horse race, when she raced at Charleston racetrack?
9. Who was the first female athlete to win $100,000 or better in a single year?
10. On October 24, 1901, 43-year-old Annie Edson Taylor became the first person to accomplish what feat?

Great Mistakes

1. What was the name of the jockey who during the 1957 Kentucky Derby misjudged the finish line and raised himself up in the saddle of Gallant Man? (Iron Siege passed him, winning the race.)
2. On June 20, 1980, Delta airline pilot Willie B. McWilliam landed his airliner at McDell Air Force Base. At what airport did he think he was landing?
3. In 1970, the Texas House of Representatives passed a bill praising what individual? Tom Moore, Jr., set up the sting.

Female Firsts (Answers)

1. Joan Rivers
2. U.S. Air Force Academy
3. *Time* magazine
4. She became the first female member of the House of Commons.
5. Law bar
6. Ann Myers
7. Judy Rankin
8. Barbara Jo Rubin
9. Billie Jean King (1971)
10. She became the first person to survive going over Niagara Falls in a barrel.

Great Mistakes (Answers)

1. Willie Shoemaker
2. Tampa, Florida
3. Albert DeSalvo (the Boston Strangler)

4. What newspaper ran the November 2, 1948, election night headline DEWEY DEFEATS TRUMAN, when in actuality Truman defeated Thomas Dewey?

5. What British Prime Minister's policy of appeasement lead to Hitler's domination of most of Europe?

6. The Ford Motor Company lost $250,000,000 while they produced 109,466 of these cars.

7. What is the name of the Minnesota Viking defensive end who picked up a fumbled ball and ran 66 yards into the wrong end zone in a game on October 28, 1964?

8. While announcing the 1947 Preakness Race, "Mr. Horse Racing" Clem McCarthy mistakenly announced that Jet Pilot had won. What horse actually won the race?

9. What Oklahoma State guard came off the bench to tackle Iowa State quarterback, Buck Hardeman, in a game on November 24, 1973?

10. What Alabama fullback came off the bench to tackle Dick Moegle of Rice in the 1954 Cotton Bowl?

Kidnappings

1. Frank "Edward" Lay and 26 children were kidnapped on their school bus in what small California town on July 15, 1976?

2. What was the name of the young boy kidnapped and murdered by Nathan Leopold, Jr., and Richard Loeb in 1924?

3. What radical organization kidnapped newspaper heiress Patty Hearst from her home on February 4, 1974?

4. After 42 days of captivity, U.S. Army Brigadier General James Dozier was finally rescued by police (February 1982). In what European country did this occur?

5. Barry W. Keenan, Joseph Clyde Amsler, and John W. Irwin were the three men who kidnapped what entertainer on December 8, 1963, asking a ransom of $240,000?

6. Although the case is still controversial, even today, who was tried and executed for the kidnapping/murder of Charles Lindbergh's 20-month-old son in 1932?

7. What wealthy brewer did Alvin "Old Creepy" Karpis and Fred Hunter kidnap in 1936?

8. What comic strip detective decided to become a police officer after robbers killed his girlfriend's (Tess Trueheart) father and kidnapped her?

4. *Chicago Daily Tribune*
5. Neville Chamberlain
6. Edsels
7. Jim Marshall
8. Faultless
9. S. L. Stephens
10. Tommy Lewis

Kidnappings (Answers)

1. Chowchilla
2. Bobby Franks
3. SLA (Symbionese Liberation Army)
4. Italy
5. Frank Sinatra, Jr.
6. Bruno Hauptmann
7. William Hamm, Jr.
8. Dick Tracy

9. What 20-year-old American heir was kidnapped in May 1973, while in Italy, and held until a $3,000,000 ransom was paid?

10. The F.B.I. captured what notorious gangster for the kidnapping of oilman Charles Urschel in July 1933?

Korean War

1. What general commanded UN forces after MacArthur was relieved of command?

2. Name the river bordering China and Korea that UN forces could not cross.

3. Name the city that served as the last foothold of UN forces on Korea in the early days of the war?

4. What coastal city was assaulted at high tide by MacArthur in one of his greatest tactical manuevers?

5. Who was the highest-scoring American jet ace of the Korean War?

6. Who is listed as the most-decorated American soldier of the Korean War?

7. What North Korean reservoir was a site of an epic Marine Corps battle?

8. What jet fighter was the mainstay of the U.S. Air Force in Korea?

9. What Russian jet fighter was most encountered in the skies over Korea?

10. What is the name of the village where truce talks are still ongoing?

11. What famous hill was captured after a number of assaults by U.S. Marines, only to be given back to the North Koreans after the armistice?

12. James Michener authored a novel based on fact about a bombing mission of the war. What is it?

13. What parallel was established at the end of World War II as the demarcation line between North and South Korea?

14. Who was the President of South Korea at the outbreak of hostilities in July 1950?

15. What acronym did the United Nations' forces use to identify South Korean forces?

16. Name the airfield west of Seoul that was one of the primary targets for the North Koreans?

9. Eugene Paul Getty (grandson of J. Paul Getty)
10. George "Machine Gun" Kelly

Korean War (Answers)

1. Matthew Ridgeway
2. Yalu River
3. Pusan
4. Inchon
5. Capt. Joseph McConnell (with 16 aircraft shot down)
6. Anthony Herbert
7. Chosin Reservoir
8. F-86
9. The Mig-15
10. Panmunjom
11. Pork Chop Hill
12. *The Bridges of Toko Ri*
13. 38th parallel
14. Syngman Rhee
15. ROK (for Republic of Korea)
16. Kimpo

17. What is the name of the valley used on the main invasion route to Seoul from the north?
18. Name the Russian-trained president of North Korea?
19. Who was the first jet ace of the Korean War?
20. What was the name given to the buffer zone between North and South Korea, established by the truce?

Marriages

1. Although Miles Standish wanted her hand, whom did Priscilla Mullins marry?
2. This married couple claims to have been taken onboard a U.F.O. on September 19, 1961. Who are they?
3. When Robert Gibson and Rhea Seddon got married, on May 30, 1981, they both shared the same occupation. What was it?
4. In 1876, who married sharpshooter Frank Butler?
5. In 1952 what did Emil and Dana Zatopek accomplish individually that was a first for a married couple?
6. What couple was married on Johnny Carson's "Tonight Show" on the evening of December 17, 1969?
7. Five U.S. Presidents have been married twice, but only one has been divorced. Name him.
8. Who conducted the marriage of actress Lucille Ball to her second husband, Gary Morton, on November 19, 1961?
9. What occurred in Montreal, Canada, on March 15, 1964, and again in Botswana, Africa, on October 10, 1975?
10. What Hollywood couple married each other, divorced, each married and divorced someone else, and finally remarried?

Medals of Honor

1. Who are the only father and son to both win the Congressional Medal of Honor?
2. What two men were awarded Medals of Honor when they flew over the North Pole in 1926?
3. What Marine Corps general won two Medals of Honor?
4. What two President's sons are recipients of the Congressional Medal of Honor?

17. Uijongbu Valley
18. Kim Il Sung
19. Major James Jabarra
20. DMZ (Demilitarized Zone)

Marriages (Answers)

1. John Aldin
2. Barney and Betty Hill
3. Both are U.S. astronauts
4. Sharpshooter Annie Oakley
5. They both won Gold Medals at the Olympics—Emil in the marathon and Dana in the javelin throw
6. Tiny Tim and Miss Vickie
7. Ronald Reagan
8. Norman Vincent Peale
9. The marriage of Richard Burton and Elizabeth Taylor
10. Robert Wagner and Natalie Wood

Medals of Honor (Answers)

1. General Arthur MacArthur and his son Douglas MacArthur
2. Richard E. Byrd and his pilot Floyd Bennett
3. General Smedley D. Butler
4. Webb Hayes and Theodore Roosevelt, Jr.

5. What composer won the medal in 1936 for composing the World War I song "Over There"?

6. What entertainer has been awarded the medal? (Both his and Cohan's are kept at New York City's Lambs Club)

7. For what Civil War mission were the first six medals awarded?

8. Why was the group's leader, James J. Andrews, not awarded the medal?

9. One of General George A. Custer's brothers had won two medals of honor. He died with his brother at the Little Big Horn. What was his name?

10. What two television series captains have won the Medal of Honor? One commanded a space ship, the other a cavalry fort.

Military Quotes

1. Who said, during the capture of Mobile Bay in 1864, "Damn the torpedos, full speed ahead!"

2. Who exclaimed, "I only regret that I have but one life to lose for my country!" just before the British hanged him for being a spy?

3. When the British requested that U.S. Navy commander John Paul Jones surrender in 1779, what did he reply?

4. As he was dying, during a battle, Captain James Lawrence, commander of the U.S.S. *Chesapeake*, gave his men what famous command?

5. General Douglas MacArthur uttered what famous line as he retreated 3,000 miles away from the Philippines to Australia?

6. During the Revolutionary War at Bunker Hill, what famous command did Isarel Putnam give his men with regard to the approaching British soldiers?

7. What Union Civil War general once stated, "War is hell"?

8. At the Battle of Lake Erie, during the War of 1812, who stated "We have met the enemy and they are ours"?

9. What British general made the following statement: "Put your faith in God, but keep your powder dry"?

10. At the beginning of the battle of Trafalgar, on October 21, 1805, what famous order did Viscount Horatio Nelson give to his men?

5. George M. Cohan
6. Bob Hope (for his U.S.O. work)
7. To James J. Andrew's men, who went behind Confederate lines to destroy their railroad lines
8. He was a civilian.
9. Tom Custer
10. Captain James T. Kirk ("Star Trek") and Captain Wilton Parmenter ("F Troop")

Military Quotes (Answers)

1. Admiral David Farragut
2. Nathan Hale
3. "I have not yet begun to fight."
4. "Don't give up the ship."
5. "I shall return."
6. "Don't fire until you see the whites of their eyes."
7. General William Tecumseh Sherman
8. Oliver Hazard Perry
9. General Oliver Cromwell
10. "England expects that every man will do his duty."

Nobel Prizes

1. In what six categories is the Nobel Prize awarded?
2. What two U.S. Presidents have won the Nobel Peace Prize?
3. What category was introduced in 1969?
4. Who was the youngest man to win the Nobel Peace Prize?
5. On what date each year are the Nobel Prizes awarded?
6. What American novelists won the Nobel Prize for Literature in 1954 and 1962?
7. Who was the first woman to win the Nobel Prize for Literature?
8. Who is the only male to win two Nobel Prizes in different categories?
9. Max Born, who in 1954 shared a Nobel Prize for Physics, is the grandfather of what Grammy winner?
10. Who is the only woman to have won two Nobel Prizes?

Nuclear Age

1. What was the code name for the day the first atom bomb was detonated at Alamogordo, New Mexico (July 16, 1945)?
2. Name the U.S. government code name for the development of the atom bomb in World War II?
3. What isotope of uranium is used to produce nuclear energy?
4. What was the name of the world's first nuclear submarine?
5. Name the world's first nuclear merchant ship?
6. What is the oldest nuclear reactor constructed for commercial use in the United States?
7. Where was the world's first controlled nuclear chain reaction?
8. What did the Germans use in World War II as a medium for a nuclear chain reaction?
9. What was the number of the B-29 bomber *Enola Gay?*
10. At what time did the Hiroshima bomb detonate?
11. What American scientist masterminded the development of the atom bomb?
12. What was the second country to develop the atom bomb?
13. What was the code name for the development of peaceful applications of nuclear energy?

Nobel Prizes (Answers)

1. Peace, Economics, Medicine/Physiology, Literature, Physics, Chemistry
2. Woodrow Wilson (in 1919) and Theodore Roosevelt (in 1906)
3. Economics
4. Martin Luther King (at age 35)
5. December 10
6. Ernest Hemingway and John Steinbeck, respectively
7. Pearl Buck (in 1938)
8. Linus C. Pauling (Chemistry, 1954; Peace, 1962)
9. Olivia Newton-John
10. Marie Curie (Physics, 1903; Chemistry, 1911)

Nuclear Age (Answers)

1. Day of Trinity
2. Manhattan Project
3. U-235
4. U.S.S. *Nautilus*
5. S.S. *Savannah*
6. Dresden Unit #1 in Illinois dating to 1960
7. University of Chicago—December 2, 1942
8. Heavy water, or deuterium
9. #83
10. 8:15 A.M.
11. J. Robert Oppenheimer
12. Great Britain
13. Operation Plowshares

14. What was the nickname given to the atom bomb dropped on Nagasaki?

15. At what Pacific atoll were several nuclear bombs detonated in 1946 to test their effectiveness on war material?

16. Paul Tibbets piloted the *Enola Gay* over Hiroshima on August 6, 1945. Who was the copilot?

17. What Tennessee town sprang up as the key research site of the Manhattan Project?

18. Name the U.S. Army officer in command of the development of the atom bomb.

19. Name the U.S. Navy cruiser that delivered the atom bombs to Taiwan?

20. What was the explosive yield of the bomb dropped on Hiroshima?

Political Firsts

1. From 1946 to 1952, who served as the first secretary general of the United Nations?

2. Who, in 1867, became the first prime minister of Canada?

3. Who became the first Republican candidate for President when he ran in 1856?

4. Sir Robert Walpole was the first pime minister of what country?

5. David Ben-Gurion, born David Green in 1886, became the first prime minister of what country?

6. On April 4, 1887, Susanna Medora Satler became the first female to hold what office in the United States?

7. She was the first Jewish woman to be elected as a U. S. representative. She was also the founder of the New Democratic Coalition. Name her.

8. Who became the first female to hold a Presidential cabinet position when President Franklin D. Roosevelt appointed her the secretary of labor?

9. Who, in 1949, became the first president of Indonesia?

10. Who became prime minister of Britain in 1783 at the age of 24, the youngest man to hold that position?

14. Fat Man
15. Bikini
16. Captain Robert Lewis
17. Oak Ridge
18. General Leslie Graves
19. U.S.S. *Indianapolis*
20. The equivalent of 20,000 tons of TNT

Political Firsts (Answers)

1. Trygve Lie (born in Oslo, Norway)
2. John A. MacDonald
3. John Charles Fremont
4. Britain (he served from 1721–1742)
5. Israel
6. Mayor (she became mayor of Arzonia, Kansas)
7. Bella Abzug
8. Frances Perkins
9. Sukarno
10. William Pitt

Political Quotes

Who said?
1. "A black, a woman, two Jews, and a cripple. . . ."
2. "The great black nigger, uh, educator—uh, excuse me for making that—the great black educator, the negro education."
3. "We may be finding that in some blacks when it (controversial choke hold) is applied the veins or arteries do not open as fast as they do on normal people."
4. "I've committed adultery in my heart many times."
5. What U.S. Naval commodore and hero coined the expression "Our country, right or wrong"?
6. What American patriot and former governor of Virginia uttered the immortal words "Give me liberty or give me death"?
7. Revolutionary War general John Stark is credited with coining the phrase that became the motto of the state of New Hampshire. What is the four-word statement?
8. Which secretary of defense (President Eisenhower's) uttered the infamous line "What's good for General Motors is good for the country and vice versa"?
9. Which statesman once said, "There never was a good war or a bad peace"?
10. Who once observed, "Politicians are the same all over. They promise to build a bridge even when there is no river"?

Revolutionary War

1. What was the nickname given to a heroine of the Revolutionary War who carried water to soldiers on a battlefield in a pitcher?
2. Who was king of England during the American Revolution (he was known as the tyrant king)?
3. What German troops were employed by the British to garrison parts of the colonies?
4. The British troops were given nicknames according to the coats they wore. What was this nickname?
5. What was the name of the standard musket used by the British army?

Political Quotes (Answers)

1. Interior Secretary James Watt (1983)
2. Texas Agriculture Commissioner Reagan Brown (1982)
3. Los Angeles Police Chief Daryl Gates (1982)
4. Presidential candidate Jimmy Carter in a *Playboy* magazine interview
5. Stephen Decatur
6. Patrick Henry
7. "Live free or die."
8. Charles Wilson
9. Benjamin Franklin
10. Nikita Khrushchev

Revolutionary War (Answers)

1. Molly Pitcher
2. George III
3. Hessians
4. Redcoats
5. Brown Bess

6. What was the treasonable act of Benedict Arnold?
7. What was the name given to the militiamen commanded by Ethan Allen and where were they from?
8. Who was the first person to sign the Declaration of Independence?
9. Who was known as the Swamp Fox because of his adeptness at eluding British troops by escaping into swamps?
10. What relative of Robert E. Lee fought against the British in the Revolutionary War?
11. What general commanded British forces in the American colonies at the outbreak of hostilities in 1775?
12. What name was applied by American patriots to English sympathizers in the colonies?
13. Name the treaty that ended the American Revolution.
14. What was the name of the flagship of John Paul Jones?
15. Who was America's representative in Paris during the Revolution?
16. Who delivered the British surrender at Yorktown, ending the war?
17. Name the British officer who was in command at the skirmish of Lexington, Massachussetts.
18. What was Paul Revere's occupation?
19. What German officer came to the colonies to teach Washington's army the art of soldiering and later became the first inspector general?
20. What was the name and denomination of the Old North Church, from whose belfry lanterns signaled the approach of the British in 1775?

Space Exploration

1. What was the name of the first U.S. artificial satellite?
2. Who was the first American to walk in space?
3. Who was the first woman in space?
4. What was the name of Alan Shephard's spacecraft?
5. What was the first animal into space?
6. Name the first space shuttle to orbit the earth?
7. What was the number of the Apollo mission to the moon that nearly ended in disaster when an onboard explosion destroyed most of the equipment?

6. He sold the plans of the defenses of West Point to the British.
7. Green Mountain Boys, from Vermont
8. John Hancock
9. Francis Marion
10. Lighthorse Harry Lee
11. General Thomas Gage
12. Tories
13. Treaty of Paris
14. *Bon Homme Richard*
15. Benjamin Franklin
16. Lord Cornwallis
17. Major Pitcairn
18. Silversmith
19. Baron Frederick von Steuben
20. Christ Church, Episcopalian

Space Exploration (Answers)

1. *Explorer I*
2. Edward White
3. Valentina Tereshkova (June 16, 1963)
4. *Freedom 7*
5. The Russian dog Laika (aboard Sputnik II)
6. Columbia
7. Apollo XIII

8. Neil Armstrong was first to walk on the moon. Who was second?
9. Who was the astronaut that remained in orbit around the moon for the first landing?
10. What was the first spacecraft ever to go into space a second time?
11. Name the book written by the original astronauts about their selection and training.
12. Who was known as the voice of mission control for NASA?
13. What was the code name for the U.S. attempt to orbit the earth?
14. Who rode *Friendship 7* for three orbits of the earth on February 20, 1962?
15. Who was the second person to orbit the earth?
16. Name the last mission of the Apollo Space Program in 1974.
17. What was the name of the Russian space mission that linked up with a U.S. Apollo flight in 1974?
18. Name America's first woman into space.
19. Who was America's second man in space?
20. Why weren't early Russian spacecraft controlled by the cosmonauts?

Supreme Court

1. Which member of the U.S. Supreme Court has his portrait on the $10,000 bill?
2. What special prosecutor authored the 1976 book *The Role of the Supreme Court in American Government?*
3. Because of accusations that he was involved in questionable practices, who was forced to resign from the Supreme Court in 1969?
4. It was during the funeral of what Supreme Court Chief Justice that the liberty bell cracked when it was rung?
5. What associate justice was called "The Great Dissenter"?
6. Who headed the official investigation into the assassination of President John F. Kennedy?
7. What associate Supreme Court judge once played pro football for the Pittsburgh Pirates and the Detroit Lions and is now a member of the Football Hall of Fame?
8. Who was the first Chief Justice of the U.S. Supreme Court?
9. Who was the first black to serve on the U.S. Supreme Court?
10. Selected and confirmed in 1981, she was the first female associate justice of the Supreme Court. Name her.

8. Buzz Aldrin
9. Mike Collins
10. Space shuttle *Columbia*
11. *We Seven*
12. Chris Craft or John "Shorty" Powers
13. Project Mercury
14. John Glenn
15. Russian Cosmonaut Titov
16. Skylab
17. Soyuz
18. Sally Ride
19. Gus Grissom
20. The Russians were afraid they might defect on reentry.

Supreme Court (Answers)

1. Salmon P. Chase
2. Archibald Cox
3. Abe Fortas
4. John Marshall
5. Oliver Wendell Holmes, Jr.
6. Chief Justice Earl Warren
7. Byron "Whizzer" White
8. John Jay
9. Thurgood Marshall
10. Sandra Day O'Connor

Treaties

1. In what U.S. city was the treaty ending the Russo-Japanese War signed on September 5, 1905?
2. Who drafted the Treaty of Paris?
3. John Adams's son John Quincy Adams was the chief negotiator for the treaty that ended the war of 1812. What was the treaty called?
4. What treaty will cede Hong Kong back to China from British control?
5. What U.S. Navy commodore negotiated the Treaty of Kanagawa with Japan, which opened the trade route for both countries?
6. In what city did the Vietnamese peace talks in the 1960s take place?
7. What American Indian who ate with the Pilgrims at the first Thanksgiving made a treaty with the white men that he faithfully kept?
8. A treaty signed in September 1951 ended the United States' occupation of what country?
9. What Indian tribe fought a war against the United States in 1835–1842 and finally signed a peace treaty in 1975?
10. What is the name of the treaty signed on June 28, 1919, which ended World War I?

Trials/Cases

1. In 1971, what young U.S. Army lieutenant went on trial, accused of the murder of 109 Vietnamese civilians in March 1968?
2. Erin Fleming was sued by the Bank of America in 1983, which claimed that she had abused the actor whom she lived with. Who was he?
3. Football coach Knute Rockne's cousin Judge Russell Rockne Leggett heard the murder case of Jean Harris, who had been accused of the murder of what diet doctor?
4. What name was given to the nine young black men who went through several trials when two white girls, Victoria Price and Ruby Bates, accused them of rape?

Treaties (Answers)

1. Portsmouth, New Hampshire
2. John Adams
3. The Treaty of Ghent
4. The Treaty of Nanking
5. Matthew Perry
6. Paris
7. Massasiot
8. Japan
9. Seminoles
10. Treaty of Versailles

Trials/Cases (Answers)

1. Lt. William L. Calley
2. Groucho Marx
3. Herman Tarnower (author of the *Scarsdale Diet*)
4. Scottsboro Boys

5. Who was the first man to go on trial in the United States for raping his wife (Greta, on October 10, 1978)?

6. In 1954, F. Lee Bailey won an acquittal for what physician on trial for the murder of his wife?

7. Tom Hayden, Abbie Hoffman, and Jerry Rubin were three members of a larger group of men who went on trial for inciting riots in 1968. What name was the group known by?

8. Who took her case all the way to the Supreme Court, arguing that her son should not have to pray in public schools? This led eventually to a ban on prayer in public schools in 1963.

9. Who was found guilty on January 26, 1971, after the jury deliberated for 42 hours and 40 minutes?

10. For what crime was Lizzie Borden tried and convicted in 1892?

United States Accessions

1. How much did the United States pay Spain for the Philippine Islands?

2. Secretary of State William H. Seward purchased what land mass from Russia in 1867? (It was soon called Seward's Folly.)

3. Who purchased Manhattan Island from the Indians for the equivalent of $24?

4. From what country did the United States purchase the Virgin Islands in 1917 for $25,000,000?

5. In 1819 the United States paid Spain $5,000,000 for what land mass?

6. How much did the United States pay Napoleon for the Louisiana Territory in 1803?

7. Beginning on April 22, 1889, the U.S. government offered land for $1.05 an acre. What was the acquisition of the land called?

8. What strip of land was purchased by the United States from Mexico in 1853?

9. In 1898 the United States acquired what two Pacific islands? (One is now an independent country.)

10. In 1899 the United States made two more acquisitions, one in the Caribbean and the other in the South Pacific. Name both.

5.   John Rideout (He was acquitted.)
6.   Dr. Sam Sheppard
7.   Chicago 7
8.   Madalyn O'Hair
9.   Charles Manson
10. None—she was tried for a double murder but was acquitted.

United States Accessions (Answers)

1. $20,000,000
2.   Alaska
3.   Peter Minuit
4.   Denmark
5.   Florida
6. $15,000,000 (averaging 2¢ an acre)
7.   Oklahoma Land Rush
8.   Gasden Purchase
9.   Hawaii and the Philippines
10. Puerto Rico and Guam

War Ships

1. On what British vessel did President Franklin D. Roosevelt and Prime Minister Winston Churchill sign the Atlantic Charter in 1941?
2. In December 1907, a fleet of American battleships departed the United States for an around-the-world voyage to spread U.S. prestige. What was the name of the fleet?
3. What U.S. heavy cruiser was sunk by the Japanese submarine I-58 on July 30, 1945, and yet a number of crew members survived only to die from exposure and shark attacks?
4. What was the name of the first U.S. aircraft carrier, which was commissioned on March 20, 1922? (It was the converted coal carrier *Jupiter*.)
5. What is the name of the U.S. Navy vessel that on June 8, 1967, was attacked by Israeli fighters, which killed 34 members of the crew?
6. What was the name of the very first U.S. Navy vessel?
7. From what U.S. aircraft carrier did Col. Doolittle lead his B-25's to bomb Tokyo on April 18, 1942?
8. What two ironclads met in a five-hour battle on March 9, 1862?
9. What U.S. warship was nicknamed Old Ironsides because cannonballs seemed to bounce off her sides?
10. What was the name of the U.S. gunboat sunk by Japanese airplanes on December 12, 1937, on the Yangtze River?

Watergate

1. What two words were substituted for any swear words used by President Nixon or his advisers on the Watergate tapes?
2. What was the name of the janitor who discovered the Watergate break-in? He played himself in the 1976 movie *All the President's Men*.

Name the authors of the following Watergate-related autobiographies:
3. *Ends of Power*
4. *Will*

War Ships (Answers)

1. *Prince of Wales*
2. The Great White Fleet
3. U.S.S. *Indianapolis*
4. U.S.S. *Langley*
5. U.S.S. *Liberty*
6. *Hannah* (a schooner)
7. U.S.S. *Hornet*
8. *Merrimack* and the *Monitor*
9. U.S.S. *Constitution*
10. *Panay*

Watergate (Answers)

1. Expletive Deleted
2. Frank Wills
3. H. R. Haldeman
4. G. Gordon Liddy, Jr.

5. *Born Again*
6. *Mo*
7. *The Whole Truth: The Watergate Conspiracy*
8. *All the President's Men* and *The Final Days*
9. *The Right and the Power*
10. *Blind Ambition*

World War I

1. One of the U.S. Army's youngest generals commanded the 42nd Rainbow Division. He later became much more famous commanding an entire theater in World War II. Name him.
2. What Tennessee sharpshooter won the Congressional Medal of Honor for killing 32 and capturing 128 Germans?
3. What was the name of the biplane used by the U.S. Army to train its aviators?
4. What famous battle in 1918 halted a major German offensive toward Paris and marked the beginning of the Allied offensives ending the war?
5. Who was the highest-scoring American ace of the war?
6. What two German generals (later Field Marshalls) became known as an unbeatable team owing to successes against Russia?
7. A U.S. Army colonel commanded the fledgling tank corps in France, later becoming famous for tank warfare in World War II. Name him.
8. A major naval battle of the war, fought in 1915, saw neither side the victor, yet convinced the German Navy to avoid direct confrontations with the Royal Navy. What was it?
9. What French general was the Allied Supreme Commander on the Western front?
10. What treaty allowed Russia to drop out of the war?
11. What was the highest medal awarded by Germany?
12. What American politician fought in Italy as a pilot?
13. What color was the aircraft of German ace Baron von Richtofen?
14. The Germans, at one point, attempted to enlist the aide of Mexico against the United States through a telegram that was intercepted and revealed. What did it become known as?
15. What weapon of war, when invented, was deemed so horrible that no war could ever be fought again?

5. Charles Colson
6. Maureen Dean
7. Sam J. Erwin, Jr.
8. Robert Woodward and Carl Bernstein
9. Leon Jaworski
10. John Dean

World War I (Answers)

1. Douglas MacArthur
2. Alvin York
3. Jenny
4. Battle of the Marne
5. Eddie Rickenbacker, with 26 German aircraft downed
6. Hindenburg and Lindendorff
7. George S. Patton
8. Battle of Jutland
9. Ferdinand Foch
10. Brest-Litovsk
11. Blue Max
12. Fiorello La Guardia
13. Red, thus the name the Red Baron
14. The Zimmerman Telegram
15. Machine gun

16. What American general commanded U.S. ground forces in France?
17. What famous female spy was executed by the Germans in 1917?
18. Name the day and hour the armistice ending World War I was signed.
19. What U.S. artillery piece fired the last shot of the war?
20. Who commanded and led some of the first zeppelin bombing raids on London in World War I?

World War II

1. Who was head of the Gestapo and is still listed as a wanted war criminal?
2. Who was known as the Flying Tailor because of the multitude of uniforms he wore in public?
3. What was the password used by Allied forces during the D-day landings?
4. What designator did the Japanese give to the attack on Pearl Harbor?
5. What Japanese admiral masterminded the early victories of the Imperial Navy until he was killed by U.S. Army Air Force fighter aircraft?
6. Name the pocket battleship of the German Navy scuttled at Montevideo, Uruguay in 1939?
7. What type of aircraft did Doolittle use to bomb Tokyo in the first attack on the Japanese mainland of World War II?
8. Who went by the code title "Naval Person" in correspondence with Churchill during the war?
9. What invasion site in Italy was called the "largest self-sustained POW camp in the world" by the Germans?
10. Pappy Boyington flew a fighter distinguished by its gull-shaped wing. What was it?
11. Where did the first U.S. Navy admiral killed in World War II die?
12. What was the name of the German car invented by Porsche to be Hitler's car for the people?
13. What U.S. fighter shot down more Japanese aircraft than any other fighter?
14. Hitler's cadre were called Zrorin Shirts. What were the followers of Mussolini called?

16. John Pershing
17. Mata Hari
18. 11 A.M. November 11, 1918—the 11th hour of the 11th day of the 11th month
19. The Calamity Jane
20. The inventor, Count von Zeppelin

World War II (Answers)

1. Heinrich Müller
2. Herman Göring, head of the Luftwaffe
3. Mickey Mouse
4. Plan Z
5. Yamamoto
6. *Graf Spee*
7. B-25
8. Franklin D. Roosevelt
9. Anzio, because it was completely surrounded and immobilized
10. F-4U Corsair
11. Pearl Harbor, aboard the U.S.S. *Arizona* (Admiral Kidd)
12. Volkswagen
13. P-38 Lightning
14. Black Shirts

15. What was the nickname, immortalized in songs and movies, given to the American female factory workers?

16. What famous Pacific battle was the first defeat for the Japanese Navy in modern history?

17. What famous leader used the code name Colonel Warden Thugheart in World War II?

18. Name the only five European countries to remain neutral throughout World War II?

19. What was the name given to Hitler's last offensive on the Western Front in World War II?

20. What German aircraft manufacturer made the jet fighter ME-262?

Years

1. In what year will Hong Kong revert to Communist China's rule?

2. How did George Orwell determine what the year of the title of his 1948 futuristic novel *1984* would be?

3. What is the only year in which there was a Triple Crown winner in both baseball and horse racing?

4. When Abraham Lincoln referred to "four score and seven years ago" in his 1863 Gettysburg address, what year was he referring to?

5. Name one of the only two years in which the United States has had three Presidents?

6. The Statue of Liberty holds in her left hand the Book of Laws. What date is inscribed on the books?

7. In what year did the United States enter World War I?

8. In what year did the United States celebrate its centennial?

9. What will be the next year that Halley's Comet will be seen from the earth?

10. In what year did the Pilgrims first land in the new world?

15. Rosie the Riveter
16. Battle of Midway
17. Churchill
18. Ireland, Spain, Portugal, Switzerland, and Sweden
19. Battle of the Bulge
20. Messerschmitt

Years (Answers)

1. 1998
2. He just reversed the 4 and the 8.
3. 1937 (Joe Medwick and War Admiral)
4. 1776 (Score = 20, 4 × 20 & 80 & 7 = 87, 1863 − 87 = 1776)
5. 1841 and 1881
6. 1776
7. 1917
8. 1876
9. 1986
10. 1620

Pastimes and Sports

Amusement Parks

1. On August 12, 1965, Mary Adams became the 50 millionth visitor to enter what world-famous amusement park?
2. In 1927, Garnet Carter introduced what new outdoor game in Lookout Mountain, Tennessee?
3. What popular Southern California amusement park did the developer of the boysenberry, Walker Knott, found that is today the third-largest in the U.S.?
4. In what state is Disneyworld located?
5. What was the first foreign country to open its own Disneyland?
6. What is the name of country music's first amusement park (there are now three), and where is it located?
7. What Southern California amusement park is the home of such giant trolls as Bloop, Bleep, and Blip?
8. What was the original name considered by Walt Disney for his new park Disneyland?
9. Freddie Cannon recorded a hit record in 1962 that was titled for what amusement park?
10. One of San Francisco's historic sites was torn down in the 1970s. What was the name of this amusement park that was only a few hundred yards from the Pacific Ocean?

Annual Events

1. In what U.S. city does the annual All-American Soap Box Derby take place?
2. The Tournament of Roses Parade takes place each January 1st in what Southern California location?
3. Beaver, Oklahoma, is the site of what annual World Championship contest?

Amusement Parks (Answers)

1. Disneyland
2. Miniature golf
3. Knott's Berry Farm
4. Florida
5. Japan
6. Opryland, Nashville, Tennessee
7. Magic Mountain Amusement Park
8. Mickey Mouse Park
9. "Palisades Park"
10. Playland, at the Beach

Annual Events (Answers)

1. Akron, Ohio
2. Pasadena
3. World Championship Cow Chip Throwing Contest

4. Dipping Springs, Texas, has been the annual site since 1973 of what country singer's Fourth of July picnic?
5. What California town is the host of the annual World's Wrist Wrestling Championship, which has been held each year since 1953?
6. In what small U.S. town would you think that the National Fence-Painting Contest is held each year?
7. Raleigh, Mississippi, is the setting each year for what event?
8. In what New Jersey town is the annual National Marbles Tournament held?
9. Stuttgart, Arkansas, is the site of what annual event associated with hunting?
10. To what California mission do the swallows return each year on St. Joseph's Day (March 19)?

Auto Racing

1. Ralph DePalma won the 1915 Indianapolis 500, but he did not win by driving across the finish line. As a matter of fact, he wasn't even in his Mercedes. How did he finish?
2. What make of automobile did Gaston Chevrolet drive, when he won the 1920 Indianapolis 500 automobile race?
3. What trophy is presented to the winner of the Indianapolis 500 race?
4. What British automobile race driver won seven Grand Prix in 1963?
5. Who is the first woman licensed in the U.S. to drive top-fueled dragsters? Her nickname is "Cha Cha."
6. Who has won the Daytona 500 seven times, from 1964 through 1981?
7. Who was the first woman to race in the Indy 500, finishing 29th in 1977?
8. What does N.A.S.C.A.R. stand for?
9. Ray Harroun drove his car to become the first winner in 1911 of the Indianapolis 500. What was the automobile he drove?
10. What early race driver drove an automobile called the "999," which was built by Henry Ford?

4.   Willie Nelson's
5.   Petaluma
6.   Hannibal, Missouri
7.   National Tobacco-Spitting Contest
8.   Wildwood
9.   World Duck-Calling Championship
10. Capistrano

Auto Racing (Answers)

1.   He pushed his car by hand, the last mile and a half across the finish line.
2.   Monroe
3.   Borg Warner Trophy
4.   Jim Clark
5.   Shirley Muldowney
6.   Richard Petty
7.   Janet Guthrie
8.   National Association of Stock Car Auto Racing
9.   Marmon Wasp
10. Barney Oldfield

Baseball Stadiums

1. What baseball stadium was the site of the first night game ever played in the major leagues?
2. A record number of 23,900 people attended the premiere of the 1970 film *Brewster McCloud*. Where did it take place?
3. Zackary Taylor Davis was the designer of what two Chicago stadiums built in 1910 and 1914, respectively?
4. The deepest part of what stadium is nicknamed "Death Valley"?
5. What is the fully enclosed playing field in Seattle, Washington, named?
6. What major league baseball park was never the site of a no-hitter?
7. What ball park has a 315-foot-high fence called the "Green Monster"?
8. Who was the first person to hit the public address system speaker hanging from the roof of the Astrodome in a regular game in 1974?
9. What three rivers meet near a junction close to Pittsburgh's Three River Stadium?
10. What ball park has never had lights installed for night games?

Baseball Autobiographies

1. Bob Uecker's 1982 autobiography, written with Mickey Herkowitz, was humorously titled what?
2. *Seeing It Through* is the title of the 1970 autobiography of what baseball player hit by tragedy?
3. *Me and the Spitter* is the autobiography of what major league pitcher who has been known to throw a spitball?
4. *Day with the Giants* is the title of the 1952 autobiography of the actress-wife of New York Giants manager Leo Durocher. Name her?
5. *Fear Strikes Out*, the 1957 movie, was based on the autobiography of what ball player?
6. Reggie Jackson's 1975 autobiography has what one-word title?
7. Jim Bouton wrote an updated edition of his autobiography *Ball Four*. What was its title?

Baseball Stadiums (Answers)

1. Crosley Field (The Reds beat the Phillies 2 to 1.)
2. Houston Astrodome
3. Comiskey Park and Wrigley Field
4. Yankee Stadium
5. King Dome
6. Forbes Field
7. Boston's Fenway Park
8. Philadelphia Philly Mike Schmidt
9. Allegheny, Monogahela, and Ohio
10. Wrigley Field in Chicago

Baseball Autobiographies (Answers)

1. *Catcher in the Wry*
2. Tony Conigliaro
3. Gaylord Perry
4. Lorrain Day
5. Jimmy Piersall
6. *Reggie*
7. *Ball Four plus Ball Five*

8. *Baseball Had Done It* was the title of what famous black baseball player's autobiography?
9. *My Turn at Bat* is the title of what Hall of Famer's life story?
10. What manager's autobiography is titled *Number 1*?

Bats

1. Who was sentenced to six months in jail for attacking television executive Sheldon Saltman with a baseball bat?
2. What U.S. President was at bat at a sandlot baseball game when he was informed that he had won the nomination for the Presidency?
3. A Hillerich & Bradsby Model T-85 Louisville Slugger baseball bat became the center of a controversy on July 25, 1983. Why?
4. What Boston Red Sox player's autograph was on the Louisville Slugger baseball bat Shelley Duvall hit Jack Nicholson with in the 1980 movie *The Shining?*
5. Whose bat did Willie Mays borrow the day he hit four home runs in a single game on April 30, 1961?
6. When he hit his 60th home run in 1927, what baseball player used a bat nicknamed Big Bertha?
7. What member of Baseball's Hall of Fame used the shortest baseball bat in major league history? It measured just 21½ inches long.
8. How many eyes watched Casey at the bat in Ernest Thayer's poem?
9. What major league catcher's name was on the bat used by Hank Aaron to hit his record-breaking 715th home run on April 18, 1974?
10. What is the nickname given to baseball bats manufactured by the Louisville, Kentucky, bat factory for Hillerich & Bradsby?

Beauty Contests

1. Where was the site of the first Miss America Pageant, which took place in 1921?
2. What actress, who was Miss Chicago in 1949, was a runner-up in the Miss America contest?

8. Jackie Robinson's
9. Ted Williams's
10. Billy Martin's

Bats (Answers)

1. Motorcycle stunt rider Evel Knievel
2. Abraham Lincoln
3. It was the bat that Kansas City Royal George Brett had too much pine tar on, causing the invalidation of his home run. (The decision was later reversed.)
4. Carl Yastrzemski's
5. Fellow Giant Joe Amalfitano's
6. Babe Ruth
7. Wee Willie Keeler
8. 10,000
9. Del Crandall's
10. Louisville Sluggers

Beauty Contests (Answers)

1. Atlantic City, New Jersey
2. Cloris Leachman

3. Miss New York, Deborah Ann Fountain, was disqualified from the 1981 U.S.A. contest for what reason?

4. In 1984 Vanessa Williams became the first black to garner what title?

5. Anita Bryant, the singer of such hit songs as "Paper Roses" and "My Little Corner of the World" was a runner-up in what beauty contest in 1959?

6. The mother of what novelist once held the beauty contest title of Miss Alabama?

7. Jo Carroll Dennison, Miss America of 1942, was the one-time wife of what TV comedian?

8. Victoria King, who once held the title of Miss New Jersey, is the sister of what television actor?

9. Who was Margaret Gorman?

10. What 5-feet 11-inch actress was the second runner-up for Miss America? She entered as Miss California 1969.

Black Sports Firsts

1. Who became the first black player to play in a professional hockey game when on November 15, 1950, he signed a contract with Atlantic City?

2. On June 6, 1952, Zack Clayton became the first black to referee a heavyweight title bout. The fight occurred between challenger Ezzard Charles and what boxing champion?

3. Who became the first black to play in the National Hockey League (as a forward for the Boston Bruins), on January 18, 1958?

4. Who (in 1947) became the first black to play major league baseball in modern times?

5. Who was the first black to become the heavyweight boxing champion of the world?

6. In 1975, who became the first black to win at Wimbledon?

7. What is the name of the first black umpire to appear in a major league game?

8. What is the name of the first black stock car champion, portrayed by Richard Pryor in the 1977 film *Greased Lightning?*

9. Who became the first black basketball player to appear in the NBA when he signed for the New York Knickerbockers in 1950?

 3. Padding her swimsuit
 4. Miss America
 5. Miss America
 6. Truman Capote
 7. Phil Silvers
 8. Michael Landon
 9. The first winner of the Miss America contest in 1921
10. Susan Anton

Black Sports Firsts (Answers)

 1. Arthur Dorrington
 2. Jersey Joe Walcott
 3. Willie O'Ree
 4. Jackie Robinson
 5. Jack Johnson
 6. Arthur Ashe
 7. Emmett Ashford
 8. Wendell Scott
 9. Nathaniel "Sweetwater" Clifton

10. In 1924, DeBart Hubbard became the first black to win an Olympic Gold Medal for the United States. For what event did he receive his medal?

Bowling

1. How many pins are used in the game of bowling as it is played in bowling alleys throughout the world?
2. What two pins are left for a railroad split?
3. What first did Emma Fahning accomplish on March 4, 1930?
4. What is the maximum legal weight of a bowling ball?
5. By what name is the side gutter opposite the hand delivering the ball called?
6. What city has the largest bowling alley in the world, with 252 lanes?
7. What is the distance from the foul line to the headpin?
8. Who was the first bowler to win $100,000 or better in a single season?
9. What are the two biggest manufacturers of bowling alley equipment?
10. In 1913, William J. Knox became the first ABC bowler to do what?

The Circus

1. In what Florida City is the Circus Hall of Fame located?
2. What was the last name of the brothers Albert, August, Alfred, Charles, John, and Henry who founded their first circus in 1882?
3. When the Ringling Brothers joined with Barnum and Bailey what was the circus's full title?
4. What song, if played by the circus band, alerts all the performers that there is danger?
5. What is the name given to the laborers who set up and take down the tents and seats each time the circus moves?
6. Who played the lead role of Corky on the 1956–1958 TV series "Circus Boy"?
7. Celeste Geyer is the real name of what one-time circus fat lady?
8. What is the theme song of the Ringling Brothers-Barnum and Bailey Circus's "Greatest Show on Earth"?

10. Long jump

Bowling (Answers)

1. Ten
2. 7–10, 8–10, or 4–6
3. She became the first female to bowl 300 in a sanctioned game.
4. 16 pounds
5. Brooklyn
6. Tokyo, Japan (Tokyo World Lanes Center)
7. 60 feet
8. Earl Anthony
9. AMF and Brunswick
10. Bowl a 300 game

The Circus (Answers)

1. Sarasota
2. Ringling
3. The Ringling Brothers—Barnum and Bailey "Greatest Show on Earth"
4. "Stars and Stripes Forever"
5. Roustabouts
6. Mickey Braddock (aka Mickey Dolenz)
7. Dolly Dimples (she weighs 550 pounds.)
8. "Here Comes the Clowns"

9. In 1956, what ended the tradition of the Ringling Brothers and Barnum and Bailey Circus history?
10. When this entrepreneur died in 1959, his last words were "How were the circus receipts today at Madison Square Garden?" Name him.

Consecutive Records

1. Between January 24, 1971, and January 29, 1974, how many consecutive basketball games did the UCLA Bruins win?
2. Between June 1, 1925, and May 2, 1939, in how many consecutive major league baseball games did Lou Gehrig of the New York Yankees appear?
3. In 1982, the New York Islanders set a National Hockey League record when they won how many consecutive games?
4. What is the NBA record number of consecutive free throws (made by Calvin Murphy between December 27, 1980 and February 28, 1981)?
5. How many consecutive games did the Atlanta Braves win at the beginning of the 1982 baseball season, setting a major league record?
6. What NBA basketball team set a record in 1973 when they lost 20 consecutive games?
7. What NHL team won 28 consecutive games in the 1977–1978 hockey season?
8. Who threw 33⅔ innings of scoreless baseball games over the 1960, 1961, and 1962 World Series?
9. What football player set a NFL record for consecutive games played?
10. Bill McGowan appeared in 2,541 consecutive major league baseball games, beating Lou Gehrig's record by 411 games. What is different about his record?

Dances

1. By the virtue of a congressional act, what is designated as the official folk dance of the United States?

9. Last performance given under a circus tent
10. P. T. Barnum

Consecutive Records (Answers)

1. 88
2. 2,130
3. 15
4. 78
5. 13
6. Philadelphia 76ers
7. Montreal Canadians
8. Whitey Ford
9. Jim Marshall
10. Bill McGowan is an umpire

Dances (Answers)

1. Square dance

2. Although Chubby Checker's version of "The Twist" became a huge success, who originally sang the song, the year before in 1959?

3. In 1958, The Diamonds titled their hit record for a dance craze, which helped to make it even more popular. Name the song.

4. Two of the greatest male dancers to ever grace the stage are Fred Astaire and Gene Kelly, who only danced together once in films. Their routine appeared in the 1946 movie *Ziegfeld Follies* and was later reshown in *That's Entertainment*. What was the name of the routine?

5. What two things are communicated when a worker bee dances for the other bees after returning to the hive?

6. Television comedian Soupy Sales invented what dance?

7. What dance was once outlawed in French nightclubs such as the Moulin Rouge?

8. What popular dance of the Roaring Twenties was introduced by black singer Elsabeth Welch in the 1923 movie *Runnin' Wild?*

9. The title of the first song to win the Academy Award was also the name of what popular dance of the early 1930s?

10. What type of popular solo dancing developed on street corners in the early 1980s?

Fads/Jokes

1. Nutritionist Horace Fletcher introduced, in the early 1900s, "Fletcherizing," which applied to the way people eat their food. What did he advocate?

2. Because of the popularity of this new item, there became a shortage in plastic piping throughout the United States in 1958. Name it.

3. Kids swallowed what items by the dozens during the 1930s?

4. What award did Dan Rowan and Dick Martin hand out on their TV series "Laugh In"?

5. Peter Hodgson introduced what versatile substance that could be formed into various shapes?

6. What fad did Gary Dahl create in the 1970s that made him a millionaire?

7. The University of Houston once elected what rock star as homecoming queen?

2. Hank Ballard
3. "The Stroll"
4. The Babbitt and the Bromide
5. The direction and the distance of food
6. The Mouse
7. The can-can
8. The Charleston
9. The Continental
10. Break dancing

Fads/Jokes (Answers)

1. That a person should chew each bite 30 times before swallowing
2. Hula Hoop
3. Goldfish
4. Fickle Finger of Fate
5. Silly Putty
6. Pet Rocks
7. Alice Cooper

8. What television series introduced the fad of coonskin hats in the 1950s?
9. Shipwreck Kelly was famous for doing what feat in the 1920s and 1930s?
10. Al Capp's *Li'l Abner* comic strip introduced Sadie Hawkins Day as an annual event when what occurs?

Football Bowl Games

Give the location of the following bowl games:
1. Cotton Bowl
2. Blue-Gray Bowl
3. Tangerine Bowl
4. Liberty Bowl
5. Sun Bowl
6. Pig Bowl
7. Orange Bowl
8. Hula Bowl
9. Sugar Bowl
10. Rose Bowl

Gambling

1. The opposite sides of a die add up to what?
2. On a typical slot machine how many coins are paid out when three bells are lined up?
3. What are the 38 numbers on a roulette wheel?
4. What are the first three places in a horse race called in betting terms?
5. How many numbers are there on a keno card?
6. How many numbers are there on a Bingo card?
7. Craps is the name given to what three numbers if they come up on the first throw of the dice?
8. What are the only two states where gambling casinos are legal?
9. What is the minimum bet allowed at a race track?
10. Italian-American Charles A. Ponzi created what gambling scheme, in 1920, that is illegal today?

8. "Davy Crockett" (on "Disneyworld")
9. Flagpole sitting
10. Women propose marriage to men

Football Bowl Games (Answers)

1. Dallas, Texas
2. Montgomery, Alabama
3. Orlando, Florida
4. Memphis, Tennessee
5. El Paso, Texas
6. Sacramento, California
7. Miami, Florida
8. Honolulu, Hawaii
9. New Orleans, Louisiana
10. Pasadena, California

Gambling (Answers)

1. 7
2. 18 coins
3. 1 through 36 + 0 and 00
4. Win, place, and show
5. 80
6. 24 (The center is free.)
7. 2, 3, or 12
8. Nevada and New Jersey
9. $2.00
10. Pyramids

11. By what more popular name is Las Vegas odds-maker Dimitrios Synodinos known?
12. What actor once won the collie dog, Lassie, in a poker game from its owner Rudd Weatherswax?
13. Who was the New York gambler blamed for rigging the 1919 World Series?
14. What TV series featured a man who ran an off-shore gambling casino onboard ship?
15. What other type of animals are bet on at raceways besides the horse?
16. What is the lowest combination that makes a payoff on a slot machine?
17. What is another name for 21?
18. What type of gambling was the subject of the 1973 Paul Newman-Robert Redford movie *The Sting?*
19. What gambling object was invented about 1244 B.C.?
20. What form of gambling is conducted in some states in the country, while it is still illegal in others?

Games

1. William and Isaac Fields invented what popular game in 1892, which has been used by people interested in the occult ever since?
2. When Alfred Mosher Butts created this board game in 1932 he originally called it Lexico. What is it called today?
3. There are exactly 43,252,003,274,489,856,000 positions that this game can be twisted into. Name it.
4. What is the most valuable property in the game of Monopoly, and what is the rent charged with a hotel on it?
5. What are the two most valuable letters in the game of Scrabble, each being worth 10 points?
6. Who is the only actual person whose portrait appears on the money in the board game of *Life?*
7. English mapmaker John Spilsbury invented what puzzle in 1760?
8. What popular board game swept the Christmas market of 1983?
9. Name the six chess pieces?
10. Arthur Wynne is credited with creating what game on December 21, 1913, that made its debut in the New York *World?*

11. Jimmy the Greek
12. John Wayne
13. Arnold Rothstein
14. "Mr. Lucky"
15. Greyhound dogs
16. One cherry (gives out 2 or 3 coins)
17. Blackjack
18. Horseracing
19. Dice
20. Lotteries

Games (Answers)

1. Ouija
2. Scrabble
3. Rubik's Cube
4. Boardwalk—$2,000
5. *Q* and *Z*
6. Art Linkletter
7. Jigsaw puzzle
8. *Trivial Pursuit*
9. Pawn, knight, bishop, castle (rook), queen, and king
10. Crossword puzzle

Heisman Trophy Winners

1. Who is the only Heisman Trophy Winner to play major league baseball?
2. Who was the first winner in 1935 of the Heisman Trophy?
3. The Heisman Trophy has been won the most by players from what college?
4. What Heisman Trophy winners went on to play football for the United States Football League?
5. Who is the only player to have won the Heisman Trophy twice?
6. What organization presents the annual Heisman Trophy?
7. Who was the first Heisman Trophy winner for West Point Military Academy in 1945?
8. The next year, another West Pointer won the trophy. Name him.
9. Rick Nelson's one-time father-in-law won the trophy in 1940. Name him.
10. Which actor won the Heisman Trophy for Southern California in 1968?

Horse Racing

1. Clyde Van Dusen won the Kentucky Derby in 1929. What was the name of the horse's trainer?
2. In her 22 races, Native Dancer only lost once. Who is the only horse to have beat her (in the 1953 running of the Kentucky Derby)?
3. What famous racehorse in the grandfather of Sea Biscuit?
4. In 1978 what horse became the only one to finish in the runner-up position in all three Triple Crown races? Who finished first?
5. What jockey was nicknamed Banana Nose?
6. Name the annual steeplechase held at Aintree, England, since 1839? The track comprises 30 jumps over a 4-mile, 856-yard course.
7. Don Meade rode the winning horse in the 1933 Kentucky Derby. Strangely, this became the only race that the horse would ever win. Name him.
8. On Whirlaway, in 1941, and on Citation, in 1948, who became the only jockey to win the Triple Crown twice?

Heisman Trophy Winners (Answers)

1. Vic Janowicz (He played for the Pittsburgh Pirates.)
2. Jay Berwanger
3. Notre Dame
4. Herschell Walker, Mike Rozier, & Steve Young
5. Archie Griffin (1974 and 1975)
6. Downtown Athletic Club in New York City
7. Doc Blanchard
8. Glenn Davis
9. Tom Harmon
10. O. J. Simpson

Horse Racing (Answers)

1. Clyde Van Dusen
2. Dark Star
3. Man of War
4. Alydar, Affirmed
5. Eddie Arcaro
6. Grand National
7. Broker's Tip
8. Eddie Arcaro

9.   Azra was the winner of the 18th Kentucky Derby, run in 1892.
     After the place and show horses came in, how many other horses
     were left?
10. When he crossed the finish line first on Middleground in 1950, at
     the age of 16 years and 10 months, who became the youngest
     jockey to win the Kentucky Derby?

Mascots

1.   El Cid was the name of what college's mascot goat?
2.   Benzoo is the Bengal tiger mascot of what professional football
     team?
3.   Until his death in 1976, at age 20, what was the name of the
     mascot mule of the Oakland A's baseball team?
4.   Chesty Pagett is the bulldog mascot of what organization?
5.   Nathaniel Ulysses Turtle is the 9,954-year-old (as of 1984)
     mascot of what society?
6.   Handsome Dan is the mascot of what college football team?
7.   Mach I was the first mascot falcon of what school in 1955?
8.   What cute little bear was the mascot for the 1980 Russia Olympics?
9.   What was the mascot of the 1984 summer Olympics?
10. What animal is the mascot of the U.S. Army Academy at West
     Point?

Olympics

1.   In the 1980 Winter Olympics he won five Gold Medals, while
     setting five Olympic and one world record. Name him.
2.   Prior to playing Tarzan in two films, what future pro football
     player won the decathlon in the 1936 Olympics?
3.   Name the Ethiopian runner who is the only person to have won
     the Olympic marathon twice (1960 and 1964), which he ran
     barefoot the first time.
4.   The 1981 movie *Chariots of Fire* recounted the story of this
     British runner who won the 100-meter race in the 1924 Olympic
     Games. Name him.
5.   When the Olympics were revived in Greece in 1896, what coun-
     try won the first medal?

9.   None (Only three horses ran.)
10.   Bill Boland

Mascots (Answers)

1.   Annapolis's Naval Academy
2.   Cincinnati Bengals
3.   Charlie O
4.   U.S. Marine Corps
5.   Turtle Organization
6.   Yale
7.   U.S. Air Force Academy
8.   Misha
9.   Sam the Eagle
10.   Mule

Olympics (Answers)

1.   Eric Heiden
2.   Glenn Morris
3.   Abebe Bikila
4.   Harold Abrahams
5.   United States—James Connolly

6. Who is the only American athlete to have won a Gold Medal in both the Summer and the Winter Olympics? (He was a light heavyweight boxer in 1920 and a bobsledder in 1932.)

7. Who is the only person to have won the Olympic decathlon twice?

8. What Olympic Gold Medal-winner is the father of an Academy Award-winning actress?

9. What two black athletes gave the black power salute during the playing of "The Star-Spangled Banner" during the medal presentation at the Olympics in Mexico City in 1968?

10. Who was the only person to compete in the 1976 Olympics in Montreal in the equestrian riding event who was not given a sex test?

11. The brother of what member of Baseball's Hall of Fame finished several places behind Jesse Owens in the 200-meter race at the 1936 Olympics in Berlin?

12. What two Olympic decathlon champions have appeared on the front of Wheaties breakfast cereal boxes?

13. In what year were the first Olympic Games held in Greece?

14. What 1976 Olympic gymnast was the inspiration for Barry DeVorzon's hit song "Nadia's Theme"?

15. Who received a Bronze Medal for skiing in the 1924 Olympics 50 years after the event, when an error in scoring was finally discovered?

16. Who were the four members of the 1960 American Olympic basketball team who went on to become NBA Rookies of the Year?

17. Actor Rex Harrison's son, Noel Harrison, was a participant in both the 1952 and the 1956 Olympics. What was his sport?

18. What figure-skater-turned-actress finished first in the women's figure skating at both the 1932 and 1936 Winter Olympics?

19. Who won the Gold Medal for heavyweight boxing for the 1972 Munich, 1976 Montreal, and 1980 Moscow Olympics?

20. Who won the Gold Medal for the discus throw in 1956, 1960, 1964, and 1968 and is the only athlete to have won the same Olympic track and field event four times in a row?

6. Eddie Eagan
7. Bob Mathias
8. John B. Kelly (Grace Kelly)
9. Tommie Smith and John Carlo
10. Princess Anne
11. Mick Robinson—the brother of Jackie Robinson
12. Bob Mathis and Bruce Jenner
13. 776 B.C.
14. Nadia Comaneci
15. Anders Haugen
16. Oscar Robertson, Jerry Lucas, Walt Bellamy, and Terry Dischinger
17. Skiing
18. Sonja Henie
19. Teofilo Stevenson (Cuba)
20. Al Oeter

Parades

1. What is the first country to march in the Olympic parade at the opening-day ceremonies?
2. What is the last country to march in the Olympic parade at the opening-day ceremonies?
3. What is the only country that does not dip its flag during the Olympic parade?
4. Which city boasts the largest Thanksgiving Day Parade, which has been held there annually since 1926?
5. What state song is played when the horses are paraded before the running of the Preakness in May of each year?
6. When this parade was telecast on January 1, 1954, it became the first coast-to-coast color show ever telecast. Name it.
7. What popular parade takes place on a Tuesday each year?
8. In a circus parade, what is the last object in the parade?
9. What parade takes place in New York City in March of every year?
10. What musician received the largest ticker-tape parade in the history of New York City, on May 20, 1958?

Players on a Team

Give the minimum number of players on the following teams:
1. Major league baseball (be careful!)
2. U.S. professional football team
3. Basketball team
4. Field hockey team
5. Roller derby team
6. Water polo team
7. Hurling team
8. Cricket
9. Soccer
10. Canadian football team

Parades (Answers)

1. Greece
2. Host country
3. The United States
4. New York City
5. "Maryland, My Maryland"
6. Tournament of Roses Parade
7. New Orleans Mardi Gras Parade
8. Calliope
9. St. Patrick's Day Parade
10. Van Cliburn

Players on a Team (Answers)

1. National League = 9, American League = 10 (designated hitter)
2. 11
3. 5
4. 11
5. 5
6. 4
7. 15
8. 11
9. 11
10. 12

Previous Team Names

1. What football team was previously known as the Frankford Yellow Jackets?
2. What football team was known as the Portsmouth Spartans?
3. By what name were the Houston Astros known between 1962 and 1964?
4. What baseball team was once known as the Bridegrooms, in 1890?
5. What football team began as the Decatur Staleys?
6. After the original Baltimore Orioles moved to New York, they went through several name changes. What is the ball club's name today?
7. Both of Los Angeles's pro football teams maintained the second part of their team names when they moved there from previous cities. Name them both.
8. The Dallas Texans, of the AFL, changed both their name and home when they moved. What was their new name?
9. The Philadelphia Phillies' owner changed his team's name in 1944 to what? (However, it never caught on.)
10. What major league baseball team has previously been known by such names as the Beaneaters, the Doves, and the Pilgrims?

Sports

1. What is the name of the fourth wood in a golf club set?
2. Name the three races in horse racing's Triple Crown.
3. In archery, how many arrows are used in a York round?
4. How high is a badminton net?
5. What color uniform does the home team wear in basketball?
6. What is listed as the most popular participant sport in the United States?
7. Name the area immediately behind the pins in bowling?
8. How many riders are on a field in a polo tournament?
9. What is the difference between rowing and sculling?
10. Name the three types of skiis?
11. What would you be playing if you practiced the American twist service or a reverse twist?

Previous Team Names (Answers)

1. Philadelphia Eagles
2. The Detroit Lions
3. Colt 45's
4. Brooklyn Dodgers (L.A. Dodgers)
5. Chicago Bears
6. New York Yankees
7. Cleveland Rams and Oakland Raiders
8. Kansas City Chiefs
9. Blue Jays
10. Boston Braves

Sports (Answers)

1. Cleek
2. Kentucky Derby, Preakness, and Belmont Stakes
3. 144 (or a dozen dozen)
4. Five feet at the center
5. White or a light color
6. Fishing
7. The pit
8. Eight—four to a team
9. Rowing uses both hands on one oar, whereas sculling uses an oar in each hand
10. Downhill, cross country, and jumping
11. Tennis

12. What sport is played on a surface divided into defending zones, neutral zones and attacking zones?

13. What is the oldest organized sport in America?

14. What is the national sport of China?

15. What three sporting events are won by moving backwards?

16. In baseball, what are the six ways a batter can get on base without getting a hit?

17. What major league baseball player once played basketball for the Harlem Globetrotters?

18. What British game was part of the Olympic Summer Games for just one Olympiad—1900 in Paris?

19. Who was the first American to capture the world chess title?

20. Who served from 1920 until his death in 1944 as the first commissioner of baseball?

Sports Announcers

1. What TV sports announcer had to apologize on national television because a week previously he referred to Richard M. Nixon as "Tricky Dick"?

2. *Like It Is* is the 1974 title of one of this sportcasters books. Name this lawyer turned sports announcer.

3. On August 5, 1921, Harold Arlin became the first person to announce a baseball game over the radio, doing the play-by-play for a contest in which the Pirates beat the Phillies 8 to 5. Over what radio station was the game broadcast?

4. When Mickey Thompson hit his 1951 pennant-winning home run what announcer screamed, "The Giants have won the pennant, the Giants have won the pennant, the Giants have won the pennant, the Giants have won the pennant!"?

5. What expression did Yankee announcer Phil Rizzuto exclaim when Bucky Dent hit his game-winning home run to beat the Red Sox in the 1978 divisional play-off?

6. What major league sports announcer described a home run by stating, "It's going, going, gone!"

7. Who became the first female major league baseball play-by-play announcer when she was signed by the Chicago White Sox on January 4, 1977?

8. In 1921, from the Polo Grounds, who was the announcer for the first broadcast of a World Series game?

12. Ice hockey
13. Lacrosse, which was played by Iroquois Indians and adopted by early French settlers
14. Ping-Pong (table tennis)
15. Tug of war, backstroke (in swimming), and sculling
16. Error, base on balls, catcher drops a third strike, hit by pitch, fielder's choice, or interference by catcher
17. Bob Gibson
18. Cricket
19. Bobby Fisher
20. Kenesaw Mountain Landis

Sports Announcers (Answers)

1. "Dandy" Don Meredith
2. Howard Cosell
3. Pittsburgh's KDKA
4. Russ Hodges
5. "Holy cow! Holy Cow! Holy Cow!"
6. Mel Allen
7. Mary Shane
8. Grantland Rice

9. What sports announcer can be heard announcing a Yankee game on Meat Loaf's 1978 hit single "Paradise by the Dashboard Light"?
10. What player and manager of the Cleveland Indians later became a sportscaster for the team?

Sports Equipment

1. In 1929, Clint Benedict of the Montreal Maroons became the first hockey player to wear what?
2. What was the name of the business that provided the first uniforms used by the Green Bay Packers football team?
3. Charles C. Write wore what piece of equipment for the first time in 1875?
4. What major league baseball player, at one time, warmed up with a sledgehammer in the on-deck circle?
5. What are the colors for the helmets of both the Annapolis and West Point football uniforms?
6. In 1969, what did New York Yankee catcher Elston Howard introduce to the on-deck circle?
7. What team introduced the use of batting helmets in 1941?
8. Skeet shooters should be grateful to George Ligowski for inventing what in September 1880?
9. In baseball, what is an Iron Mike?
10. What is the highest number shown on a dart board?

Sports Firsts

1. Who became the first Australian aborigine to play professional tennis on the pro tour?
2. Who became the first player selected in an AFL college draft in 1959?
3. Who was baseball's first free agent?
4. On November 30, 1963, Army quarterback Rollie Stichweh made television history during a game. How?
5. On April 6, 1973, New York Yankee Ron Blomberg became the very first player to do what?
6. In 1855, Charles Blondin became the first person to cross what body of water on a tightrope?

9. Phil Rizzuto
10. Lou Boudreau

Sports Equipment (Answers)

1. He became the first goalie to wear a face mask.
2. Acme Packing Company
3. A baseball glove
4. Willie Stargell
5. Gold
6. Doughnut weights
7. Brooklyn Dodgers
8. Clay pigeon
9. An automatic pitching machine
10. 20

Sports Firsts (Answers)

1. Evonne Goolagong
2. Don Meredith
3. Andy Messersmith
4. He was the first athlete to be featured on an instant replay.
5. He became the first designated hitter after the rule was put into effect.
6. Niagara Falls

7. Who was the first pitcher to hit a home run in a World Series game?
8. In 1936, what became the first racetrack to use a photo finish?
9. In a game on September 5, 1906, what first in football did St. Louis University's Brandbury Robinson introduce in a game against Waukeska, Wisconsin?
10. In 1951, what catcher became the first major league player to wear glasses while he played baseball?

Sports Nicknames

Identify the following players, teams, or arenas:
1. Golden Jet—hockey
2. The Black Babe Ruth—baseball
3. Black Pearl—soccer
4. Hitless Wonders—baseball
5. Little Miss Poker Face—tennis
6. Three-Fingered—baseball
7. The Flying Fin—track and field
8. The Big Train—baseball
9. The Cinderella Man—boxing
10. Night Train—football
11. Golden Bear—golf
12. The Bronx Bull—boxing
13. Mr. Inside and Mr. Outside—football
14. The Brat—tennis
15. The House that Ruth Built—baseball
16. Louisville Lip—boxing
17. Broadway Joe—football
18. Mustache Gang—baseball
19. What three opponents did Muhammad Ali nickname the Rabbit, the Bear, and the Turtle?
20. Dr. J—basketball

Sports Quotes

1. Whom was heavyweight champion Joe Louis speaking about when he stated, on June 18, 1941, "He can run, but he can't hide"?

7. Jim Bagby of the Cleveland Indians
8. Hialeah
9. The first forward pass
10. Clint Courtney

Sports Nicknames (Answers)

1. Bobby Hull
2. Josh Gibson
3. Péle
4. 1906 Chicago White Sox
5. Tennis champion Helen Wills Moody
6. Mordecai Brown
7. Paavo Nurmi
8. Walter Johnson
9. James J. Braddock
10. Dick Lane
11. Jack Nicklaus
12. Jake LaMotta
13. Felix "Doc" Blanchard and Glenn Davis
14. John McEnroe
15. Yankee Stadium
16. Muhammad Ali
17. Joe Namath
18. Oakland A's
19. Floyd Patterson, Sonny Liston, and Joe Frazier
20. Julius Irving

Sports Quotes (Answers)

1. Billy Conn

2. When explaining how to get hits, what major league player exclaimed, "Keep your eye clear, and hit 'em where they ain't, that's all!"?

3. Who is credited with the line "When the going gets tough, the tough get going"?

4. Who made the following boast: "Float like a butterfly—sting like a bee"?

5. Whose philosophy consists of advice such as "Never look back because someone may be gaining on you"?

6. The man that said, "Say it ain't so Joe," was talking about whom?

7. George Leigh-Mallory's answer was "Because it is there." What was the question?

8. Finish this famous line: "Sometime when the boys are up against it and the pressure's really on Notre Dame, tell them to _____"?

9. Who made the witty remarks "I want to thank everybody who made this necessary" and "You can't think and hit at the same time"?

10. On the evening of September 23, 1926, when Louella Parsons asked Jack Dempsey the question "But how did it happen?" the defeated Dempsey gave what classic reply?

Sports Terms

1. What is one stroke above par in golf called?

2. What is one stroke under par in golf called?

3. What is two strokes under par in golf called?

4. What was the point after touchdown called in the defunct World Football League? (It had to be scored by a run or a pass.)

5. What name is given when a hockey player scores three or more goals in one game?

6. What object is hit in the game of badminton?

7. What are the three weapons used in fencing?

8. What sport was originally known as sphairistike?

9. What is it called in football when a member of the offensive team is tackled behind his own goal line, resulting in 2 points for the defensive team?

10. What term is used for a score of zero in the game of tennis?

2. Wee Willie Keeler
3. Knute Rockne
4. Muhammad Ali
5. Satchel Paige
6. Shoeless Joe Jackson
7. Why he and his partner wanted to climb Mt. Everest
8. "Win one for the Gipper" (said by George Gipp to Knute Rockne)
9. Yogi Berra
10. "I guess I forgot to duck"

Sports Terms (Answers)

1. Bogey
2. Birdie
3. Eagle
4. Action point
5. Hat trick
6. Shuttlecock
7. Foil, épée, and saber
8. Tennis
9. A safety
10. Love

Sports Times

1. In a rodeo what is the minimum time that a bareback rider on a saddle horse must stay on his animal to qualify?
2. How many minutes does a 15-round boxing match take, counting the time between rounds?
3. What two boxers were involved in the boxing match of September 22, 1927, called "The Long Count" because the referee took so long to begin his count on one of the fighters?
4. How many seconds does an offensive team, in basketball, have to bring the ball across the division line?
5. Without overtime how long does a football game take to play?
6. What is the duration of a professional basketball game?
7. What is the count made by the referee in wrestling to determine a fall?
8. How many time-outs is a team allowed in the game of basketball?
9. What is the time duration of a half in professional soccer?
10. When Roger Bannister became the first person to run a sub-4-minute mile on May 6, 1954, what was his exact time?

Sportswriters

1. What sportswriter won an Academy Award for his 1942 one-reel short subject titled *Amphibious Fighters?*
2. Sportswriter Arthur Robinson coined what term to describe the top of the line-up of the 1927 New York Yankees?
3. In 1933, *Chicago Tribune* sportswriter Arch Ward originated the idea for what annual game?
4. What sportswriter wrote a syndicated column titled "On the Line"?
5. What sports columnist was born in Green Bay, Wisconsin, in 1905, and wrote for such papers as the *New York Herald-Tribune* and *The New York Times?* (He has also authored a number of sports books.)
6. Name the sportswriter who became known as the professional amateur because he tried his hand playing many pro sports?

Sports Times (Answers)

1. 8 seconds
2. 59 minutes—45 minutes of boxing plus 14 minutes between rounds
3. Jack Dempsey and Gene Tunney
4. 10 seconds
5. 60 minutes (although it may take 3 hours to play the 1 hour)
6. 48 minutes
7. 3 count
8. 5
9. 45 minutes
10. 3:59.4

Sportswriters (Answers)

1. Grantland Rice
2. Murderer's Row
3. All-Star baseball game
4. Bob Considine
5. Red Smith
6. George Plimpton

7. What sportswriter and sportscaster appeared as himself in such films as *The Pride of the Yankees* (1942) and *Spirit of West Point* (1947)?

8. What New York City sportswriter was once a frontier lawman?

9. On July 1, 1892, George Bechel became the first sportswriter to be slugged by a major league baseball player. What Chicago Cubs outfielder hit him?

10. Who was the sportswriter for the *New York Daily News* who wrote such novels as *The Snow Goose* and *The Poseidon Adventure?*

Swimmers

1. What Australian swimmer, crippled in her youth, was portrayed by Esther Williams in the 1952 movie *Million-Dollar Mermaid?*

2. In 1926, who became the first woman to swim the English Channel?

3. In 1950 and in 1951, Florence Chadwick became the first woman to accomplish what feat?

4. What U.S. swimmer won seven Gold Medals in the 1972 Summer Olympics after previously winning two in the 1968 Summer Olympics?

5. What Hawaiian swimmer won the 100-mile freestyle in the 1912 and 1920 Olympics?

6. What two Olympic Gold Medal winners for swimming went on to play Tarzan in films?

7. Where is the Swimming Hall of Fame?

8. What swimming stroke did Australian Dick Cauill help to create?

9. When the Swimming Hall of Fame was opened in 1965, who was the first member elected?

10. How long is a regulation Olympic-sized pool?

Teams

1. What is the name of the U.S. Navy's flight demonstration team based at Pensacola, Florida?

2. What were the two college teams that competed in the very first episode of G. E. College Bowl telecast on January 4, 1959?

7. Bill Stern
8. Bat Masterson
9. Jimmy Ryan
10. Paul Gallico

Swimmers (Answers)

1. Annette Kellerman
2. Gertrude Ederle
3. She became the first woman to swim the English Channel in both directions (France to England in 1950 and England to France in 1951).
4. Mark Spitz
5. Duke Kahanamoku
6. Johnny Weissmuller and Buster Crabbe
7. Fort Lauderdale, Florida
8. The crawl
9. Johnny Weismuller
10. 50 meters long

Teams (Answers)

1. Blue Angels
2. Northwestern (winner) and Brown

3. What is the name of the precision parachute team of the United States Army?

4. The New York Knickerbockers was organized in 1845 and was the first professional team in what sport?

5. The book *The Boys of Summer* is about what professional baseball team?

6. What country flies a 9-plane aerobatic team called the Snowbirds?

7. What is the last name of the popular black brothers Fayard and Howard, dancing team of the 1950s?

8. The Derrick Dolls are the cheerleaders for what football team?

9. What team featured the defensive backs called the Fearsome Foursome—Merlin Olsen, Lamar Lundy, Deacon Jones, and Roosevelt Grier?

10. What is the only U.S. college to have lost its entire 11-man football team during World War II?

Tennis

1. What Australian-born tennis player won the Grand Slam of tennis twice (1962 and 1969)?

2. Who took part in the tennis match called the Battle of the Sexes, held at the Houston Astrodome on September 20, 1973?

3. What gifts did the opponents in question 2 give each other?

4. Until 1927, what four countries competed for the Davis Cup?

5. Who introduced the catch line "Tennis anyone?" which originated in the 1923 Broadway comedy play *Meet the Wife?*

6. What is the women's equivalent of the Davis Cup?

7. What three opens constitute the Grand Slam of Tennis?

8. Who, in 1951, became the only mens doubles team ever to win the Grand Slam of Tennis?

9. Who was the first woman to win the Grand Slam, in 1953?

10. Who, in 1938, was the first player to win the Grand Slam of Tennis?

3. Golden Knights
4. Baseball
5. The Brooklyn Dodgers
6. Canada
7. Nicholas Brothers
8. Houston Oilers
9. Los Angeles Rams
10. Montana State

Tennis (Answers)

1. Rod Laver
2. Billie Jean King and Bobby Riggs
3. King gave Riggs a piglet; Riggs gave King an inflatible "Sugar Daddy"
4. Australia, Britain, New Zealand, and the United States
5. Humphrey Bogart
6. Federation Cup
7. United States, British, French, and Australian
8. Frank Sedgeman and Ken McGregor
9. Maureen Connolly
10. Don Budge

Track and Field

1. Who broke the four-minute mile on May 6, 1954, at Oxford, England?
2. In what West Virginia city can the National Track and Field Hall of Fame be found?
3. What track and field athlete has won more Olympic medals than anyone, with nine gold and three silver (he won five of the Gold Medals in 1924)?
4. Wearing number 261, Katharine Switzer was the first woman to run in what marathon in 1967?
5. What child polio victim became the first woman to win three gold medals in the Olympics for track in 1960?
6. What Polish Olympic Gold Medal track star, who became the first female to run 100 yards in less than 11 seconds, was discovered to have been a man after he died?
7. What is the maximum official weight of a shot put?
8. Yale University track man Charles Sherrill introduced what first in track on May 12, 1888?
9. Who won four Gold Medals and set three Olympic records at the 1936 Summer Olympics in Berlin?
10. Who set an Olympic long jump record in 1968 when he jumped 29 feet 2½ inches, beating the previously held record by 21¾ inches?

Video Games

1. What is the first breakfast cereal to be named for a video game?
2. What is the second breakfast cereal to be named for a video game?
3. What was the first game manufactured by Atari, which appeared in December 1975?
4. What is the name of the man who attempts to rescue the blond girl in the game Donky Kong?
5. What game was a spin-off of Pac Man?
6. What are the annual awards called for the year's best electronic game (video or computer)?

Track and Field (Answers)

1. Roger Bannister
2. Charleston
3. Paavo Nurmi
4. Boston Marathon
5. Wilma Rudolph
6. Stella Walsh
7. 16 pounds
8. The crouching start
9. Jesse Owens
10. Bob Beamon

Video Games (Answers)

1. Pac Man
2. Donkey Kong
3. Pong
4. Mario
5. Ms. Pac Man
6. Arkies

7. Pac Man inspired a 1981 hit song by Buckner and Garcia. Name it.

8. Name the tasteless video game introduced in 1982 in which General Custer rapes an Indian maiden.

9. What 1982 Walt Disney movie with hundreds of special effects was about a video game?

10. What was the first video game to be based on a cartoon character who originated in the 1930s?

Wrestlers

1. This professional wrestler weighed over 600 pounds and dressed like a farmer. He can be seen in the 1962 movie *Requiem for a Heavyweight*. Name him.

2. What is the professional name of Peter Falk's two female wrestlers in the 1981 movie *All the Marbles?*

3. What 6-feet 5¾-inch heavyweight boxing champion turned to wrestling after he lost the title in 1934?

4. In an exhibition bout on April 5, 1982, what comedian did 234-pound pro-wrestler Jerry Lawler hospitalize when he slammed his head into the mat?

5. What popular wrestler of the 1950s wore gold bobby pins in his hair?

6. What popular wrestler of the 1950s was nicknamed "The Strangler"?

7. Whom did Japanese wrestler Antonio Inok "fight" to a draw in Tokyo on June 26, 1976, after 15 rounds?

8. In what Oklahoma City is the National Wrestling Hall of Fame located?

9. Name the Harvard student who won the U.S. national title in wrestling, rowed in the British Henley Regatta, and came in third in the Inveray Pro Am Golf Tournament, despite the fact that he is blind?

10. What 6-feet 8-inches tall, 325-pound professional wrestler played the role of Thunderlips in the 1982 movie *Rocky III?*

7. "Pac Man Fever"
8. Custer's Revenge
9. *Tron*
10. Popeye

Wrestlers (Answers)

1. Haystack Calhoun
2. California Dolls
3. Primo Carnera
4. Andy Kaufman
5. Gorgeous George
6. Ed Lewis
7. Muhammad Ali
8. Stillwater
9. Tom Sullivan
10. Hulk Hogan

Yachts

1. On July 13, 1949, movie producer David O. Selznick married a
   young actress on the 30-ton yacht *Manona*. Who was the starlet
   he wed?
2. What is the name of the British royal family's yacht?
3. In July 1893, who underwent a secret operation for the removal of
   a growth in his mouth onboard the yacht *Oneida?* The account of
   the operation wasn't revealed publicly until 1917.
4. What was the name of Ernest Hemingway's 40-foot vessel,
   which he named after a character in his novel *For Whom the Bell
   Tolls?*
5. What was the name of the Presidential yacht that Elvis Presley
   bought in 1964?
6. Although he owned several, what was the name of actor Humphrey Bogart's favorite yacht?
7. Actor Sterling Hayden wrote a novel about his yacht, which also
   furnished the book's title. Name the yacht.
8. What Hollywood producer and director called the Father of the
   Western mysteriously died on William Randolph Hearst's yacht
   Oneida?
9. Name either one of actor Errol Flynn's yachts.
10. What Hollywood actor owned the yacht *Carrie B?*

Yachts (Answers)

1. Jennifer Jones
2. *Britannia*
3. President Grover Cleveland
4. *Pilar*
5. *Potomac*
6. *Santana*
7. *Wanderer*
8. Thomas H. Ince
9. *Sirocco* or *Zacca*
10. Spencer Tracy

People

Artists

1. He illustrated many books on birds, such as *The Birds of America*. A society for the preservation of wildlife was named in his honor. Who was he?
2. This artist designed the color schemes on each of Brandiff Airlines' aircraft. Each plane had a different design. Who is he?
3. Painter Anna Mary Robertson titled her 1952 autobiography *My Life's History*. By what more popular name is she known?
4. What world-famous artist founded the Cubist movement?
5. When W. Somerset Maugham authored his 1919 novel *The Moon and Sixpence*, about what French artist was he writing?
6. What is the first name of the crippled French artist who painted scenes of Parisian life from his favorite hangout, the Moulin Rouge nightclub?
7. What U.S. painter (1836–1910) created some beautiful scenes of the New England life of sailors and fishermen?
8. What American painter became popular for his pop art portraits of such subjects as Campbell Soup cans and Marilyn Monroe?
9. *At the Piano* and *The Little Girl in White* are two paintings by what artist?
10. Who is the Spanish artist whose surrealistic paintings feature such items as melted clock faces?

Assassins

1. On May 13, 1981, what world-famous figure did Mehmet Ali Agca attempt to assassinate?
2. What is the name of the son of late Soviet premier Leonid Brezhnev, who in 1983 allegedly shot and wounded Brezhnev's successor, Yuri V. Andropov?

Artists (Answers)

1. John Audubon
2. Alexander Calder
3. Grandma Moses
4. Pablo Picasso
5. Paul Gauguin
6. Henri (de Toulouse-Lautrec)
7. Winslow Homer
8. Andy Warhol
9. James Whistler
10. Salvador Dali

Assassins (Answers)

1. Pope John Paul II
2. Yuri Brezhnev

3. What U.S. President did anarchist Leon F. Czolgosz shoot and kill, at the Pan-American Exposition in Buffalo, New York, on September 6, 1901?
4. Who killed Macbeth?
5. The assassination of Archduke Francis Ferdinand of Austria by what assassin began World War I?
6. What poker hand was James Butler "Wild Bill" Hickok holding when Jack McCall shot him in the back, killing him on August 2, 1876?
7. Who was the first man to attempt to assassinate a U.S. President, when on January 30, 1835 both of his guns misfired?
8. What was the name of the man who shot and killed Rev. Martin Luther King in Memphis on April 4, 1969?
9. What is the name of the young man who shot President Ronald Reagan on March 30, 1981?
10. What U.S. President was shot at twice in the same month and in the same state in 1975, by two females? Name the would-be assassins.

Babies

1. What famous first did Elizabeth Jordon Carr experience when she was born on December 28, 1981?
2. In an episode of the 1914 serial *The Perils of Pauline*, a baby was thrown from a train only to be caught by Pearl White. Who played the baby?
3. What was the name of the baby girl of Rhett Butler and his wife Scarlett O'Hara Butler in Margaret Mitchell's *Gone with the Wind?*
4. Brooke Shields and rock musician Dr. John both posed for what commercial product when they were babies?
5. Emilio Marcos Palma, an Argentine baby, in January 1978, became the first baby ever born on what continent?
6. On July 4, 1979, Donald Duck presented Teresa Salcedo with the first birth certificate ever given for being born where?
7. What nickname was given to Marie Perry, daughter of Admiral Robert Perry, when she was born in the Arctic Circle in 1893?
8. Whose grandson played the baby Swee' Pea in the 1980 movie *Popeye?*

3. William McKinley
4. Macduff
5. Gavrilo Princip
6. Aces and eights (2 pair)
7. Richard Lawrence (He tried to assassinate President Andrew Jackson.)
8. James Earl Ray
9. John Hinckley
10. Gerald Ford—Lynette "Squeaky" Fromm (September 5) and Sara Jane Moore (September 22)

Babies (Answers)

1. She became the first test tube baby to be born in the United States.
2. Milton Berle
3. Bonnie Blue Butler (or Eugenia Victoria Butler)
4. Ivory soap
5. Antarctica
6. Disneyland
7. Snow Baby
8. Director Robert Altman's (played by Westey Van Hurt)

9. What is the name of the world's first test tube baby who was delivered by cesarean section on July 26, 1978?

10. What was the name of the 11-week-old baby who appeared in the 1942 British movie *In Which We Serve?*

Brothers

1. He had a brief ring career and took up the name Rahamon Ali when he changed to the Muslim faith. Whose brother is he?

2. Brothers John and William introduced the first flaked breakfast cereal in 1895. What was their last name?

3. One brother co-hosts TV's "Today" show, while the other co-anchors ESPN's "Sports Center." Give their last name?

4. Hank Aaron, Johnny Cash, Dick Smothers, and Waylon Jennings all have brothers with what same first name?

5. Richard Henry Lee and Francis Lightfoot Lee are the only brothers to have signed what document?

6. These brothers not only had their own bands but they also had their own television series. Who were they?

7. Actor Robert Mitchum has a brother who has also appeared in a number of films. Name him.

8. What two brothers hold the major league record for the most home runs hit by brothers?

9. What was the name of Moses' brother who took over leading the Israelis after Moses' death?

10. Whose brother was Charles Thorpe?

11. What are the first names of the two Baer brothers of boxing fame?

12. What are the first names of the two acting Beery brothers?

13. Band leader Glenn Miller had a younger brother who also led an orchestra in the 1940s. Name him.

14. What was the last name of the five brothers who perished on board the U.S. cruiser *Juneau* when it was torpedoed by a Japanese submarine on November 13, 1942?

15. What twin brothers created the *Guinness Book of World Records* in 1956?

16. Who is the actor brother of Tom Conway?

17. Name the only two brothers to have both held boxing crowns. One was welterweight champion in 1927–1929, the other held the middleweight title in 1933.

9.   Louise Joy Brown
10. Juliet Mills

Brothers (Answers)

1.   Muhammad Ali's
2.   Kellogg
3.   Gumbel (Bryant and Greg, respectively)
4.   Tommy
5.   The Declaration of Independence
6.   Dorsey brothers (Tommy and Jimmy)
7.   John Mitchum
8.   Aaron brothers (Hank with 755 and Tommy with 13)
9.   Aaron
10. He was the twin brother of athlete Jim Thorpe. He died in childhood.
11. Buddy and Max
12. Noah and Wallace
13. Herb Miller
14. Sullivan brothers
15. McWhirter brothers (Norris and Ross)
16. George Sanders
17. Joe and Vince Dundee

18. Whose brother, Neil, starred in the 1967 movie *Operation Kid Brother,* (which bombed)?
19. Who were the two 19th-century scientific twin brothers who made explorations in both stratospheric baloons as well as bathyscaphic driving vehicles?
20. The 1980 film *The Long Riders* had an unusual distinction of featuring four sets of actual brothers. Give their last names.

Children

1. What was the name of the first child of English parents to be born in the American colonies (August 18, 1587)?
2. Fourteen-year-old Sara Brown traveled with Richard Nixon, Gerald Ford, and Jimmy Carter to whose funeral in 1981?
3. Shirley Temple's mother always insisted that her actress-daughter had an exact amount of curls set in her hair each day. How many?
4. In November 1983, 4-year-old Kil Woo and 7-year-old Gi Sook traveled in *Air Force One* with President Ronald Reagan and First Lady Nancy Reagan to the United States. What was the reason for the trip?
5. With her leg in a cast, in 1975, 11-year-old Karen Stead became the first girl to win what annual contest?
6. Who was the only child of King Henry VIII and Anne Boleyln?
7. Who was the first successful child actor?
8. What black comedian named his film company Black Rain after his daughter, Rain, who was born in 1969?
9. Singer Sonny and Cher's daughter, for which they named a 1969 movie, was given what unusual name?
10. When their son was born in 1974, what did actor David Carradine and actress Barbara Hershey name him?

Courageous People

1. What is the name of the man who ran across Canada after he had had a leg amputated? (He ran with an artificial leg in order to make money to fight cancer.)

18. Sean Connery's
19. Piccard (Auguste and Jean)
20. The Carradines (David, Keith, and Robert), the Keaches (James and Stacy), The Quaids (Dennis and Randy), and the Guests (Nicholas and Christopher).

Children (Answers)

1. Virginia Dare
2. Egyptian President Anwar Sadat's
3. 56
4. They traveled to the United States to undergo heart surgery.
5. All-American Soap Box Derby in Akron, Ohio
6. Queen Elizabeth I
7. Jackie Coogan
8. Richard Pryor
9. Chastity
10. Free

Courageous People (Answers)

1. Terry Fox

2. Who hid in an Amsterdam house with her family for over two years, beginning in 1942? (She eventually died in a concentration camp.)

3. Isa Yukihiro, paralyzed from the waist down, climbed what 12,388-foot mountain in August of 1978?

4. On December 13, 1982, while out jogging, who freed 67-year-old Jessie Dye from a burning automobile, saving her life, after which he continued jogging?

5. This happy-go-lucky, stand-up comic is a victim of cerebral palsy, but her handicap doesn't get in her way. Who is this comic?

6. On February 2, 1983, U.S. Marine Captain Charles B. Johnson did what that got him front-page coverage in newspapers back home?

7. What handicapped actor's 1949 autobiography *Victory in My Hands* was written after he had lost both hands in a dynamite explosion?

8. On July 7, 1977, 41-year-old Chinese Communist Fan Yuan-Yen defected to Taiwan and was paid $700,000 when he arrived. Why?

9. What person has physically touched President Franklin D. Roosevelt, Mark Twain, Enrico Caruso, and Carl Sandburg (and it wasn't to shake their hands)?

10. What Hollywood actor was one of the most decorated American soldiers during World War II?

Creators

1. Francis Bellamy created what patriotic pledge in 1892 in order to celebrate Columbus Day?

2. Who is the creator (as well at narrator) of the TV series "The Waltons"?

3. Who created the television soap operas "All My Children," "One Life To Live," and "Loving"?

4. Who created the TV series "I Dream of Jeannie"?

5. What writer of fiction created the TV series "Checkmate"?

6. What actor created the short-lived 1975 TV series "We'll Get By"?

7. Who created daylight savings time?

8. For what reason did Sanford Fleming create the time zone in 1879, which was adopted in 1883?

2. Anne Frank
3. Mt. Fuji
4. Heisman Trophy-winner Herschel Walker
5. Jerry Jewell
6. He stood in front of three Israeli tanks, armed with only his pistol, in order to halt their advance.
7. Harold Russell
8. He flew a MIG-19 in his escape.
9. Helen Keller, in order to read their lips
10. Audie Murphy

Creators (Answers)

1. Pledge of Allegiance
2. Earl Hammer, Jr.
3. Agnes Nixon
4. Sidney Sheldon
5. Eric Ambler
6. Alan Alda
7. Benjamin Franklin
8. So that time could be universal for railroad use

9. Charles Bogle was a pseudonym used by whom when he wrote the story for the 1939 movie *You Can't Cheat an Honest Man?*
10. Who created the American dish chicken a la king?

Criminals

1. While doing research on convicted murderer Gary Gilmore, author Norman Mailer befriended this convict, author of the book *In the Belly of the Beast.* Name him.
2. What convicted perjurer authored the 1957 book *In the Court of Public Opinion?*
3. In 1973, convicted murderer Cotton Adamson married what actress while he served his term in prison?
4. What convicted robber, kidnapper, and rapist, known as "The Red Light Bandit," authored a number of books, such as *Cell 2455, Death Row,* in 1954 before he was executed in 1960?
5. Alfred Packer is the only man in the United States to have been convicted of what crime?
6. On June 7, 1939, Eugene Weidmann became the last person in France to be executed by what means?
7. On March 19, 1831, in New York City, Edward Smith became the first man to commit what crime?
8. By what name is confessed killer David Berkowitz better known?
9. What couple went on a murderous Nebraska crime spree in 1958? (The 1973 movie *Badlands* was based on their exploits.)
10. What infamous bank robber was nicknamed "Willie the Actor"?

Daughters

1. On April 13, 1933, President Franklin D. Roosevelt selected Ruth Bryan Owens as the first female foreign minister for the United States. Who was her father?
2. Liz, the daughter of what golf pro, became, in 1983, the first female to caddy in a Master's Tournament?
3. William Bankhead, the Speaker of the House from 1936 to 1940, was the father of what actress?
4. Who is tax expert S. Jay Lasser's actress daughter?
5. Soul singer Carla Thomas is the daughter of what soul-singing father?

9. W. C. Fields
10. Thomas Jefferson

Criminals (Answers)

1. Jack Henry Abbott
2. Alger Hiss
3. Sue Lyon
4. Caryl Chessman
5. Cannibalism
6. Guillotine
7. Bank robbery (he robbed the City Bank of New York)
8. Son of Sam or the 44-Caliber Killer
9. Charles Starkweather and Carol Ann Fugate
10. Willie Sutton

Daughters (Answers)

1. William Jennings Bryan
2. Tom Watson
3. Talullah Bankhead
4. Louise Lasser
5. Rufus Thomas

6. When she defected to the United States in 1967, Svetlana Alliluyeva changed her name to Lana Peters. Who was her father?
7. What actress is the daughter of a well-known ventriloquist?
8. Whose daughter was Linda Morgan, the "Miracle girl" who was lifted from the *Andrea Doria* to the *Stockholm*, when both ships collided on July 26, 1956?
9. Actress Liza Minnelli is the daughter of what actress and what director?
10. Anastasia was believed by some to have been the surviving daughter of what royal couple?

Explorers

1. Jean Baptiste Point Du Sable was nicknamed the father of what city because he built the first trading post on its site, in the 1770s?
2. Although Sir Edmund Hillary and Tenzing Norkay are credited as the first to conquer Mt. Everest, what mountain climber may have reached the summit first (but he and all of his party were killed during either the climb or the descent in 1924)?
3. What three flags did Edmund Hillary and Tenzing Norkay place atop Mt. Everest on May 28, 1953?
4. What famous conquistador accompanied Balboa on his "discovery" of the Pacific Ocean in 1513, and later conquered the Inca Empire in Peru (1531–1535)?
5. What Italian journeyed to China in 1271, where he studied under the Kublai Khan for 16 years?
6. What Norwegian explorer was the first person to reach the North Pole in 1911?
7. What Portugese explorer discovered the Cape of Good Hope?
8. Which explorer discovered Florida while searching for the elusive Fountain of Youth?
9. America was named for what Italian navigator and explorer?
10. Who explored and conquered Mexico and Cuba for Spain between 1511 and 1521?

6.   Joseph Stalin
7.   Candice Bergen (daughter of Edgar Bergen)
8.   News commentator Edward P. Morgan
9.   Judy Garland and Vincent Minnelli
10. Russian Czar Nicholas II and his wife Alexandra

Explorers (Answers)

1.   Chicago
2.   George Leigh Mallory
3.   Great Britain, India, and Nepal
4.   Francisco Pizarro
5.   Marco Polo
6.   Ronald Amundsen
7.   Bartholomew Dias
8.   Juan Ponce De León
9.   Amerigo Vespucci
10. Hernando Cortez

Fathers

1. Milton Ager who wrote the music to the classic song "Ain't She Sweet" is the father of what journalist?
2. Actor Keenan Wynn's 1960's autobiography featured his famous father's name in the title. Give the title.
3. On November 25, 1983, heavyweight champion Larry Holmes defeated a young fighter named Marvis in only 2 minutes and 57 seconds of the first round. Who is Marvis's father?
4. In 1983, the autobiography *Going My Own Way* was published. Name both the author and his famous father?
5. Academy Award-winning cinematographer Floyd Crosby is the father of what rock singer?
6. Musician Ernest Gold is the father of another rock singer. Name him.
7. What President's father swore him into office at his inauguration?
8. Clarence A. Crane, the father of author Hart Crane, created what candy?
9. General Richard "Light Horse Harry" Lee was the father of what Civil War general?
10. The father of what singer once set a world aviation speed record in a B-58 Hustler bomber?

Fathers-in-law

1. Pat Boone's father-in-law is a member of the Country Music Hall of Fame. Name him.
2. Who was the father-in-law of Jefferson Davis, President of the Confederate States of America?
3. Actor Richard Widmark is the father-in-law of what famous baseball pitcher?
4. Singer Ricky Nelson was the son-in-law of what college football star?
5. Comic Dan Rowen is the father-in-law of what actor?
6. Writer Eugene O'Neill was the father-in-law of what silent-film comic?
7. The son-in-law of what U.S. president is also the grandson of what other U.S. president? (Name all three.)

Fathers (Answers)

1. Shana Alexander
2. *Ed Wynn's Son*
3. Former heavyweight Champion, Joe Frazier
4. Gary Crosby, son of Bing Crosby
5. David Crosby, of Crosby, Stills, and Nash
6. Andrew Gold
7. Calvin Coolidge's
8. Life Savers
9. Robert E. Lee
10. John Denver

Fathers-in-law (Answers)

1. Red Foley
2. Zachary Taylor, future president of the United States
3. Sandy Kofax
4. Tom Harmon
5. Peter Lawford
6. Charles Chaplin
7. David Eisenhower, son-in-law of Richard Nixon, grandson of Dwight Eisenhower

8. Composer Franz Liszt was the father-in-law of what other composer?
9. Western actor Buck Jones was the father-in-law of what Hollywood actor?
10. Producer George Abbott is the son-in-law of what actor?

Founders

1. After her 13-year-old daughter had been killed by a hit-and-run drunk driver, this Sacramento, California, woman founded M.A.D.D. (Mothers Against Drunk Drivers). Who is she?
2. James Macie, an illegitimate English scientist, left his estate to the United States when he died, in order to establish what famous institution?
3. What two actors founded Del Mar Race Track near San Diego, in 1937?
4. A man named Charles founded what jewelry store in Manhattan on September 18, 1837, which today bears his last name?
5. Nicknamed Angel of the Battlefield, what Civil War nurse founded the American Red Cross in 1881?
6. Golf enthusiast Patty Beg founded what association in 1951?
7. William H. Donaldson founded what trade magazine in 1894 that is still being sold weekly today?
8. American Revolutionary War brigadier general Henry Knox established what military school in 1779?
9. What huge firm did Thomas Watson found in 1924?
10. What social reformer founded, with Ellen Gates Starr, Chicago's Hull House?

Gangsters

1. What Chicago crime boss used the pseudonym of Al Brown?
2. He was called the Lord High Executioner of the Mafia until he was shot and killed while sitting in a barber's chair on October 25, 1957?
3. What member of the Mafia testified at a congressional hearing, where he revealed the structure of the Mafia organization?

8. Richard Wagner
9. Noah Beery, Jr.
10. Tom Ewell

Founders (Answers)

1. Candy Lightner
2. The Smithsonian
3. Bing Crosby and Pat O'Brien
4. Tiffany's
5. Clara Barton
6. The Ladies Professional Golf Association
7. *Billboard*
8. West Point
9. I.B.M.
10. Jane Adams

Gangsters (Answers)

1. Alphonse Capone
2. Albert Anastasia
3. Joe Valachi

4. Lester Gillis is the real name of what youthful-looking 5-feet ¾-inch tall robber and killer?

5. Mobster Louis Buchaller, head of the much feared Murder, Inc., was known by what nickname?

6. What gangster taught Charles Manson to play the guitar while they both were in prison (together)?

7. George "Bugs" Moran was almost killed on what day of the year, but was saved when he was five minutes late (although several of his gang were machine gunned to death)?

8. Lloyd, Herman, Fred, and Arthur were the gangster sons of whom?

9. What object did 1930s gangster Jack "Machine Gun" McGurn place in the hands of his victims?

10. Who was the F.B.I.'s first public enemy number one?

Generals

1. What U.S. general was the first American ever to participate in the Olympic Pentathlon in 1912?

2. Who is the only U.S. general to be awarded the Nobel Peace Prize?

3. What U.S. Army general won the 1932 Pulitzer Prize for his book *My Experiences in the World War?*

4. What hero of the War of 1812 was nicknamed "Old Fuss and Feathers"?

5. Nicknamed "Hap," he commanded the U.S. Army Air Corps during World War II. Name him.

6. Who became the first black U.S. Air Force general, in 1954?

7. Name the general who served in both the Union and the Confederate services during the Civil War. (He was also pallbearer for both Robert E. Lee and Ulysses S. Grant.)

8. What American general served as the leader of the Flying Tigers in China during World War II?

9. Who became the first black U.S. Army general in 1940?

10. In 1867, white Union general Oliver Otis _____ founded what Negro college which bears his name?

11. What U.S. Vice-President served as a Confederate general during the Civil War?

12. While pretending to negotiate a surrender, on April 11, 1873, Indian leader Captain Jack shot and killed what U.S. cavalry officer? (The only general killed while fighting Indians.)

4. Baby Face Nelson
5. Lepke
6. Alvin "Creepy" Kapis
7. St. Valentine's Day (February 14, 1929) at the Saint Valentine's Day Massacre
8. Ma Barker
9. A nickel
10. John Dillinger

Generals (Answers)

1. General George S. Patton
2. General George C. Marshall
3. General John Joseph Pershing
4. General Winfield Scott
5. General Henry "Hap" Arnold
6. General Benjamin Oliver Davis, Jr.
7. Simon Bolivar Buckner
8. General Claire Lee Chennault
9. General Benjamin Oliver Davis
10. Howard (University)
11. John C. Breckinridge
12. General Edward Canby

13. What U.S. Army general holds the record of serving 69 years, 8 months in the U.S. military—longer than any other man?

14. What Union Civil War general later authored the classic novel *Ben Hur?*

15. Why was George Custer, who served as a general during the Civil War, only a lieutenant colonel when he was killed at the Little Big Horn?

16. Who was the first U.S. soldier to hold the rank of lieutenant colonel (which was created by Congress in March of 1864)?

17. Name the brigadier general who retired in 1983 at the age of 45, who had won the Heisman Trophy in 1958 when he played for West Point?

18. What U.S. army general was captured by the North Koreans during the Korean War?

19. Who was the last U.S. President to have been an Army general?

20. Who was the first U.S. President to have been an Army general?

Girl Friends

1. Chorus girl Betty Compton was the girl friend of what New York City mayor?

2. Nicknamed "the girl on the red velvet swing," who was the mistress of architect Harry Thaw?

3. Oola is the girl friend of what caveman?

4. Virginia Hill was the girl friend of what gangster?

5. Who was Tarzan's girl friend and eventual wife in novels and motion pictures? First and last names.

6. In his youth, as Superboy, who did high-school student Clark Kent have as his girl friend?

7. Petunia is the girl friend of what cartoon character?

8. What are the names of Archie Andrews's two girl friends?

9. Who was Running Bear's girl friend (they both drowned) in the Johnny Preston 1959 hit song "Running Bear"?

10. Margaret Wade is the "girl friend" of what comic strip/TV character?

13. General Omar N. Bradley—a 5-star general never officially retires
14. Lew Wallace
15. He was given a brevet promotion only for the duration of the war.
16. Ulysses S. Grant
17. Peter Dawkins
18. William Dean
19. Dwight D. Eisenhower
20. George Washington

Girl Friends (Answers)

1. Jimmy Walker
2. Evelyn Nesbit
3. Alley Oop
4. Bugsy Siegel
5. Jane Porter (or Parker)
6. Lana Lang
7. Porky Pig
8. Veronica and Betty
9. Little White Dove
10. Dennis the Menace

Godfathers

1. Who is the godfather of actor Robert Cummings?
2. Liza Minnelli's godfather is one of a pair of songwriting brothers. Who is he?
3. What Pulitzer Prize-winning author is the godfather to Steven Bryant the son of actor Humphrey Bogart and actress Lauren Bacall?
4. What popular British playright is the godfather to actor Raymond Massey's son Daniel, who is also an actor?
5. Who won an Oscar for Best Actor playing Vito Corleone in the 1972 movie *The Godfather?*
6. Who won an Oscar for Best Supporting Actor playing Vito Corleone in the 1974 sequel movie *The Godfather Part II?*
7. Who authored the best-selling novel *The Godfather?*
8. Who is called the Godfather of Soul?
9. Who was comic Joseph Keaton's godfather, who gave him his stage nickname of Buster?
10. Founded in Omaha, Nebraska, what restaurant chain uses the name of Godfather?

Guests

1. Who was the first white performer on the television music show *Soul Train?*
2. What atheist who took her case to the Supreme Court, thus ending school prayer programs in public schools, was the first guest on "Donahue," November 6, 1967?
3. What New York Yankee became the first mystery guest on the TV quiz show "What's My Line"?
4. What baseball great became the first mystery guest to appear twice (1951–1953) on TV's "What's My Line"?
5. Food expert J. E. Rodale had a heart attack and died on June 8, 1971, while a guest on "The Dick Cavett Show" on TV. His last words were "I'm so healthy that I expect to live on and on." What magazine was Rodale the editor of?
6. In 1973 Diana Ross became the first entertainer to be invited to perform by the empress of what Far East country?

Godfathers (Answers)

1. Aviator Orville Wright
2. Ira Gershwin
3. Louis Bromfield
4. Noel Coward
5. Marlon Brando
6. Robert DeNiro
7. Mario Puzo
8. James Brown
9. Magician Harry Houdini
10. Godfather's Pizza

Guests (Answers)

1. Elton John
2. Madelyn Murry O'Hair
3. Phil Rizzuto
4. Leo Durocher
5. *Prevention* magazine
6. Japan

7.   What baseball player was the first guest on Edward R. Murrow's "Person To Person" TV series when it debuted on October 2, 1953?

8.   What guest walked off TV's "Today" show when host Jane Pauley asked her the wrong questions?

9.   What guest on Edward R. Murrow's TV series "Person To Person," in February 1959, appeared in his pajamas?

10. What rock group did Secretary of the Interior James Watt, turn down as the guest performers at the July 4, 1983, concert in Washington, DC? (He later reversed himself after First Lady Nancy Reagan said the group was one of her favorites.)

Husbands

1.   Name actor John Derek's three actress wives, all of whom he photographed for *Playboy* magazine.

2.   Jim Dougherty was the first husband of what Hollywood actress?

3.   Millionaire shoe magnate Harry Karl (Karl Shoes) was once married to Joan Cohn, the widow of Harry Cohn, and to two other actresses, one of them twice. Name both of his actress wives.

4.   What is the name Phyllis Diller calls her husband in her comedy routines?

5.   Mickey Hargitay, Mr. Universe, was once married to what Hollywood actress?

6.   What Hollywood writer has been married to such actresses as Joan Bennett, Hedy Lamarr, and Myrna Loy?

7.   NFL quarterback Terry Bradshaw was once married to what figure-skating star?

8.   In 1943, Cleveland Rams quarterback Bob Waterfield married his childhood sweetheart, who became what actress?

9.   Who was the husband of Xanthippe?

10. Who has been the husband of two of the Gabor sisters?

Judges

1.   What is the name of the female judge who swore in Lyndon Johnson as the new President after the death of John F. Kennedy in Dallas on November 22, 1963?

7. Roy Campanella
8. Margaret Trudeau
9. Cuban leader Fidel Castro
10. The Beach Boys

Husbands (Answers)

1. Ursula Andress, Linda Evans, and Bo Derek
2. Marilyn Monroe
3. Marie McDonald (twice) and Debbie Reynolds
4. Fang
5. Jayne Mansfield
6. Gene Markey
7. Jo Jo Starbuck
8. Jane Russell
9. Socrates
10. Actor George Sanders

Judges (Answers)

1. Sarah Hughes

2. Who, in 1967, became the first black to serve on the Supreme Court?
3. Who, in 1981, became the first woman to serve on the Supreme Court?
4. Who is the only President of the United States to also have served on the Supreme Court?
5. Using the pen name of Robert Traver, what best-selling novel did Michigan Supreme Court Justice John D. Voelker write (which was filmed in 1959)?
6. This frontier judge, who sat in his saloon court in Langtry, Texas, was nicknamed "The Law West of the Pecos"?
7. Who was nicknamed the "Hanging Judge" because in his 21 years on the bench he sentenced 172 men to be hanged, hanging the first six men who faced him?
8. This judge not only sentenced singer Arlo Guthrie to jail for littering, but he later portrayed himself in the 1969 movie *Alice's Restaurant*. Name him.
9. What District of Columbia judge presided over the Watergate scandal trials from 1972 until 1974?
10. On the very last televised episode of Perry Mason, who played the judge?

Kings

1. Who was the first king of Israel?
2. What English king signed the Magna Carta in 1215?
3. Who was the last monarch of France (who was deposed in 1871)?
4. In 1936, what king of England abdicated his throne so that he could marry the American Mrs. Wallis Warfield Simpson?
5. What king of Egypt built Egypt's largest pyramid at Giza?
6. What king led the Knights of the Round Table?
7. Queen Isabella I and what husband king financed Christopher Columbus's first voyage to the New World in 1492?
8. What sport did British monarch King Edward IV outlaw in 1477?
9. King Louis XIV of France had what named after him in the New World?
10. What French king did Joan of Arc help to defeat the British?

2. Thurgood Marshall
3. Sandra Day O'Connor
4. William Howard Taft
5. *Anatomy of a Murder*
6. Judge Roy Bean
7. Isaac Charles Parker
8. Judge James Hannon
9. Judge John J. Sirica
10. Creator Earle Stanley Gardner

Kings (Answers)

1. Saul
2. King John
3. Napoleon III (Louis Napoleon Bonaparte)
4. King Edward VIII
5. King Cheops
6. King Arthur
7. King Ferdinand
8. Cricket
9. The State of Louisiana
10. King Charles VII

Lawyers

1. What criminal lawyer has authored such books as *My Life in Court*, in 1962, and *The Jury Returns*, in 1966?
2. What real-life lawyer of the Army-Joseph McCarthy hearings played Judge Weaver in the 1959 movie *Anatomy of a Murder?*
3. Two of this attorney's books are titled *The Defense Never Rests* (1971) and *For the Defense* (1975). Who is he?
4. This lawyer and politician was one of the prosecuting attorneys at the famous Scopes Monkey Trial of 1925, dying a few days after the trial's end. Name him.
5. This San Francisco-based lawyer had defended such individuals as Martha Mitchell, Lenny Bruce, and Jack Ruby. Who is he?
6. Who defended John Scopes at the Scopes Monkey Trial in Dayton, in 1925?
7. What American lawyer authored the classic adventure autobiography *Two Years Before the Mast*, about his youth?
8. Called the Hollywood lawyer, he defended many of the film industries' most well-known celebrities, such as Errol Flynn (when he was tried for rape)?
9. Hollywood attorney Jerry Giesler was once employed as the office boy for what other prominent lawyer?
10. Name the feminist and lawyer who ran for the President of the United States twice, in 1884 and 1888? (She was the first woman to plead a case before the U.S. Supreme Court.)

Military Commanders

1. What Revolutionary War hero commanded the Green Mountain Boys?
2. Who was the commanding general of the U.S. Army Air Force during World War II?
3. Who commanded the U.S. forces in Vietnam from 1964 until 1968?
4. What American lawyer commanded the Israeli Army in 1947 until he was killed by his own soldiers by mistake?
5. Who was the first U.S. President to hold the title of commander-in-chief?
6. Who was the commander of the Rough Riders in Cuba during the Spanish-American War?

Lawyers (Answers)

1. Louis Nizer
2. Joseph Welch
3. F. Lee Bailey
4. William Jennings Bryan
5. Melvin Belli
6. Clarence Darrow
7. Richard Henry Dana
8. Jerry Giesler
9. Earl Rogers
10. Belva Ann Lockwood

Military Commanders (Answers)

1. Ethan Allen
2. General Henry "Hap" Arnold
3. General William C. Westmoreland
4. David "Mickey" Marcus
5. Franklin D. Roosevelt
6. Col. Leonard Wood (Theodore Roosevelt was *second* in command)

7. Who commanded the United Nations forces during the Korean War (1952–1953)?
8. Who was the Japanese admiral who was the commander-in-chief of the Japanese fleet during World War II?
9. Who was the one-eyed commander of the Israeli Army during its six-day war with Egypt?
10. Who was the supreme commander of the allied forces during World War II?

Military Heroes

1. Rev. Jesse Jackson went to Syria in January 1984 in order to free what American Navy pilot who had been shot down over Syria in December 1983?
2. Who is the only American to have won the four highest U.S. decorations: Congressional Medal of Honor, Distinguished Service Cross, Distinguished Service Medal, and the National Security Medal?
3. What U.S. Army general replied, "Nuts," to the Germans' request that he surrender at Bastogne during the Battle of the Bulge in December 1944?
4. What Pulitzer Prize-winning war correspondent was killed by a Japanese machine gun on the island of Le Shima on April 18, 1945?
5. What is the name of the handicapped British pilot who flew without legs during World War II?
6. Sgt. Anthony Herbert was the most decorated U.S. soldier in what war?
7. Who was the fighter pilot who flew 313 missions in Korea? (This colonel and clergyman previously flew in World War II.)
8. What first did J. T. Callahan achieve on January 23, 1946?
9. What Hollywood actor was a well-decorated soldier during World War II? (He went on several desert raid missions in Africa and became the first actor to be awarded a Silver Star.)
10. Using his Springfield rifle, what future NCO killed 25 and captured 132 Germans at Argonne during World War I?

7. Mark Clark
8. Isoroku Yamamoto
9. Moshe Dayan
10. General Dwight D. Eisenhower

Military Heroes (Answers)

1. Lt. Robert Goodman, Jr.
2. William "Wild Bill" Donovan
3. General Anthony McAuliffe
4. Ernie Pyle
5. Douglas Bader
6. Korean
7. Dean Hess
8. He became the first U.S. Navy chaplain to be awarded the Medal of Honor.
9. Douglas Fairbanks, Jr.
10. Sgt. Alvin York

Mothers

1. Patricia Priest and Beverly Owen both played Marilyn Munster on the TV series "The Munsters." Who was Patricia's mother?
2. Who has authored such books as *Angel Unaware, Dearest Debbie,* and *Salute To Sandy,* about her children who had died at an early age?
3. Her murdering and robbing sons were named Lloyd, Arthur, and Fred, whom she helped to live a life of crime until her death in 1935. Name her.
4. By what name was Elizabeth Foster better known?
5. During a Mother's Day game at Comisky Park in 1939, whose mother was hit on the head and knocked unconscious by a foul ball?
6. Anna Jarvis began what holiday, which was finally officially adopted in 1914?
7. Who was called the Mother of the American Revolution?
8. Who is the mother of actor Larry Hagman?
9. What was the nationality of Sir Winston Churchill's mother?
10. Who is the mother of recording artist and record producer Terry Melcher?

Outlaws

1. What gang was responsible for the first train robbery in the United States?
2. This outlaw was the husband of the woman outlaw Belle Starr. Who was he?
3. This pair of bank robbers and killers were shot to death in their automobile by Texas Rangers in 1934. Who were they?
4. Pat Garrett shot and killed what 21-year-old western outlaw accused of killing one man for every year of his age?
5. Policeman John Selman shot to death what outlaw in El Paso's Acme Saloon on August 19, 1895?
6. What western outlaw died on his 27th birthday?
7. What western outlaw and train robber was pardoned by President Theodore Roosevelt in 1907 and later appeared in films?

Mothers (Answers)

1. Ivy Baker Priest, former treasurer of the United States
2. Dale Evans, wife of Roy Rogers
3. Arizona Kate "Ma" Barker
4. Mother Goose
5. Pitcher Bob Feller
6. Mother's Day
7. Mercy Otis Warren
8. Mary Martin
9. American
10. Doris Day

Outlaws (Answers)

1. The Reno Brothers
2. Sam Starr
3. Bonnie (Parker) and Clyde (Barrow)
4. Billy the Kid
5. John Wesley Hardin
6. Sam Bass
7. Al Jennings

8. What was the name of the California stagecoach robber who was supposedly killed and beheaded by Texas Ranger Harry Love?
9. Name the two James brothers?
10. What two outlaws traveled to Bolivia where they continued their holdups, only to be killed in 1911?

Photographers

1. Margaret Bourke-White photographed the first cover of what major publication in 1936?
2. He took thousands of photographs of the American Civil War, hiring others so that he could record this part of history on film. Name him.
3. He just happened to have his camera with him at Dallas's grassy knoll on November 22, 1963. What is the name of the man who filmed the assassination of President John F. Kennedy?
4. Name the photographer that Jacqueline Kennedy got a court injunction against so that he had to stay clear of her by a certain distance.
5. In 1947, who invented the first Polaroid camera?
6. Photographer Paul Goresh photographed singer John Lennon on the last night of his life (December 8, 1980), autographing his album *Double Fantasy*. This became the last photo of Lennon alive. Who was Lennon autographing the album for?
7. What famous pop artist often uses an enlarged photograph as the basis for his celebrity portraits?
8. Photographer Tom Howard's illegal photographs of her electrocution at Sing Sing Prison in January 1928 made front page news in the *New York Daily News*. Who was she?
9. What word did *New York Journal* photographer James Kane coin in 1912 when referring to a sexy photograph?
10. What award is presented to photographers by *Photoplay* magazine for the year's best picture?
11. What is the name of the photographer who, on May 27, 1949, took the famous nude photographs of Marilyn Monroe that were used on calendars titled "Golden Dreams" and "A New Wrinkle"?
12. What photographer won a Pulitzer Prize for his classic photo of the marines raising the U.S. flag on Iwo Jima during World War II?

8. Joaquin Murrieta
9. Jesse and Frank
10. Butch Cassidy and the Sundance Kid

Photographers (Answers)

1. *Life* magazine
2. Matthew Brady
3. Abraham Zapruder
4. Ron Galella
5. Edwin Land
6. Mark David Chapman
7. Andy Warhol
8. Ruth Snyder
9. Cheesecake
10. Gold Medal Award
11. Tom Kelley
12. Joe Rosenthal

13. On May 6, 1937, Al Gold was the camerman who filmed this tragic event—a film just about everyone has seen. What was the event?

14. AP photographer Eddie Adams won the Pulitzer Prize for taking what famous Vietnam War photo?

15. Photographer Roger Wrenn took what famous photograph of General Douglas MacArthur during World War II?

16. On January 10, 1911, Maj. A. H. "Jimmie" Erickson became the first person to take photographs from what?

17. What tragic event did 24-year-old Michael Laughlin photograph in Chicago on May 25, 1979?

18. John Plumber became the first photographer to photograph what U.S. President?

19. What did the initials *T.B.I.* on the early Kodak camera stand for?

20. What was the name of the Frenchman who, in 1826, took the first photograph using light alone?

Pilots

1. On November 29, 1929, Bert Balchon flew what famous explorer over the South Pole (the first flight ever over the pole)?

2. Name the pilot who was killed with his passenger, humorist Will Rogers, when their airplane crashed at Barrow, Alaska, on August 15, 1935?

3. The pilot of the B-25 *The Ruptured Duck*, one of Lt. Col. Doolittle's bombers in his raid on Tokyo, later wrote the book *Thirty Seconds over Tokyo*, on which the 1944 movie was based. Name the pilot.

4. Who piloted the Ben X-1, when on October 14, 1947, it became the first airplane to officially exceed the speed of sound?

5. Name the pilot of the B-29 *Enola Gay*, which on August 6, 1945, dropped the atomic bomb on the Japanese city of Hiroshima?

6. What was the name of the Canadian pilot who, on April 21, 1918, shot down German ace Manfred von Richtofen, better known as the Red Baron?

7. What pilot got his nickname "Hollywood Pilot" because he flew many couples to Las Vegas, where they were married?

8. Who was Amelia Earhart's copilot on her last flight, June 1–2, 1937, before her disappearance?

13.   The crashing of the Hindenberg
14.   A South Vietnamese police chief, executing a Vietcong officer
      in civilian clothes
15.   MacArthur wading ashore in the Philippines in October 1944
16.   An aircraft (He was flying over San Diego.)
17.   The crash of an American Airlines DC-10
18.   James Polk
19.   Time, bulb, instantaneous
20.   Joseph Niepce

Pilots (Answers)

1.   Richard Byrd
2.   Wiley Post
3.   Ted Lawson
4.   Major Charles E. Yeager
5.   Major Paul Tibbets
6.   Roy Brown
7.   Paul Mantz
8.   Fred Noonan

9. What pilot claimed to have flown the wrong way across the Atlantic Ocean in July 1938 (only after he was denied permission to make the flight)?
10. What stunt flier was killed when the *Phoenix* crashed after takeoff in the 1966 movie *Flight of the Phoenix*?

Pirates

1. What Scottish-born pirate captained the 284-ton 34-gun vessel *Adventure Galley*?
2. *The Albatross* was the pirate ship of Captain Geoffrey Thorpe in the 1940 film *The Sea Hawk*. Who played the swashbuckler?
3. Captain Flint was the captain of the pirate ship *Walrus* in what classic novel?
4. West Indies pirate Edward Teach was known by what more familiar name?
5. What is the name of Captain James Hook's pirate vessel in James Barries's *Peter Pan?*
6. What insignia is shown on the traditional pirate's flag?
7. In what 1870 Gilbert and Sullivan opera about pirates did Linda Ronstadt make her Broadway debut?
8. What actual pirate aligned himself with General Andrew Jackson in 1815 in order to defeat the British at the Battle of New Orleans?
9. In 1739 Spanish pirates cut the ear off of what English captain?
10. What do the pirates call home?

Religious People

1. What religious figure became the youngest man to win the Nobel Prize for Peace?
2. What major league baseball player became a practicing evangelist after leaving baseball in 1890?
3. The wife of the U.S. Senate chaplain authored a biography about her husband titled *A Man Called Peter*, which was filmed in 1955. What was her husband's name?
4. What evangelist is a cousin of country singer Jerry Lee Lewis and Mickey Gilley?
5. Who is the only religious personality to have won an Emmy for his own TV show?

9. Douglas "Wrong Way" Corrigan
10. Paul Mantz

Pirates (Answers)

1. Captain William Kidd
2. Errol Flynn
3. *Treasure Island* by Robert Louis Stevenson
4. Blackbeard
5. *The Jolly Roger*
6. Skull and crossbones
7. *The Pirates of Penzance*
8. Jean Laffite
9. Robert Jenkins
10. Pittsburgh's Riverfront Stadiun (of course)

Religious People (Answers)

1. Rev. Martin Luther King
2. Billy Sunday
3. Peter Marshall
4. Jimmy Swaggart
5. Bishop Fulton J. Sheen

6. Who became head of the Southern Christian Leadership Conference upon the death of Rev. Martin Luther King, Jr., in 1968?

7. Name the two Catholic priests/brothers who went to jail during the 1960s because they destroyed government records in order to protest the Vietnam War?

8. In the 1930s who preached her international doctrine of Four Square Evangelism from her Le Angelus Temple in Los Angeles?

9. What priest founded Boy's Town near Omaha, Nebraska, on December 1, 1917?

10. In 1873, Belgian Catholic missionary Father Francois de Veuster helped the lepers on the Hawaiian Island of Molokai. By what other name do we know him?

11. What actor was once a child evangelist who eventually rejected the ministry to become an actor?

12. What clergyman wrote the best-selling book *The Power of Positive Thinking?*

13. What U.S. Episcopalian priest died in the Judean desert in 1969, during an expedition?

14. What Nobel Prize-winning author in literature is the daughter of missionaries?

15. John Knox helped to establish what church in his homeland of Scotland?

16. What religious following did George Fox organize in 1668?

17. She often stated that she was the only woman to found a religious movement. What church did Mary Morse Baker Eddy organize in 1879?

18. What religion did the mysterious L. Ron Hubbard organize in the early 1950s?

19. In 1972, Sally Priesand was chosen to be the first U.S. female to hold what religious position?

20. What British clergyman founded the colony of Rhode Island after being banished for his religious beliefs?

Royalty

1. Who was the first wife of Henry VIII of England?

2. The official residence of English crowned heads is Buckingham Palace. Who was the first to occupy it?

3. What is the highest British order of knighthood?

4. Who was the first woman to rule alone as Queen of England?

6. Ralph Abernathy
7. Daniel and Philip Berrigan
8. Aimee Semple McPherson
9. Father Edward J. Flanagan
10. Father Damien
11. Marjoe Gortner
12. Norman Vincent Peale
13. Bishop James Pike
14. Pearl Buck
15. Presbyterian Church
16. Quakers (the Society of Friends)
17. Christian Science Church
18. Scientology
19. Rabbi
20. Roger Williams

Royalty (Answers)

1. Catherine of Aragon
2. Queen Victoria in 1837
3. Order of the Garter
4. Mary I, daughter of Henry VIII

5. Who is the longest-ruling monarch in history?
6. Who is the longest-ruling monarch of more modern times?
7. What was the name of the Italian ruling family?
8. What country is ruled by the House of Orange?
9. What was the name of the Civil War of the English nobility?
10. Who ruled the Austro-Hungarian Empire at the outbreak of World War I?
11. What English King had the shortest reign?
12. The rulers of Russia were given a title equivalent to Caesar. What is it?
13. What Russian ruler set the country on the road to modernization in the 1700s?
14. What was the family name of the last czars of Russia?
15. Who was Kaiser of Germany during World War I?
16. In early California history, who was the self-avowed Emperor of San Francisco?
17. What relative of Napoleon was crowned Emperor of Mexico until overthrown and shot by Mexican nationalists?
18. What famous Queen of Egypt is famous for her regal profile?
19. Who was Emperor of Rome at the time of the birth of Christ?
20. What color robe did Roman emperors wear that has become the color of royalty?

Rulers

1. Confederate general Nathan Bedford Forrest served as the first head of what organization after the end of the Civil War?
2. What is the full name of the last czar to rule Russia?
3. Who was the first Christian emperor of Rome?
4. Who was the ruler of Judea who had John the Baptist beheaded at the request of Salome?
5. Actress Sophia Loren was the sister-in-law of the son of what world ruler?
6. Who was the Roman emperor from 54 A.D. to 68 A.D., who committed suicide?
7. On June 11, 1923, what future European ruler was awarded the Order of Knight Grand Cross of the Order of Bath from Britain's King George V?
8. What Babylonian emperor built the Hanging Gardens of Babylon?

5. Pepi II of Egypt, 90 years
6. Louis XIV King of France, who ruled for 72 years
7. House of Savoy
8. The Netherlands
9. War of the Roses
10. Emperor Franz Joseph
11. King Edward V (77 days in 1483)
12. Czar
13. Peter the Great
14. Romanovs
15. Wilhelm II
16. Emperor Norton
17. Maximilian
18. Nefertiti
19. Augustus Caesar
20. Purple

Rulers (Answers)

1. The Ku Klux Klan (He was their first Grand Wizard.)
2. Nicholas Romanov II
3. Constantine
4. Herod Antipas
5. Benito Mussolini
6. Nero
7. Benito Mussolini
8. Nebuchacdnezzar

9. What Cuban president did Fidel Castro overthrow in 1959?
10. Who was the Mongol conqueror who conquered Northern China, Southern Russia, and Iran and was named ruler of the Mongols in 1206?

Sailors

1. What Portugese sailor was the first man credited with circumnavigation of the globe? (However, he died before his ships completed the journey.)
2. In 1970, Capt. Arlene Duerk of the Navy Nurse Corps achieved what rank that no other woman in the history of the world's navies had reached?
3. What American admiral defeated the Spanish fleet at Manila Bay in 1898 (during the Spanish-American War)?
4. Who is the only man to have been an admiral in both the U.S. and the Russian navies?
5. What U.S. admiral won a Pulitzer Prize in 1920 with his book *The Victory at Sea*?
6. Who is Samuel L. Gravely, Jr.?
7. What is the name of the British sailor on the packages of Player Cigarettes?
8. On April 12, 1979, Lt. Beverly G. Kelly became the first woman to do what?
9. By what nickname is a British sailor known?
10. Scottish sailor Alexander Selkirk became the inspiration for what novel?

Saints

1. St. Andrews is the patron saint of what country, which has named a famous golf course in his honor?
2. The location named after this country's patron saint, St. Denis, is also the location of the tombs of what country's kings?
3. Who is the patron saint of Britain?
4. This patron saint drove the snakes out of his favorite country. Name him and the country.
5. The Vatican's basilica (whose dome was designed by Michelangelo) is named in honor of what saint?

9.   Fulgencio Batista
10. Genghis Khan

Sailors (Answers)

1.   Ferdinand Magellan
2.   She became the first female admiral
3.   Admiral George Dewey
4.   John Paul Jones
5.   Admiral William Sims
6.   First black United States Admiral (he was promoted on April 27, 1971)
7.   Hero
8.   Command a U. S. Navy (or Coast Guard) vessel, when she commanded the Coast Guard *Cape Newagen*
9.   Jack Tar
10. Robinson Crusoe (he was left on an island for four years.)

Saints (Answers)

1.   Scotland
2.   France's
3.   St. George
4.   St. Patrick of Ireland
5.   Saint Peter

6. London's large-domed cathedral, designed in the 17th century by Sir Christopher Wren, is named in honor of what saint?
7. What patron saint of travelers was de-canonized as a saint by the Catholic Church in 1969?
8. Who was the first U.S.-born saint (canonized in 1975)?
9. What breed of animal is named after an 11th-century saint?
10. Saint Vladimir is the patron saint of what country?

Scholars

1. Mary Lyon founded the first women's college in the United States. Name this Maryland school (established in•1837)?
2. What famous scholar translated *The Tales of the Arabian Nights* (16 volumes) during the years 1885–1888?
3. What country singer and composer was a Rhodes scholar in his youth?
4. Singer Neil Diamond majored in biology at New York University in hopes of becoming a doctor. For what did he win a scholarship?
5. Who authored six volumes of standard textbooks for public schools called Eclectic Readers? (He died in 1836.)
6. What brother of a U.S. President served as the president of Kansas State University, Pennsylvania State University, and Johns Hopkins University?
7. What U.S. educator, who organized Boston's Academy of Music in 1833, composed the hymn "Nearer My God to Thee"?
8. Who proved to be Socrates' best student?
9. What English historian wrote 12 volumes titled *A Study in History*?
10. What female historian won a Pulitzer Prize in History for her 1971 biography *Stilwell and the American Experience in China, 1911–1945*?

Sculptors

1. Daniel Chester French sculpted what President's statue in Washington, DC (dedicated in 1922)?
2. *The Bronco Busters* is just one of a number of sculptures by what talented illustrator, painter, and sculptor of the American West?

6. Saint Paul
7. St. Christopher
8. Elizabeth Ann Seton
9. Saint Bernard (dog)
10. Russia

Scholars (Answers)

1. Mt. Holyoke College
2. Sir Richard Burton
3. Kris Kristofferson
4. Fencing
5. William McGuffey
6. Milton Eisenhower, brother of Dwight D. Eisenhower
7. Lowell Mason
8. Plato
9. Arnold Toynbee
10. Barbara Tuchman

Sculptors (Answers)

1. Statue of Lincoln at the Lincoln Memorial
2. Frederic Remington

3. What two American gold pieces did Irish-born Augustus Saint-Gaudens design?

4. What is the name of James Earl Fraser's sculpture of an Indian on a horse, both with their heads down and ready to collapse?

5. Who sculpted *The Hand of God*, which is on display at the Metropolitan Museum of Art in New York City?

6. Thomas Schomer sculpted a statue of what fictitious boxing champion, (which was presented to the City of Philadelphia)?

7. What is the name of the 19½-foot-tall statue that sits on the capital building in Washington, DC?

8. What is the only sculpture signed by Michelangelo?

9. When completed, Stone Mountain, Georgia, will feature the sculptures of what three men?

10. Who sculpted the heads of four U.S. Presidents on Mt. Rushmore between 1927 and 1941?

Sisters

1. In 1942, two sisters were nominated for Best Actress for films they appeared in during 1941. Name both sisters.

2. In 1967, two sisters were again nominated for Best Actress for a film each appeared in during 1966. Name the sisters.

3. Actor Warren Beatty's sister is a superstar actress in her own right, name her.

4. Adeline Gehrig was the National Women's Foil Champion for 1920 through 1923. She was the sister of whom?

5. Georganne LaPierre, who played Heather Grant on TV's *General Hospital*, is the sister of what singer/actress?

6. What were the names of the three Brontë sisters?

7. Name the three Gabor sisters.

8. What are the first names of the two Gish sisters?

9. U.S. novelist Mary McCarthy, who wrote *The Group*, in 1963, is the sister of what actor?

10. In 1954, Juanita Ruz immigrated to the United States. She is the sister of what well-known person?

3. $10 and $20 gold pieces
4. *End of the Trail*
5. Auguste Rodin
6. Rocky Balboa
7. *Freedom*
8. The *Pieta*
9. Jefferson Davis, Robert E. Lee, Stonewall Jackson
10. Gutzon Borglum

Sisters (Answers)

1. Joan Fontaine and Olivia DeHavilland (Joan won.)
2. Vanessa Redgrave and Lynn Redgrave (Neither won.)
3. Shirley MacLaine
4. Baseball's Lou Gehrig
5. Cher
6. Charlotte, Emily, and Anne
7. Magda, Zsa Zsa, and Eva
8. Dorothy and Lillian
9. Kevin McCarthy
10. Cuban premier Fidel Castro

Spies

1. On February 10, 1962, Russian spy Col. Rudolph Abel was exchanged in Germany for Yale student Frederick L. Pryor and what other American held prisoner in the Soviet Union?
2. By what more famous name is World War II spy Elyesa Bazna known?
3. What Swedish-born actress spied for the Allies against the Axis powers during World War II? (She was Adolf Hitler's favorite actress.)
4. Born Gertrud Margarote Zelle, this Dutch dancer was executed by the French in 1917, who tried her for spying. What was her better-known name?
5. What husband and wife were put to death in the United States on June 19, 1953, after being convicted of espionage?
6. What British novelist and playwright spied for the British during World War I?
7. The Germans made two landings on the East Coast of the United States from submarines in June 1942. How many of the spies landed and how many were executed by the U.S. after their capture?
8. What major league baseball player, who traveled with his team, the New York Yankees, to Japan in the 1930's, was acting as a spy for the federal government?
9. What wife of a U.S. President was accused of being a spy? (The accusation was never proved.)
10. Hollywood biographer Charles Higham raised quite a controversy when his book was published in the 1970s. What prominent Hollywood actor did Higham claim was actually a Nazi spy?

Teachers

1. In what novel, by Margaret Landon, did an English teacher travel to Siam in the 1860s in order to teach the children of royalty?
2. What French music teacher created the raised-dot system of reading for the blind?

Spies (Answers)

1. Francis Gary Powers
2. Cicero
3. Greta Garbo
4. Mata Hari
5. Julius and Ethel Rosenberg
6. Somerset Maugham
7. Eight landed—six executed (two cooperated with authorities)
8. Moe Berg
9. Mary Todd Lincoln (Four of her brothers fought for the South.)
10. Errol Flynn *(Errol Flynn: The Untold Story)*

Teachers (Answers)

1. *Anna and the King of Siam* (not *The King and I*—that was the title of the musical film)
2. Louis Braille

3. After teaching in the Chicago public school system for 14 years, what black teacher quit her job to establish her own school—the Westside Preparatory School? (Her name is part of a 1981 TV movie based on her life.)
4. What is the name of the courageous teacher who taught a blind and deaf girl named Helen Keller?
5. What schoolteacher was actually put on trial for teaching evolution?
6. What was the name of the American educator who was the first black to ever earn a Ph.D. from Harvard?
7. What U.S. politician, teacher, and lawyer founded the Fulbright Scholarship program?
8. What subject did Mr. Chips (Chippings) teach in James Hilton's novel *Good-bye Mr. Chips?*
9. What is the title of Bel Kaufman's best-selling book about the New York City public school system?
10. Prior to becoming a rock superstar, Gordon Sumner was a teacher. By what name is he better known today?

Time Magazine's Man of the Year

1. What religious leader was the recipient of *Time* magazine's Man of the Year Award for 1979?
2. *Time* conferred their Man of the Year Award on the freedom fighters of what country in 1956?
3. Who was the first *Time* magazine Man of the Year in 1927?
4. What, not who, was *Time* magazine's Man of the year for 1982?
5. In 1975, 12 people were selected—what group did they represent?
6. In 1968, what Apollo crew (number) won the title?
7. In 1937, what husband-and-wife team won the award?
8. In 1960, what group of 15 people became *Time* magazine's Man of the Year?
9. In 1962, who became the only pope to win the title?
10. What world leader was *Time* magazine's Man of the Year for both 1939 and 1942?

3. Marva Collins *(The Marva Collins Story)*
4. Annie Sullivan
5. John Scopes
6. W.E.B. DuBois
7. J. William Fulbright
8. Latin
9. *Up the Down Staircase*
10. Sting

Time Magazine's Man of the Year (Answers)

1. Ayatollah Ruhollah Khomeini of Iran
2. Hungry
3. Charles Lindbergh
4. The Computer
5. Women
6. *Apollo 8* astronauts
7. General and Mme. Chiang Kai-Shek
8. Scientists
9. Pope John XXIII
10. Joseph Stalin

Translators

1. What is the literal translation of the words "Mardi Gras"?
2. What does "Cave canem" mean?
3. What does "Pravda" (name of the Soviet Union's leading newspaper) mean in English?
4. What does the Japanese word "kamikaze" mean?
5. What does "Caveat emptor" translate as?
6. Translate "Costra Nostra" into English.
7. What is the meaning of the French expression "coup de grace"?
8. What name was given to the lightning war conducted by Germany at the beginning of World War II?
9. "Exitus acta probat," was the family motto of George Washington. What does it translate as?
10. Doris Day's hit song "Que Sera Sera" translated as what?

Wives

1. Sara Barg had been married to what two superstar country singers?
2. She authored the book *My Luke and I* with cowriter Joseph Durso about her late husband. What was Eleanor's famous husband named?
3. All three of what TV host's wives' first names began with the letter *J?*
4. Country singer Merle Haggard's first and thrid wives both had what same name?
5. Who has been the wife of actors Charlie Chaplin, Burgess Meredith, and of writer Erich Maria Remarque?
6. What author of the best-seller *Forever Amber* was married to both All-American/sportswriter Robert Herwig and bandleader Artie Shaw?
7. Anne Hathaway was the wife of what noted author?
8. Actresses Lana Turner, Ava Gardner, and Evelyn Keyes have all been married to what same bandleader?
9. Name singer Frank Sinatra's four wives.
10. What are the names of King Henry VIII's six wives?

Translators (Answers)

1. Fat Tuesday
2. Beware of dog.
3. Truth
4. Divine Wind
5. Let the buyer beware.
6. Our thing
7. The finishing stroke
8. Blitzkrieg
9. The end justifies the means.
10. "Whatever Will Be, Will Be"

Wives (Answers)

1. Mac Davis and Glen Campbell
2. Lou Gehrig
3. Johnny Carson's (Jody, Joanne, and Joanna)
4. Leona
5. Paulette Goddard
6. Kathleen Windsor
7. William Shakespeare
8. Artie Shaw
9. Nancy Sinatra, Ava Garner, Mia Farrow, Barbara Marx
10. Catherine of Aragon, Anne Boleyn, Jane Seymour, Anne of Cleves, Catherine Howard, Catherine Parr

World Leaders

1. Name the president of Zimbabwe, who in 1983 passed a law making it a crime to make fun of his name.
2. It has been stated that this world leader was given a tryout for the Washington Senators baseball team and appeared in bit parts in several Hollywood films. Name him.
3. What field marshal /doctor/president was the dictator of the African county of Uganda from 1971 to 1979?
4. In 1978, what two world leaders jointly were awarded the Nobel Peace Prize?
5. Name the father and the daughter who both served as prime minister of the same country. (The father was the first to serve.)
6. Name the concert pianist who once served as the prime minister of Poland (1919 to 1921).
7. Who became Prime Minister of Britain in 1783 at the age of 24?
8. After 16 years as the Canadian prime minister, who stepped down as head of his country in 1984?
9. What world leader had a capital city renamed in his honor?
10. What are the two capitals of China?

World Leaders (Answers)

1. President Canaan Banana
2. Fidel Castro
3. Idi "Dada" Amin
4. Anwar Sadat of Egypt and Menachem Begin of Israel
5. Jawaharlal Nehru and Indira Nehru of India
6. Ignace Jan Paderewski
7. William Pitt
8. Pierre Trudeau
9. Ho Chi Minh (Ho Chi Ming City in Vietnam)
10. Taipei (Republic of China) and Peking (People's Republic of China)

Writers and

the Written Word

American Indians of Fiction

1. Peter Pan rescued what Indian princess from the claws of Captain Hook?
2. Injun Joe was an evil character in what 1876 novel?
3. What cigar store wooden Indian did Hank Williams compose and record a song about?
4. Who was the pretty Indian maiden on TV's "Howdy Doody Show"?
5. In James Fenimore Cooper's classic novel, what was the name of the last of the Mohicans?
6. In Longfellow's poem *Hiawatha's Wedding Feast*, what is the name of Hiawatha's bride?
7. What is the name of the faithful sidekick of ex-Texas Ranger, John Reid?
8. What was the name of the Navajo Indian sidekick of Red Ryder?
9. What was the name of the person who accepted Marlon Brando's Oscar for Best Actor for his role in *The Godfather?*
10. What Indian maiden is "Running Bear" in love with in Johnny Preston's 1959 hit recording?

The American Novel

1. In what southern county does William Faulkner place most of his novels?
2. What is Gatsby's first name in Fitzgerald's *The Great Gatsby?*
3. Who is the father of Hester Pryne's illegitimate daughter in Hawthorne's *The Scarlet Letter?*
4. With what line is "Bartleby the Scrivener" most closely associated?
5. What is the name of the title character in Mark Twain's *A Connecticut Yankee in King Arthur's Court?*

American Indians of Fiction (Answers)
1. Princess Tiger Lily
2. *The Adventures of Tom Sawyer*
3. "Kaw-Liga"
4. Princess Summerfall Winterspring
5. Uncas
6. Laughing Water
7. Tonto (John Reid is the Lone Ranger)
8. Little Beaver
9. Sacheen Littlefeather
10. Little White Dove

The American Novel (Answers)
1. Yoknapatawpha County
2. Jay
3. Arthur Dimmsdale
4. "I prefer not."
5. Hank Morgan

6. What is the great scientific discovery of Felix Hoeniker in Kurt Vonnegut's *Cat's Cradle?*

7. In John Steinbeck's *Travels with Charley*, who is Charley?

8. What does the term "the Sotweed Factor" refer to in John Barth's novel of the same name?

9. What is the Christian name of the title character in Thomas Berger's *Little Big Man?*

10. What is the setting for Norman Mailer's *The Naked and the Dead?*

11. What is the collective title for the Natty Bumpo novels of James Fenimore Cooper?

12. What is the title of the trilogy composed of *The Forty-Second Parallel, 1919*, and *The Big Money?*

13. Where is the House of Seven Gables located?

14. Of what nationality is the old fisherman in Hemingway's *The Old Man and the Sea?*

15. What is the name of the Neal Cassady character in Jack Kerouac's *On the Road?*

16. What are the names of the three major characters on whom James T. Farrell focused his three major cycles of fiction?

17. Who is the narrator of Nabokov's *Lolita?*

18. What is the title of Edgar Alan Poe's fragmentary novel?

19. Who is the seeker of truth in Thomas Pynchon's *The Crying of Lot 49?*

20. Who is considered to be the first American novelist?

Authors

1. What science fiction writer has written a science fiction book beginning with every letter of the alphabet?

2. In the history of films there has been only one case in which one Nobel Prize-winning author wrote the screenplay based on a novel by another Nobel Prize-winning author. What was the film?

3. In 1956, this author's hometown library in Gilmanton, New Hampshire refused to keep a copy of her novel *Peyton Place* on their shelves. Name her.

4. Although he came to Hollywood in order to write for the motion picture industry, he only received partial credit for one film— *Three Comrades* (1938). Name him.

6. Ice-nine
7. Steinbeck's dog.
8. The tobacco planters
9. John Crabb
10. A Pacific Island during World War II
11. *The Leatherstocking Tales*
12. *U.S.A.* by John Dos Passos
13. Salem, Massachusetts
14. Cuban
15. Dean Moriarty
16. Studs Lonigan, Danny O'Neill, and Bernard Carr
17. Humbert Humbert
18. *The Narrative of Arthur Gordon Pym of Nantucket*
19. Oedipa Maas
20. Charles Brockden Brown

Authors (Answers)

1. Andre Norton
2. *To Have and Have Not* (1944)—original novel by Ernest Hemingway, screenplay by William Faulkner
3. Grace Metalious
4. F. Scott Fitzgerald

5. What novelist served as President Lyndon B. Johnson's speech-writer in 1967?
6. What U.S. poet always spelled his name without using capital letters?
7. Ian Fleming dedicated his 1962 James Bond novel *The Spy Who Loved Me* to the head of the C.I.A. Who was it?
8. Who is the most filmed American writer?
9. Clarence Shephard Day, Jr., authored three books about his parents. Give the titles of all books.
10. Rosemary Rogers dedicated her first novel, *Sweet Savage Love*, to one C.E. Who is C.E.?

The Bible

1. Whose wife turned into a pilar of salt when she looked back at the destruction of the City of Sodom?
2. Where is the site of Jesus' first miracle?
3. What names are the first five books of the Bible?
4. What was the first book ever set in print (between 1450 and 1455)?
5. John 11:35 is the shortest verse in the Bible. What is it?
6. What is the name of the man whom Jesus Christ raised from the dead?
7. What are the names of Jesus' four evangelists?
8. On what mountain peak was Noah's Ark found resting after the Great Flood?
9. What animal is mentioned more often in the Bible, the cat or the dog?
10. Who spent three days and three nights in the belly of a whale?

Books

1. One of Erma Bombeck's books was made into a 1978 TV movie starring Carol Burnett. Name it.
2. In 1926 British author Sylvia Townsend Warner's novel *Lolly Willowes* became the first selection to be offered by what new company?

5.   Peter Benchley
6.   e.e. cummings (Edward Estlin Cummings)
7.   Allen Dulles
8.   Zane Grey (with over 100 films based on his works)
9.   *Life with Father*, *Life with Mother*, and *Father and I*.
10. Actor Clint Eastwood

The Bible (Answers)

1.   Lot
2.   Cana
3.   Genesis, Exodus, Leviticus, Numbers, and Deuteronomy
4.   Gutenberg Bible
5.   "Jesus wept."
6.   Lazarus
7.   Matthew, Mark, Luke, and John
8.   Mt. Ararat
9.   The dog 18 times and the cat not even once
10. Jonah

Books (Answers)

1.   *The Grass Is Always Greener Over the Septic Tank*
2.   The Book-of-the-Month Club

3. Bette Midler's second book made the best-seller list in 1983. Name it.

4. Charmian Kittredge authored a book by her late author husband that became the basis of a 1943 movie in which Susan Hayward portrayed Charmian. Who was her husband?

5. Who wrote the book *On the Origin of Species by Means of Natural Selection, or the Preservation of Favored Races in the Struggle for Life?*

6. What was the title of Pat Boone's best-selling book?

7. Ernest Poole was the first recipient in 1918 for the Pulitzer Prize for literature. Name the book.

8. What book was a best-seller for two years in a row, 1972 and 1973?

9. What is the title of the best-selling popular novel of all-time?

10. Who is the best-selling modern author of horror novels?

The British Novel

1. In what novel by Charles Dickens does the legal case of "Jaryndyce v. Jaryndyce" figure prominently?

2. In what fictitious language is Anthony Burgess's novel *A Clockwork Orange* written?

3. Who is the narrator of Emily Bronte's *Wuthering Heights?*

4. What is the full name of the author of *Lord Jim?*

5. For what famous family saga is John Galsworthy best known?

6. By what title is Jack Wilton best known?

7. In what historic setting does Graham Greene place the action of his novel *The Confidential Agent?*

8. What is the occupation of the title character in Thomas Hardy's *Jude the Obscure?*

9. Where is James Joyce's *Ulysses* set?

10. What is Lady Chatterly's first name in the famous D. H. Lawrence novel *Lady Chatterly's Lover?*

11. What is Lady Chatterly's lover's name and occupation?

12. What novel by Matthew Gregory Lewis has yielded its author his nickname?

13. In what country does *1984* by George Orwell take place?

14. Who is "the Italian" in Ann Radcliffe's novel of the same name?

15. In what literary form is Samuel Richardson's *Pamela* written?

3. *The Saga of Baby Divine*
4. Jack London
5. Charles Darwin in 1859
6. *Twixt Twelve and Twenty*
7. *His Family*
8. *Jonathan Livingston Seagull* by Richard Bach
9. *Valley of the Dolls* by Jacqueline Susann
10. Stephen King

The British Novel (Answers)

1. *Bleak House*
2. Nadsat
3. Mr. Lockwood
4. Teodor Jozef Konrad Nalecz Korzeniowski
5. *The Forsyte Saga*
6. *The Unfortunate Traveler*
7. The Spanish Civil War
8. Stone mason
9. Dublin, Ireland
10. Connie
11. Mellors the gameskeeper
12. *The Monk*
13. Oceana
14. Schedoni
15. Epistolary

16. What is the title of Mary Shelley's 1826 "end of the world" novel?
17. What is the name of the gentleman from Texas who plays a key role in the destruction of the vampire in Bram Stoker's *Dracula*?
18. In what novel does the character of Becky Sharp, an unscrupulous adventuress, appear?
19. What is the name of the famous prelude to J.R.R. Tolkien's *Lord of the Rings*?
20. What is *Zastrozzi*?

Celebrity Books

1. What actor wrote such novels as *Beams End* (1937) and *Showdown* (1946)?
2. In 1983 actress Victoria Prinicpal's exercise book was published. Give the title?
3. Under his real name of Bernard Schwartz, what Hollywood actor authored the 1977 novel *Kid Andrew Cody and Julia Sparrow?*
4. What singer wrote the book *For Every Young Heart,* in 1962?
5. *One Special Summer* is the title of the book written by what sisters when they toured Europe in the summer of 1951?
6. What was the title of Yoko Ono's 1971 best-selling book?
7. What actor authored the 1978 historical book *The Outlaw Trail?*
8. *Savrola*, written in 1900, was the only novel ever written by what well-known statesman and author?
9. What well-respected criminal attorney authored a novel titled *Secrets* (published in 1978)?
10. *Stained Glass,* one of a number of spy novels, was authored by what political writer?

Children's Stories

1. What British author wrote the children's story *The Jungle Book* in 1895?
2. What well-known author of spy stories authored the children's tale *Chitty Chitty Bang Bang*, which was filmed in 1968?
3. The former husband of actress Patricia Neal authored the 1964 book *Charlie and the Chocolate Factory* (which was filmed in 1971). Name him.

16. *The Last Man*
17. Quincy Morris
18. *Vanity Fair* by William Thackery
19. *The Hobbit*
20. A gothic novel by Percy Shelley.

Celebrity Books (Answers)

1. Errol Flynn
2. *The Body Principal*
3. Tony Curtis
4. Connie Francis
5. Jackie Bouvier and Lee Radziwill
6. *Grapefruit*
7. Robert Redford
8. Sir Winston Churchill
9. F. Lee Bailey
10. William F. Buckley

Children's Stories (Answers)

1. Rudyard Kipling
2. Ian Fleming
3. Roald Dahl

4. What noted prize-winning novelist authored the boy-horse story, *The Red Pony?*

5. What U.S. humorist authored the children's story *Charlotte's Web* in 1952?

6. What Pulitzer Prize-winning novelist authored the children's story *The Gnomemobile?*

7. What Nobel Prize-winning novelist authored the story of Bongo, the unicycling bear, which Walt Disney produced as a cartoon film?

8. Zerna A. Sharp wrote what primary reader series of books for young children?

9. What British essayist, writing with his sister, authored the children's book *Tales From Shakespeare* in 1807?

10. What British humorist created the Winnie the Pooh series of children's books?

Columnists

1. What two brothers authored the syndicated column *Matter Of Fact*, which was published by the New York *Herald-Tribune?*

2. Upon the death of columnist Drew Pearson, who took over his syndicated column?

3. What humorous columnist wrote such books as *I Am Not A Crook* (1974) and *Down the Seine and Up the Potomac* (1977)?

4. This gossip columnist had an affair with novelist F. Scott Fitzgerald, who became the subject of several of her books. Name her.

5. Elda Furry is the original name of what actress turned gossip columnist, and mother of a television actor?

6. Name the two columnists who are also twin sisters?

7. Which columnist created the characters Mehitabel the cat and Archy the cockroach in *the lives and times of archy and mehitabel* in 1927?

8. In Hollywood this actress turned columnist was Hedda Hopper's rival?

9. Name the film critic and columnist who was a member of the "Gong Show" panel, made a cameo in the 1978 movie *Superman*, and played a character who underwent a sex change in the 1970 movie *Myra Breckinridge*.

10. What columnist is a regular on TV's "60 Minutes"?

4. John Steinbeck
5. E. B. White
6. Upton Sinclair
7. Sinclair Lewis
8. Dick and Jane
9. Charles Lamb (with Mary Ann Lamb)
10. A. A. Milne

Columnists (Answers)

1. Stewart and Joseph Alsop
2. Jack Anderson
3. Art Buchwald
4. Sheilah Graham
5. Hedda Hopper, the mother of William Hopper
6. Ann Landers and Abigail Van Buren
7. don Marquis
8. Louella Parsons
9. Rex Reed
10. Andy Rooney

Columns

1. What was the name of Franklin P. Adams's *New York Herald-Tribune* newspaper column that was syndicated throughout the country?
2. Busybody was the byline used by what columnist when he wrote his first column for *Billboard* in 1919? (He later wrote a column titled *On Broadway*.)
3. What was the name of Drew Pearson's syndicated newspaper column that exposed many government scandals?
4. *At Wit's End* is the title of whose syndicated newspaper column?
5. His gossip column, *It Happened Last Night*, has been syndicated in American newspapers since 1942. Name him.
6. Who authored the *New York Daily News* column titled *Little Old New York?*
7. *My Answer* is the name of the syndicated daily column of what minister?
8. What writer and TV game show panelist authored the syndicated column *Voice of Broadway?*
9. What was the name of U.S. First Lady Eleanor Roosevelt's newspaper column?
10. *Woody Sez* was a daily column that appeared in the *People's Daily Word*. Who was its author?

Comic Books

1. What comic book character is "trapped in a world he never made"?
2. Alicia Masters is the blind girlfriend of what superhero?
3. What gang of escaped convicts are always trying to break into Uncle Scrooge's money bin?
4. The most valued comic book was first issued in June 1938, which saw the debut of Superman. What was the comic book's name?
5. Who was Richard Gere's favorite comic book hero in the 1983 movie *Breathless?*
6. In comic books of the 1950s and 1960s Red Ryder and Beaver advertised what product?

Columns (Answers)

1. *The Conning Tower*
2. Walter Winchell
3. *Washington Merry-Go-Round*
4. Erma Bombeck
5. Earl Wilson
6. Ed Sullivan
7. Billy Graham
8. Dorothy Kilgallen
9. *My Day*
10. Woody Guthrie

Comic Books (Answers)

1. Howard the Duck
2. The Thing
3. The Beagle Boys
4. *Action Comics* #1
5. Silver Surfer
6. Red Ryder: Daisy B.B. guns, and Beaver: B.B. shot

7.   Captain Marvel used the magic word "SHAZAM" to change into Billy Batson. What did Shazam stand for?
8.   What did the *D.C.* in *D.C. Comics* stand for?
9.   Name the six Blackhawks and their cook?
10. Who was introduced in *Amazing Fantasy* No. 15, August 1962?

Comic Strip

1.   What is Cathy's last name in Cathy Guisewite's comic strip *Cathy?*
2.   The registration name of what bassethound is Verwood Frederick of Ticehurst?
3.   Who in 1975 became the cartoonist to win the Pulitzer Prize for his comic strip (which debuted in *The Yale Daily News* in 1968)?
4.   Although it was ghost-written and drawn by Clayton Knight, who received credit for the newspaper comic strip *Ace Drummond?*
5.   Who created the comic strip *Abbie an' Slats,* in July 1937?
6.   Who is called the Father of the Comic Strip?
7.   What two simultaneous comic strips did Mort Walker write, both of which began in the early 1950s?
8.   What two comic strips that later became radio series, movies, and television series, both debuted on the same day, January 7, 1929?
9.   Ironically, the same thing happened again on the same day five years later, when two comic strips that would be made into a movie also debuted together. What were they?
10. In Lake Geneva, Wisconsin, there is a 14-foot tall statue to what comic strip character created by Sydney Smith?

Cookbooks

1.   What million-selling ballad singer wrote the 1982 book *Cooking for You Alone?*
2.   Name the singer who has authored several cookbooks, one of which was titled *Someone's in the Kitchen with Dinah?*
3.   The Tastemaker Award is the annual award given for what?
4.   Name the author of numerous cookbooks such as *Beard on Bread* (1973) and *Cook's Catalogue* (1975). (He has several others that bear his name.)

7. Solomon, Hercules, Atlas, Zeus, Achilles, and Mercury
8. Detective Comics
9. Blackhawk, Andre, Chuck, Hendrickson, Olaf, Stan, and Chop Chop
10. Spider Man

Comic Strip (Answers)

1. Valentine
2. Fred Basset
3. Gary Trudeau
4. Captain Eddie Rickenbacker
5. Al Capp
6. Wilhelm Busch
7. *Beetle Bailey* and *Hi and Lois*
8. *Tarzan* and *Buck Rogers*
9. *Jungle Jim* and *Flash Gordon*
10. Andy Gump (of the Gumps)

Cookbooks (Answers)

1. Johnny Mathis
2. Dinah Shore
3. Year's Most Outstanding Cookbooks
4. James Beard

5. This tall cook and TV personality authored such cookbooks as *The French Chef Cookbook* (1968) and co-wrote the best-selling *Mastering the Art of French Cooking*. Who is she?

6. What cookbook, published by Random House, had to be recalled in 1978 because one of the recipies for silky caramel slices called for putting a can of condensed milk in a crockpot?

7. What popular radio singer wrote the *Company's Coming Cookhouse* in 1958?

8. What Italian-born actress authored the 1972 cookbook *In the Kitchen with Love?*

9. Irma S. Rombauer wrote one of the all-time best-selling cookbooks in 1931 that is still selling today. Name it.

10. What commercial food brand has a popular cookbook named for it?

Documents

1. What two presidents signed the Constitution?

2. What are the first ten amendments to the U.S. Constitution called?

3. What British king signed the Magna Carta?

4. What agreement was made to set up a government when the pilgrims met in November 1620, after landing in the new world?

5. How many men signed the Declaration of Independence?

6. Who nailed his 95 theses to the castle door at Wittenberg, Germany, in 1517?

7. President Abraham Lincoln issued what edict on January 1, 1863, which freed some of the slaves?

8. What is the only crime mentioned in the U.S. Constitution?

9. What world leaders signed the Atlantic Charter on August 14, 1941?

10. What document stated that the United States would not allow any new colonization and wanted no European interference in the Americas?

5. Julia Child
6. *Woman's Day Crockery Cuisine*
7. Kate Smith
8. Sophia Loren
9. *The Joy of Cooking* (revised to *The New Joy of Cooking*)
10. Betty Crocker

Documents (Answers)

1. George Washington and James Madison
2. Bill of Rights
3. King John
4. Mayflower Compact
5. 56
6. Martin Luther
7. Emancipation Proclamation
8. Treason
9. Winston Churchill and Franklin Delano Roosevelt
10. Monroe Doctrine

Ghost Writers and Collaborators

1. Gerald Green ghost-wrote the novel *The Senator*, which was credited to what columnist?
2. Alvin Moscow ghost-wrote what political figure's book *Six Crises?*
3. Theodore C. Sorensen collaborated on what Pulitzer Prize-winning book?
4. What actor of many western films wrote the song "(Ghost) Riders in the Sky" in 1949?
5. Mystery writer Craig Rice was the actual author of the 1941 novel *The G-String Murders*, but to what celebrity was it credited to?
6. The author of the novel *The Green Berets* was the ghost-writer of Xavier Hollander's *The Happy Hooker*. Name him.
7. Who aided in the autobiography of Lillian Roth's *I'll Cry Tomorrow*, Diana Barrymore's *Too Much Too Soon*, and Sheilah Graham's *Beloved Infidel?*
8. What freelance writer actually wrote John Dean's autobiography *Blind Ambition* in 1976?
9. Mickey Herskowitz has been the unknown co-writer of what book credited to sportscaster Howard Cosell?
10. Who co-authored black nationalist leader Malcolm X's autobiography?

Journalists

1. This journalist authored two scathing biographies of men who died in the bathroom—Lenny Bruce and Elvis Presley. Name the journalist.
2. What well-known political figure once wrote *Washington Post*'s reviewer Paul Hume a nasty letter after Hume gave a critical analysis of the politician's daughter's musical performance?
3. What witty reviewer once wrote the following statement in one of her 1933 play reviews? "Katharine Hepburn runs the gamut of emotions from A to B."
4. What frontier marshal became a sports writer later in his life?
5. Henry and Louis were the first middle names of what satirist who began writing with the *Baltimore Morning Herald* in 1899?

Ghost Writers and Collaborators (Answers)

1. Drew Pearson
2. Richard Nixon
3. *Profiles In Courage* by John F. Kennedy
4. Stan Jones
5. Gypsy Rose Lee
6. Robin Moore
7. Gerald Frank
8. Taylor Branch
9. *Cosell*
10. Alex Haley

Journalists (Answers)

1. Albert Goldman
2. President Harry S. Truman
3. Dorothy Parker
4. Bat Masterson
5. H. L. Mencken

6. Kansas editor William Allen White's daughter was killed in a horse accident at the age of 16. What was her name?

7. In 1939, Hungarian journalist Ladislao Biro invented what writing utensil?

8. Name the two *Washington Post* reporters whose persistence eventually led to the exposure on the Watergate coverup?

9. This journalist authored a number of historical accounts beginning with the words "the day" in their titles, who was it?

10. *Memoirs: Sixty Years on the Firing Line* is the autobiography of what four-time Pulitzer Prize-winning journalist?

11. Her book *Etiquette,* first published in 1921, has set the standard for accepted social behavior. Who is she?

12. Who is the only American journalist buried in the Kremlin?

13. Who was a reporter for the *San Francisco Chronicle* from 1946 until 1955 and served as President John F. Kennedy's press secretary from 1961 until 1963, after which he became a U.S. senator?

14. She rivaled Emily Post in informing America on what standard of etiquette to use. Name her.

15. What popular writer for the *New York Herald-Tribune* was a member of the panel for the radio quiz show "Information Please"?

16. When *London Evening Standard* reporter Maureen Cleave interviewed John Lennon on March 4, 1966, Lennon made what remark that would cause great controversy?

17. What was the name of the *Chicago Tribune* reporter who was gunned down in Chicago by Al Capone's mob on June 9, 1930?

18. Name the New York journalist who authored such books as *The Gang That Couldn't Shoot Straight* and *The Day The Good Guys Finally Won?*

19. What newspaper publisher has been called the Father of Modern American Journalism?

20. What newspaper publisher organized the first major newspaper chain in the United States, in 1895?

Magazines

1. Walter Annenberg was the founder, in April 1953, of what famous weekly publication?

2. Hugh Hefner founded what popular magazine in 1953?

6. Mary White (subject of a 1977 TV movie)
7. Ballpoint pen
8. Carl Bernstein and Robert Woodward
9. Jim Bishop
10. Arthur Krock
11. Emily Post
12. John Reed
13. Pierre Salinger
14. Amy Vanderbilt
15. Franklin P. Adams
16. "We're more popular than Jesus now."
17. Alfred "Jake" Lingle
18. Jimmy Breslin
19. Joseph Pulitzer
20. (E.W.) Scripps

Magazines (Answers)

1. *TV Guide*
2. *Playboy*

3. What magazine (founded in 1821) has inventor Benjamin Franklin been erroneously credited with founding?

4. Gloria Steinem founded what women's magazine in 1970?

5. What film did the publisher of *Penthouse* magazine produce as a Penthouse Production?

6. Cyrus Curtis founded what woman's magazine in 1896?

7. Nat Fleischer founded what sports magazine that is still making the rounds today?

8. Inventor Alexander Graham Bell's father-in-law, Gardner Greene Hubbard, founded what popular magazine in 1888?

9. In 1947 John H. Johnson founded what black magazine?

10. In March 1983 *McCalls* magazine featured its first male centerfold in its 107-year history. Who posed with his clothes on?

11. One-time Secretary of Agriculture, Edwin Thomas Meredith, founded what magazine in 1937, which was originally named *Fruit, Gardener, and Home?*

12. In April 1972, who became the first nude centerfold for *Cosmopolitan* magazine?

13. What magazine that is still being read today was originally founded by the Southern Pacific Railroad in 1898?

14. In July 1978, who became the first male to appear on the cover of *McCalls* magazine in over 100 years?

15. What female athlete founded *Women's Sports* magazine?

16. *American Girl* is the official magazine of what organization?

17. What two people appeared on the cover of the premiere edition of *TV Guide* in April 3–9, 1953?

18. *The Ambassador* is what airline's in-flight magazine?

19. Social reformer and agitator Mary Harris Jones, who at the age of 82, was arrested for her union activities, inspired a magazine named for her. Name the publication?

20. Who became the first male to appear on the cover of *Ladies Home Journal?*

Military Autobiographies

1. What very young World War II American general authored the book *On to Berlin*, in 1978? Ryan O'Neal portrayed him in the film *A Bridge Too Far*.

2. *A Soldier's Story* is the autobiography of what U.S. Army general?

3. *Saturday Evening Post*
4. *Ms.*
5. *Caligula*
6. *Ladies Home Journal*
7. *Ring*
8. *National Geographic*
9. *Ebony*
10. Tom Selleck
11. *Better Homes and Gardens*
12. Burt Reynolds
13. *Sunset*
14. John Travolta
15. Billie Jean King
16. Girl Scouts of America
17. Lucille Ball and her baby son, Desiderio Arnez
18. TWA
19. *Mother Jones*
20. Robert Redford (he appeared with a female)

Military Autobiographies (Answers)

1. General James Gavin
2. Omar Bradley

3. Who allegedly went broke when he published General/President Ulysses S. Grant's memoirs?

4. Major Gregory "Pappy" Boyengton's autobiography was made into a TV series in 1976. Name it.

5. *To Hell and Back* was both a book and a film, written by and based on whose life?

6. Who won a Pulitzer Prize for his historical account titled "My Experiences in the World War"?

7. Before his death, General George S. Patton penned his autobiography. Give its title.

8. Whose military autobiography was titled *Crusade in Europe?*

9. *Calculated Risk* is the autobiography of what U.S. Army general?

10. *Inside the Third Reich* has become one of the most widely read World War II autobiographies. Who is the author of this best-selling book?

Newspapers

1. Give the name of London's first daily newspaper (established in 1702)?

2. Who is the *Chicago Sun Times* movie reviewer who holds the distinction of being the only film critic to win a Pulitzer Prize for Journalism (Criticisn) in 1975?

3. Roger Ebert's co-host, Gene Siskal, is a film reviewer for what other newspaper?

4. In what newspaper did Ernest L. Thayer's famous poem "Casey at the Bat" first appear on June 3, 1888?

5. What is the official newspaper of the U.S. Armed Forces called?

6. Name the woman who signed hotel registers with "Your loving home defender" and who published a newspaper called *The Hatchet?*

7. Marshall Field was the founder, in 1941, of what Chicago paper?

8. What 1872 presidential candidate founded the *New York Tribune* in 1841?

9. What newspaper magnate was so wealthy that he had a castle built in California?

10. "All the news that's fit to print," coined by Adolph S. Ochs, is the motto of what newspaper?

3. Mark Twain
4. *Baa Baa Black Sheep*
5. Audie Murphy
6. John J. Pershing
7. *War As I Knew It*
8. Dwight D. Eisenhower's
9. General Mark Clark
10. Albert Speer

Newspapers (Answers)

1. *Daily Courant*
2. Roger Ebert, who appears each week on the syndicated TV series "At the Movies"
3. *Chicago Tribune*
4. *San Francisco Examiner*
5. *Stars and Stripes*
6. Carrie Nation
7. *Chicago Sun* (later known as the *Chicago-Sun-Times*)
8. Horace Greeley
9. William Randolph Hearst
10. *New York Times*

11. Name the official Communist newspaper sold in the United States.

12. Robert L. *Ripley's Believe It or Not!* column originally appeared in what New York newspaper on December 19, 1918?

13. What newspaper did Clark Kent, Lois Lane, and Perry White work for?

14. Karl Marx was once employed by what New York paper as a correspondent?

15. For what newspaper did Ernest Hemingway once work as a reporter, and Walt Disney as an artist?

16. In what city did two newspapers, *The Examiner* and *The Mirror*, both fold on the same day in January 1962?

17. What daily newspaper has the largest circulation in the United States?

18. What national newspaper is published Monday through Friday and is one of the fastest growing in the country, the first to use color on an ongoing basis?

19. What is rather unique about the cover page of the *Wall Street Journal?*

20. Name the three biggest New York papers that bear "New York" in their title.

Original Book Titles

1. What Robert Louis Balfour Stevens's novel was originally titled *Catriona* when it was published in Great Britain in 1893?

2. Leo Tolstoi originally wanted to title his 1869 masterpiece "All's Well That Ends Well." Name it.

3. What D. H. Lawrence classic 1928 novel was written under the working title of *Tenderness?*

4. *Bar-B-Q* was the original title of what 1934 novel by James M. Cain, which has been brought to the screen twice?

5. What was the original working title of Joseph Heller's 1961 novel *Catch-22?*

6. *Before This Anger* was the working title of what best-selling historical account, (which took its author eleven years to write)?

7. L. Frank Baum originally used the working title of *The Emerald City* for which one of his classic works?

8. *Fiesta* was the original title of what Ernest Hemingway novel written in 1926?

11. *The Daily Worker*
12. *The Globe*
13. *Daily Planet*
14. *New York Tribune*
15. *Kansas City Star*
16. Los Angeles
17. *Wall Street Journal*
18. *U.S.A. Today*
19. No photographs appear on it.
20. *New York Daily News, New York Post, New York Times*

Original Book Titles (Answers)

1. *David Balfour*
2. *War and Peace*
3. *Lady Chatterly's Lover.*
4. *The Postman Always Rings Twice*
5. *Catch-18*
6. *Roots* by Alex Haley
7. *The Wizard of Oz*
8. *The Sun Also Rises*

9. What was the working title of Jane Austen's 1813 novel *Pride and Prejudice?*
10. *Twilight* was the original title of what 1929 William Faulkner novel?

Pen Names

1. Kenneth Miller is the real name of what writer of detective stories?
2. Evan Hunter sometimes writes mystery stories under what popular name?
3. A. A. Fair is a pen name of what writer when he writes books on female detective Bertha Cool?
4. Mary Westmascott was a pen name used by what British novelist when she wished to write romantic stories?
5. What Watergate principal wrote mystery novels under the name of David St. John?
6. Dr. A is the pen name of what science fiction writer when he writes books such as *The Sensuous Dirty Old Man?*
7. What pen name did American writer Fredrick Schiller Faust use when he wrote westerns as well as creating the "Dr. Kildare" series?
8. What male pen name did Janet Miriam use to write her best-selling novels?
9. What author signed his first novel *Under the Moon of Mars*, written in 1911, with the name of Norman Beau?
10. Under what male name did English novelist Mary Ann Evans write?

Philosophers

1. Name the New York City longshoreman who became a social philosopher with his book *The True Believer* and *Reflections on the Human Condition?*
2. Who authored the piece *Civil Disobedience* in 1845?
3. Who founded the philosophy of utilitarianism?
4. Who authored the book of philosophy titled *Thus Spoke Zarathustra* in 1884?

9. *First Impressions*
10. *The Sound and the Fury*

Pen Names (Answers)

1. Ross MacDonald
2. Ed McBain
3. Erle Stanley Gardner
4. Agatha Christie
5. E. Howard Hunt
6. Isaac Asimov
7. Max Brand
8. Taylor Caldwell
9. Edgar Rice Burroughs
10. George Eliot

Philosophers (Answers)

1. Eric Hoffer
2. Henry David Thoreau
3. Jeremy Benthay
4. Friedrich Nietzche

5. What Chinese philosopher is the most quoted because of his extremely logical sayings?
6. What mathematician-philosopher created what is often called the most famous sentence in philosophy: "Cogito ergo sum"?
7. What Greek philosopher spent his entire life in search of a honest man?
8. Greek philosopher Empedocles postulated that the world was made up of what four elements?
9. What nineteenth-century philosopher introduced transcendental thinking?
10. What great French philosopher gave us the quote "I do not agree with a word that you say—but I'll defend to the death your right to say it"?

Plays

1. What is the name of "the gentleman caller" in "The Glass Menagerie"?
2. What are the names of Willy Loman's sons in "Death of a Salesman"?
3. Upon what play is Larry Gelbert's "Sly Fox" based?
4. What historic event acts as the setting for Arthur Miller's "The Crucible"?
5. What is the setting for Lanford Wilson's "Talley's Folly"?
6. Upon what classic trilogy is Eugene O'Neal's "Mourning Becomes Electra" based?
7. What is the title of the sequel play that Lillian Hellman wrote after "The Little Foxes"?
8. What is the title of James Joyce's only play?
9. What is the first name of the character referred to in the title of Tennessee Williams's "Cat on a Hot Tin Roof"?
10. What is Stanley's occupation in "A Streetcar Named Desire"?
11. What two historic characters are featured in Peter Shaffer's "The Royal Hunt of the Sun"?
12. Who is the author of "The Man in the Glass Booth"?
13. What is unusual about the chronological sequence of the acts in Harold Pinter's "Betrayl"?
14. To what does the title of David Mamet's play "American Buffalo" refer?
15. What is the setting of David Rabe's "Streamers"?

 5. Confucius
 6. René Descartes (I think, therefore I am.)
 7. Diogenes
 8. Air, earth, fire, and water
 9. Immanuel Kant
10. Voltaire (François Marie Arouet)

Plays (Answers)

 1. Jim O'Connor
 2. Biff and Happy
 3. "Volpone" by Ben Jonson
 4. The Salem witch trials
 5. A deserted boathouse
 6. The Orestia
 7. "Another Part of the Forest"
 8. "Exiles"
 9. Margaret/Maggie
10. A salesman
11. Atahualpa and Francisco Pizarro
12. Actor Robert Shaw
13. The acts are placed in inverse chronological order.
14. A rare nickel
15. An army barracks

16. What is the title of the play for which Sidney Bruhl is willing to kill in Ira Levin's "Death Trap"?
17. What is the name of the slightly eccentric family in "Arsenic and Old Lace"?
18. What do "Sleuth" and "'Night Mother" have in common?
19. Upon whose works did Neal Simon base his play "The Good Doctor"?
20. Upon what famous case is the play "Inherit the Wind" based?

Poetry

1. What is the title of the collection of 44 love poems that includes the immortal "How do I love thee, let me count the ways"?
2. What two poets collaborated on the 1798 collection entitled *The Lyrical Ballads?*
3. What was John Milton's sequel to *Paradise Lost?*
4. What famous poem is featured in Lewis Carroll's *Alice's Adventures Through the Looking Glass?*
5. About whose death is Walt Whitman's "When Lilacs Last in the Dooryard Bloom'd"?
6. What poet composed the following epitaph for his own tombstone—"Cast a cold eye/On life, on death: Horseman, pass by!"?
7. Where did Emily Dickinson spend virtually all of her life?
8. To whom did Tennyson write *In Memoriam* as a tribute?
9. Who was T. S. Eliot's editor on *The Wasteland?*
10. Whom did Pope cast as the king of the dunces in *The Dunciad?*
11. Who was the famous Renaissance heretic who composed the immortal *Hero and Leander,* judged by many to be the finest epyllion of the 16th century?
12. What poem by Robert Frost was read by the author at President Kennedy's inauguration?
13. What famous artist illustrated William Blake's original editions of *The Songs of Innocence* and *The Songs of Experience?*
14. Who wrote the two famous Renaissance nondramatic poems entitled *Venus and Adonis* and *The Rape of Lucrece?*
15. Who is the author of *Verses on the Death of Dr. Swift?*
16. According to the title of Wallace Stevens's poem, who is "the only emperor"?
17. To whom did John Keats dedicate *Endymion?*

16. "Death Trap"
17. The Brewsters
18. They are both two-character/single-sex plays
19. Anton Chekhov
20. The Scopes Monkey Trial

Poetry (Answers)

1. *Sonnets from the Portuguese*
2. Samuel T. Coleridge and William Wordsworth
3. *Paradise Regained*
4. "Jabberwocky"
5. Abraham Lincoln
6. William Butler Yeats
7. Amherst, Massachusetts
8. Arthur Henry Hallam
9. Ezra Pound
10. First edition—Theobald, second edition—Colley Cibber
11. Christopher Marlowe
12. "The Gift Outright"
13. William Blake
14. William Shakespeare
15. Jonathan Swift
16. "The Emperor of Ice Cream"
17. Thomas Chatterton

18. In what stanzaic form is "The Tale of Sir Thopas" by Geoffrey Chaucer written?
19. What is the name of Ezra Pound's first book of poetry?
20. What famous American poet served with the Fighting 69th in World War I?

Pseudonyms

1. Edgar Box is a pen name sometimes used by what well-known author?
2. What performer used the name "The Cherokee Kid" when he first performed in Wild West shows and in vaudeville?
3. What author wrote two dozen books for young girls under the pen name of Edith Van Dyne?
4. Jonathan Ryder was a pseudonym of what author when he wrote two books *Trewayne* (1973) and *The Cry of the Halidon* (1974)?
5. Who used the name of Ruth Hagg when she recorded the song "I Can't Begin to Tell You" with her husband Harry James's orchestra?
6. What female comedienne authored the screenplay for the 1971 movie *Such Good Friends* under the name of Ester Dale?
7. Jeffrey Hudson and John Lange are pseudonyms of what best-selling author?
8. What is comedian Albert Brooks's real name?
9. What rock singer has been credited under the names of Apollo C. Vermouth and Paul Ramon?
10. What pseudonym did English author Hector Hugh Munro use to author his macabre stories?

Publications

1. What group's publication is titled *Last Month's Newsletter?*
2. What is the name of the almanac published by Benjamin Franklin?
3. It is the only magazine in the United States dedicated to trivia, published in Lincoln, Nebraska. What is its title?
4. Robert B. Thomas began publishing what annual book of information beginning in 1792?

18. Rhyme royal, also known as the Troilus stanza
19. *A lune spento*
20. Joyce Kilmer

Pseudonyms (Answers)

1. Gore Vidal
2. Will Rogers
3. L. Frank Baum (author of *The Wizard of Oz*)
4. Robert Ludlum
5. Actress Betty Grable
6. Elaine May
7. Michael Crichton
8. Albert Einstein
9. Paul McCartney
10. Saki

Publications (Answers)

1. Procrastinator's Club of America, Inc.
2. *Poor Richard's Almanac*
3. *Trivia Unlimited*
4. *The Farmer's Almanac*

5. What is the title of activist Phyllis Schlafly's monthly newsletter?
6. What is the best-selling (and often sued) weekly tabloid in the United States?
7. What eight-time Hugo Award-winning publication is referred to as "the newspaper of the Science Fiction field"?
8. *The Red Herring* is the official newsletter of what organization?
9. The Mystery Writers of America also have their own newsletter. What is its name?
10. In what weekly supplement does the Wallaces' *Significa* column appear?

Publishers

1. Publisher George Palmer Putnam, the founder of G. P. Putnam and Son Publishers, was married to what controversial figure?
2. Richard Simon, co-founder of the publishing firm of Simon and Schuster, is the father of a popular rock 'n' roll singer. Name her.
3. Richard Simon was also the father-in-law of a rock 'n' roll singer. Name him.
4. Canadian-born newspaper publisher William Maxwell Aiken (1879–1964) was better known by what British title?
5. Natalie Wood once portrayed the publisher of a *Cosmopolitan*-like magazine in a 1964 film titled *Sex and the Single Girl*. Name her.
6. What pop artist began publishing *Interview* magazine in 1969?
7. Julius Adler is credited with developing what U.S. newspaper into the giant it is today?
8. Who founded *Time* magazine in 1932 and *Life* magazine in 1936?
9. Who published the *New York World* and in 1903 established the most prestigious American award for journalism?
10. Dewitt Wallace and his wife, Lila Acheson Wallace, founded what magazine in Greenwich Village, New York, in 1921?

Pulitzer Prizes

1. What two brothers have both won Pulitzer Prizes, one for the biography of *Benjamin Franklin* in 1938 and the other for his *Collected Poems* in 1940?

5. *Phyllis Schlafly Report*
6. *National Enquirer*
7. *Locus*
8. Crime Writers Association
9. *The Third Degree*
10. *Parade*

Publishers (Answers)

1. Amelia Earhart
2. Carly Simon
3. James Taylor
4. Lord Beaverbrook
5. Helen Gurley Brown
6. Andy Warhol
7. *New York Times*
8. Henry Luce
9. Joseph Pulitzer
10. *Reader's Digest*

Pulitzer Prizes (Answers)

1. Carl and Mark Van Doren

2. Who has won a Pulitzer Prize in both poetry in 1951 and history in 1940?

3. Who has won both the Medal of Honor and a Pulitzer Prize?

4. What longest-running musical in Broadway history won the 1976 Pulitzer Prize?

5. What institution of learning awards the Pulitzer Prize?

6. What French writer declined his Pulitzer Prize for literature in 1964?

7. Who is the only person to have won the Pulitzer Prize in both fiction—*All the Kings Men* in 1947—and Poetry—*Promises* in 1958?

8. He helped to create NATO and in 1970 won the Pulitzer Prize in History for his work titled *Present At the Creation?*

9. Who is the only president to have won a Pulitzer Prize?

10. What was unusual about Pulitzer Prize winners James Agee's and Robert Lowell's deaths?

Shakespeare

1. What are the names of Romeo's and Juliet's families?

2. Who delivers the famous "All the world's a stage" soliloquy in "As You Like It"?

3. What is Hamlet's mother's name?

4. Who is mistakenly killed by the angry mob in "Julius Caesar"?

5. In "Henry IV Part I," who is Henry Percy better known as?

6. Who delivers an eloquent eulogy on the death of Wolsey in "Henry VIII"?

7. What are the names of King Lear's three daughters?

8. What are the names of Gloucester's two sons in the same play?

9. At the opening of "Richard III" what is Richard's title?

10. In what country does "Macbeth" take place?

11. Who succeeds Macbeth to the throne?

12. What obsolete law is revived by Lord Angelo in "Measure for Measure"?

13. Who is "The Merchant of Venice"?

14. What are the three caskets of Portia made of?

15. What non-history play does Sir John Falstaff appear in?

16. In "A Midsummer Night's Dream," what are Puck's other names?

2. Carl Sandburg
3. Charles Lindbergh
4. *A Chorus Line*
5. Columbia University
6. Jean Paul Sarte
7. Robert Penn Warren
8. Dean Acheson
9. John F. Kennedy for his *Profiles in Courage*
10. The both died of heart attacks in New York City taxicabs.

Shakespeare (Answers)

1. Montague and Capulet
2. Jacques
3. Queen Gertrude
4. Cinna the Poet
5. Hotspur
6. Thomas Cramner
7. Goneril, Regan, and Cordelia
8. Edmond and Edgar
9. Duke of Gloucester
10. Scotland
11. Malcolm
12. "Death to all seducers"
13. Antonio
14. Gold, silver, and lead
15. "The Merry Wives of Windsor"
16. Robin Goodfellow and Hobgoblin

17. What is Iago's military rank in "Othello"?
18. What is the most incriminating piece of evidence that Othello has against Desdemona?
19. In "The Taming of the Shrew," who is the shrew?
20. Who are the brother and sister twins in "Twelfth Night"?

17. Ensign
18. A handkerchief
19. Katharina, daughter of Baptista Minola
20. Sebastion and Viola

Bits and Pieces

Advertising

1. What product used the slogan "A little dab'll do ya"?
2. What cereal used the advertising slogan "Breakfast of champions"?
3. "99 44/100% Pure" was associated with what product?
4. "Does she or doesn't she?" was the popular advertising slogan for what female product?
5. Doublemint Gum has used what three-word slogan for years?
6. "Freshness never tasted so good" is the advertising slogan for which cake product?
7. What product slogan was actually borrowed from a statement once made by an American President? Name the product, slogan, and President.
8. "It's two mints in one" is the advertising slogan for what product?
9. "Take the worry out of being close" is the advertising slogan for what deodorant?
10. What breakfast cereal company uses the slogan "The best to you each morning"?
11. "You deserve a break today" is the advertising slogan of what business?
12. The father of what actor coined the slogan "The beer that made Milwaukee famous"?
13. What company uses the motto "His master's voice"?
14. What is the significance of the numbers 10-2-4 on Dr. Pepper bottles?
15. What is "The world's most honored watch"?
16. What product claimed to have the "Skin you love to touch"?
17. What did the abbreviation "LS/MFT" stand for?
18. What is the "Candy mint with the hole"?
19. What product did singer Pat Boone advertise on television while Maureen Reagan endorsed it in magazines? (The product was later found to be ineffective in clearing the skin.)

509

Advertising (Answers)

1. Brylcream hair oil
2. Wheaties
3. Ivory Soap
4. Clairol Hair Coloring
5. Double your pleasure
6. Hostess cupcakes
7. Maxwell House Coffee, "Good to the last drop," Theodore Roosevelt
8. Certs breath mints
9. Ban
10. Kellogg's cereals
11. McDonald's hamburgers
12. Robert Stack
13. RCA Victor
14. They are the suggested times to take a Dr. Pepper break
15. Longines
16. Woodbury
17. Lucky Strike means fine tobacco.
18. Life Savers
19. Acne Statin

20. Who composed the first commercial jingle "Does the Spearmint Lose Its Flavor on the Bedpost Over Night," in 1924?

Animals

1. What is the name of the Bronx Zoo buffalo, designed by James Earle Fraser, that posed for the buffalo-head nickel?
2. What is a cross between a lion and a tiger called?
3. Tico, the racoon, could be seen stealing a wallet in what TV commercial?
4. What is the only animal that will eat a skunk?
5. What is the only animal that can't jump?
6. What is the name of the lioness cub raised and eventually set free by husband and wife George and Joy Admson?
7. What are the types of camels?
8. What two animals sunburn?
9. What is the only marsupial native to North America?
10. In 1859, Thomas Austin introduced what proliferating animal in Australia?
11. In several films Tarzan can be seen wrestling a tiger. What was unusual about this?
12. What is the largest animal in the world?
13. What was the name of the elephant that showman Billy Rose built a show around?
14. How many toes does an ostrich have?
15. Ray Berwick's trained cockatoo, Lana, played what role on the TV series "Baretta"?
16. What color are the stripes on a zebra?
17. For years the mass deaths of what animal created the falsehood that they committed suicide when they became overpopulated?
18. What is a *Geococcyx californianus?*
19. What animal has a duck's bill, a beaver-like tail, and webbed feet? (The female lays eggs.)
20. If Chilean flamingos are fed a diet of shrimp, what happens to their white feathers?

20.   Billy Rose

Animals (Answers)

1.   Black Diamond
2.   Liger
3.   American Express
4.   An owl (specifically the great horned owl)
5.   Elephant
6.   Elsa
7.   Dromedary (one hump) and Bactrian (two humps)
8.   Humans and pigs
9.   Opossum
10.   Rabbits
11.   Tigers are native to India, not Africa
12.   The blue whale
13.   Jumbo
14.   Four (two on each foot)
15.   Fred
16.   Black
17.   Lemmings
18.   Roadrunner
19.   Platypus
20.   They will turn pinkish in color.

Awards

1. On whom is the life achievement award called the Ruby Slipper Award conferred?

2. Jean Henrie Durant, the founder of the Red Cross, in 1901, was the first recipient of what prestigious award?

3. What heavyset female singer became the first private citizen to receive the American Red Cross Medal of Valor?

4. Who won the 1973 Pulitzer Prize for his play *The Championship Season* and was nominated for an Oscar for Best Supporting Actor in the 1973 movie *The Exorcist?*

5. The novelist who authored such books as *Back Street* and *Imitation of Life* became the first recipient of *Photoplay* magazine's Gold Medal Award. Name her.

6. The first award of its kind was given in 1975 to the National Science Foundation, which conducted an $84,000 study to find out why people fall in love. Name the award.

7. In 1974 who won the Gordie Howe Trophy as the WHA's Most Valuable Player?

8. What is the highest military decoration awarded by the German government?

9. What critic publishes annually his list of both the best-dressed and the worst-dressed celebrities?

10. In what field are the Hugo and the Nebula awards given?

11. The Logie is what country's equivalent to the Emmy Awards?

12. The Maggie is the annual award in what field?

13. When a ribbon is awarded for places in a contest, what are the colors of the first three places?

14. Who was the first recipient in 1965 of the Screen Actor's Guild Annual Award?

15. What annual award is given to the year's best animal actors for both motion pictures and television?

16. What is Broadway's most coveted award?

17. What is Off-Broadway's most coveted award, given by the *Village Voice?*

18. What type of award is the George Foster Peabody?

19. What award is given for the previous year's best commercials?

20. In the Miss America contest, what award is given to the girl voted most popular by all the contestants?

Awards (Answers)

1. Child actors
2. Nobel Peace Prize
3. Kate Smith
4. Jason Miller
5. Fannie Hurst
6. Senator William Proxmire's Golden Fleece Award
7. Gordie Howe
8. The Iron Cross
9. Earl Blackwell
10. Science fiction
11. Australia's
12. Magazines
13. Blue (first), red (second), and yellow (third)
14. Bob Hope
15. Patsy
16. Tony Award (the Antoinette Perry Award)
17. Obie Award
18. Broadcasting
19. Clio
20. Miss Congeniality

Bells

1. "The Bell Waltz" was the theme song of what television musical series?
2. The London firm called White Chappel Bell manufactured what famous bell?
3. What is the name of the most famous bell in the United Kingdom?
4. Where is the Liberty Bell on display?
5. Maria is the young Spanish girl in what Ernest Hemingway novel with a title borrowed from John Donne's *Devotions?*
6. What was the name of the deaf bell-ringer in Victor Hugo's classic novel *The Hunchback of Notre Dame?*
7. What color are the bells on a slot machine?
8. Bing Crosby and Ingrid Bergman starred in this 1945 sequel to the film *Going My Way* (1944)?
9. What is the significance of the title *Bell, Book, and Candle?*
10. "The Browns" had a #1 hit record for four weeks in 1959 with what song about Jimmy Brown?

Candy

1. What candy bar did David L. Clark introduce in 1886?
2. What candy did E.T. eat in the 1983 Steven Spielberg movie *E. T.—The Extraterrestrial?*
3. What candy turned down Steven Spielberg's request to tie-in an add campaign with his film?
4. Mars candy introduced what candy bar in 1932, which was named for several heroes of literature?
5. What type of candy did Arte Johnson, as the "dirty old man" often offer to Ruth Buzzi, as "Gladys," on the TV series "Laugh In"?
6. Baseball superstar Hank Aaron has made television commercials for what candy bar?
7. What New York Yankee baseball player had a candy bar named for him?
8. Derry Church, Pennsylvania, was the previous name of what town where chocolate candy bars are manufactured?

Bells (Answers)

1. The Bell Telephone Hour
2. Liberty Bell
3. Big Ben in London
4. Independence Hall
5. *For Whom the Bell Tolls*
6. Quasimodo
7. Yellow
8. *The Bells of St. Mary's*
9. They are items used in an exorcism/seance.
10. "The Three Bells"

Candy (Answers)

1. Clark Bar
2. Reese's Pieces
3. M & M's
4. 3 Musketeers
5. Walnetto
6. Oh Henry
7. Reggie Jackson
8. Hershey, Pennsylvania

9. What company makes the Baby Ruth candy?
10. Name the candy that is only advertised on the Grand Ole Opry?

Casinos

1. What British agent often gambles at the private London club Blades, which was founded in the late 1700s?
2. On May 1, 1967, what world-famous couple were married at Las Vegas's Aladdin Hotel? Nevada Supreme Court Judge David Zenoff, conducted the ceremony.
3. From 1966 until his death in 1976, recluse Howard Hughes resided in a penthouse apartment in what Las Vegas hotel/casino?
4. Gangster Benjamin "Bugsy" Siegel built the first casino in 1946 on the Las Vegas strip, naming it after the nickname of his girlfriend Virginia Hill. Name the club.
5. On February 15, 1954, what actor opened at the Hotel Last Frontier with the Honey Brothers?
6. On December 8, 1963, the son of what entertainer was kidnapped from Harrah's South Lodge in Lake Tahoe, Nevada?
7. What are the three gambling centers in the United States where dozens of casinos are located?
8. What is the name of the 1960 Frank Sinatra movie in which he and a band of conspirators rob five Las Vegas casinos?
9. What is the card game most often played by James Bond when he visits private casinos?
10. Formerly the Chalforte-Haddon Hall Hotel, this casino became the first major gambling place in Atlantic City on May 26, 1978. What is its current name?

Christmas

1. What was the first state to legalize Christmas as a holiday in 1836?
2. In what year did Christmas become a national holiday?
3. Name Santa Claus's eight reindeer, as mentioned in Clement Clarke Moore's poem "A Visit from St. Nicholas."
4. Give the exact last line of Clement Clarke Moore's 1823 poem "A Visit from St. Nicholas."

9. Curtiss
10. Goo Goo

Casinos (Answers)

1. James Bond (as did his boss M)
2. Elvis Presley and Priscilla Beaulieu
3. Desert Inn
4. Flamingo
5. Ronald Reagan
6. Frank Sinatra
7. Las Vegas and Reno, Nevada; and Atlantic City, New Jersey
8. *Oceans-11*
9. Baccarat
10. Resorts International Hotel Casino

Christmas (Answers)

1. Alabama
2. 1890
3. Dasher, Dancer, Prancer, Vixen, Comet, Cupid, Donner, and Blitzen
4. "Happy Christmas to all and to all a good night."

5. Who first recorded the song, in 1949, that introduced "Rudolph the Red-Nosed Reindeer"?
6. The best-selling Christmas song is also the all-time best-selling song. Name the song and its artist.
7. Bing Crosby introduced "White Christmas" in what 1942 movie?
8. What #1-charted Christmas song when first aired in 1958 was subtitled "Christmas Don't Be Late"?
9. What are the twelve days of Christmas?
10. What are the three gifts of the Magi?

Clothing

1. When Edward R. Murrow interviewed Cuban leader Fidel Castro on TV's "Person To Person," in February 1959, what was Castro wearing?
2. What type of clothing did John B. Stetson manufacture?
3. What South Pacific lagoon that was the site of an atomic bomb test in June 30, 1946, lent its name to a piece of clothing?
4. What is the name of the one-piece garment worn by men in ancient Rome?
5. Mr. F. H. Mellinger opened his first women's apparel clothing chain in Hollywood in 1946. What did he name it?
6. Posture Foundation was the selling point of what type of shoe?
7. What sweater was named for the commander of the light brigade cavalry who led the Six Hundred at the Battle of Balaklava during the Crimean War in 1854?
8. What Hollywood producer and director invented a pushup bra to highlight actress Jane Russell?
9. What American social reformer lent her name to a piece of clothing introduced by one Elizabeth Miller?
10. What company is the biggest manufacturer of clothing in the United States?

Coins

1. In 1905, a waitress named Mary Cunningham posed for something designed by Augustus Saint-Gaudens. What was it?
2. The United States manufactures the coins for what three countries?

5. Gene Autry
6. "White Christmas" by Bing Crosby
7. *Holiday Inn*
8. "The Chipmunk Song" by the Chipmunks (David Seville)
9. First, a partridge in a pear tree; second, two turtle doves; third, three French hens; fourth, four calling birds; fifth, five golden rings; sixth, six geese a-laying; seventh, seven swans a swimming; eight, eight maids a-milking; ninth, nine ladies dancing; tenth, ten lords a-leaping; eleventh, eleven pipers piping; twelfth, twelve drummers drumming
10. Gold, frankincense, and Myrrh

Clothing (Answers)

1. Pajamas
2. Hat
3. Bikini
4. Toga
5. Fredrick's of Hollywood
6. Tennis shoes (PF Flyers)
7. Lord Cardigan
8. Howard Hughes
9. Amelia Bloomer
10. Levi Strauss and Co.

Coins (Answers)

1. Miss Liberty on the $20 gold piece
2. United States, Dominican Republic, and Panama

3. *S* is the United States mint mark for what city?

4. *D* has been the United States mint mark since 1906 for what city?

5. From 1870 until 1893, coins with the mint mark of *CC* were struck. In what capital city were they minted?

6. Except for the years 1942 and 1945, coins with no mint mark were struck in what U.S. city?

7. After Gilroy Roberts designed this coin he put his initials *GR* just under the neck of the featured President. Unfortunately the *GR* resembled a hammer and a sickle. What coin did he design?

8. John Spinnock designed what U.S. coin on which his initials, *JS*, can be found under the head of FDR?

9. Actress and model Doris Dosoher Boum posed for sculptor Herman Atkins, who put her likeness on what U.S. coin in 1916?

10. Immediately before the Kennedy half-dollar appeared, whose face appeared on the coin?

11. Sarah Longacre, the daughter of the U.S. Mint's chief engraver James Longacre, posed for what U.S. coin?

12. What was the source for the first coins minted in the United States?

13. On all U.S. coins what words are found on the front and what two sentences are found on the back?

14. What was the denomination of the last coin minted in San Francisco on March 24, 1955?

15. What mottoes were inscribed on each side of the 1¢ piece that was the first official coin minted in the United States?

16. In the 1932 movie *Scarface*, what coin did George Raft flip throughout the film?

17. To decide who would fly first on December 17, 1903, the Wright Brothers flipped a coin. Orville won and entered history. What was the coin they tossed?

18. Whose faces are depicted on a nickel and on a dime?

19. Whose faces are depicted on a quarter and a penny?

20. What is a collector of coins called?

Descriptions

1. To what country was Mark Twain referring when he called it the "Mother of history, grandmother of legend, and great-grandmother of tradition"?

3. San Francisco
4. Denver
5. Carson City, Nevada
6. Philadelphia, Pennsylvania
7. John F. Kennedy half-dollar
8. The Franklin D. Roosevelt 10¢ piece (dime)
9. Quarter
10. Benjamin Franklin's
11. The Indian-head penny
12. Martha Washington's silver service, which she volunteered
13. Liberty—In God We Trust (front), United States of America—
    E Pluribus Unum (back)
14. Penny
15. "Mind your business" and *"Fugit"*
16. Nickel (although one would think it should have been a half
    dollar or dollar piece)
17. 50 cent piece
18. Thomas Jefferson's and Franklin D. Roosevelt's, respectively
19. George Washington's and Abraham Lincoln's, respectively
20. Numismatist

Descriptions (Answers)

1. India

2. What country was Winston Churchill referring to when he called it "A riddle wrapped in a mystery inside an enigma"?

3. What one word described women in the 1973 movie *Soylent Green?*

4. After he lost many of his troops at Fredricksburg, President Abraham Lincoln said "Only _____ could have managed such a coup, wringing one last spectacular defeat from the jaws of victory." Fill in the blank.

5. Dorothy Parker once describe whose acting as "running the gamut of emotions from A to B"?

6. Of whom was Henry "Light-Horse Harry" Lee speaking when he said "First in war, first in peace, and first in the hearts of his countrymen"?

7. What did poet Carl Sandburg say "Comes on littlest feet"?

8. To whom was actress Constance Bennett referring when she remarked, "Now there's a broad with a future behind her"?

9. What television game show panelist coined the question "Is it bigger than a bread box"?

10. "The bigger they come, the harder they fall" was a description made by what heavyweight boxer about what opponent?

Dimensions

1. How long is the approach area prior to the foul line on a bowling lane?

2. How long is a tennis court?

3. How long is a shuffleboard court?

4. What is the height of a rim in basketball?

5. What is the distance between bases in baseball?

6. What measured 300 cubits by 50 cubits by 30 cubits when it was completed?

7. What sports court measures 60 feet by 30 feet?

8. What sports court measures 44 feet by 20 feet for both singles and doubles play?

9. What game is played on a playing field 110 yards by 53⅓ yards to 60 yards?

10. At 408 acres, what is the largest national cemetery in the United States?

2. Russia
3. Furniture
4. General Ambrose Burnside
5. Katharine Hepburn's
6. George Washington
7. Fog
8. Marilyn Monroe (referring to her rear in a tight-fitting dress)
9. Steve Allen
10. Said by Jim Jeffries about Bob Fitzsimmons

Dimensions (Answers)

1. 16 feet
2. 78 feet long
3. 52 feet long
4. 10 feet
5. 90 feet
6. Noah's Ark
7. Volleyball court
8. Badminton court
9. Lacrosse field
10. Arlington National Cemetery

Dogs

1. What is the wild dog of Australia called?
2. What was the name of Vice-President Richard M. Nixon's dog?
3. What is the name of Dagwood and Blondie's dog?
4. What were the names of President Lyndon B. Johnson's two pet beagles, which he would pick up by their ears?
5. Admiral Byrd's fox terrier holds the distinction of being the only dog to visit both the Arctic and Antarctic poles. What was his name?
6. Jacqueline Susann's first best-seller was written about her pet poodle. Name the book.
7. In November 1957, what Russian dog became the first canine to orbit the earth?
8. What is the average body temperature of a dog?
9. What American President had a pet Scottie named Fala?
10. What is the name of the dog that Lee Duncan found in a foxhole in France during World War I?

Drinks

1. In 1893, New Bern, North Carolina, druggist Caleb B. Brabham created what popular soft drink?
2. When G. L. Grigg first introduced this drink in 1929, he named it Bib-Label Lighthearted Lemon-Lime Soda. What is it called today?
3. On March 29, 1886, chemist John S. Pemberton developed a new drink that he called the Esteemed Brain Tonic and Intellectual Beverage. By what name do we know it today?
4. President Lyndon B. Johnson was so fond of what soft drink that he had special taps installed in the White House to dispense it?
5. What American invented root beer soft drink in 1869? Give his last name.
6. Waco, Texas, chemist R. S. Lazenby invented what soft drink at his old corner drug store in 1885?
7. What alcoholic drink is nicknamed Nelson's Blood, in the British Navy?

Dogs (Answers)

1. Dingo
2. Checkers
3. Daisy
4. Him and Her
5. Igloo
6. *Every Night Josephine!*
7. Laika
8. 101 degrees Fahrenheit
9. Franklin Delano Roosevelt
10. Rin Tin Tin

Drinks (Answers)

1. Pepsi-Cola
2. 7-Up
3. Coca-Cola
4. Fresca
5. Hires (Charles Elmer Hires)
6. Dr. Pepper
7. Rum

8. What do the winners of the Indianapolis 500 auto race traditionally drink in the winner's circle?

9. When the soft drink 7-Up was first introduced in 1929, what did the "7" and the "Up" mean?

10. For what soft drink company was Richard Nixon once a lawyer and actress Joan Crawford once a board member?

Duration

1. How long were the employees of the American Embassy in Tehran, Iran, held captive against their will?

2. What was the length of the omission in the taped conversation between President Richard M. Nixon and H. R. Halderman that secretary Rose Mary Woods testified that she accidently erased?

3. What strike lasted 57 days in 1982?

4. How long is a fortnight?

5. Name the only two major league baseball players to have played in five different decades (1893–1933 and 1949–1980)?

6. How many years did Sleeping Beauty sleep?

7. What utopian book written in 1888 by Edward Bellamy spanned the years 1887–2000?

8. What ABC television series debuted on February 5, 1969, only to be cancelled the same night as being too risque?

9. What lasted from April 3, 1860, until October 24, 1861—18 months and 21 days?

10. How long did the singer spend in prison in the Tony Orlando and Dawn hit song "Tie a Yellow Ribbon 'Round the Ole Oak Tree"?

11. How long did history's longest war, the Hundred Years' War, last?

12. Who holds the record for playing for one baseball club? This player played for the Baltimore Orioles for 23 years.

13. Who is credited as having given the longest acceptance speech in Academy Award history—sources rate it between 15 minutes and 30 minutes?

14. What was the length of Pope John Paul I's reign as head of the Roman Catholic Church?

15. How often can Halley's Comet be seen from the earth?

16. What was the duration of the Wright brothers' first successful flight, on December 17, 1903?

17. How long is a millennium?

8.   Milk
9.   "7" for 7-ounce bottles and "Up" for bottoms up
10.   Pepsi-Cola

Duration (Answers)

1.   444 days (November 1979–January 1981)
2.   18½ minutes
3.   NFL football strike
4.   14 days
5.   Ninck Altrock and Minnie Minoso, respectively
6.   100 years
7.   *Looking Backward*
8.   "Turn On"
9.   The Pony Express
10.   Three years
11.   116 years (1337 to 1453)
12.   Brooks Robinson
13.   Greer Garson when she won Best Actress for *Mrs. Miniver*
14.   34 days (He died after only a month as pope.)
15.   Every 76 years
16.   12 seconds
17.   1,000 years

18. How long is the gestation period of an elephant?
19. Who was trapped for a period of 28 years, 2 months, and 19 days before being rescued?
20. What is the average life span of a $1 bill?

Eyes

1. Who flunked his physical during World War II when he read the eye chart in the next room by mistake?
2. What Israeli Defense minister lost his left eye in 1941 when he led a Jewish company against the Vichy French in Syria?
3. Yoda, the lovable Frank Oz character introduced in the 1980 movie *The Empire Strikes Back,* had his eyes patterned after what real-life person?
4. Survivor's version of the theme song of the 1982 movie *Rocky III* went to #1 on the charts. What was its title?
5. What giant creature of Greek mythology had but one eye, in the center of his face?
6. What is the color of the glass or plastic lenses in a pair of 3-D glasses?
7. The only film that Barbra Streisand sang the title song for but did not appear in was titled what?
8. What letter can be found at the top of an optometrist's eye chart?
9. What is the name of the 100-eyed giant in Greek mythology?
10. Although he directed possibly the best 3-D movie ever made— *House of Wax* in 1953—he had only one eye, and so he could never appreciate the depth of his project. Who was he?

Fashion

1. What "less is more" fashion trend did Rudi Gernreich introduce?
2. When France's tennis team, with member René LaCoste, defeated the U.S. team in the 1927 Davis Cup, LaCoste wore what insignia on his shirt pocket that launched a line of men's clothing?
3. Katharine Hepburn played what French fashion designer on Broadway?
4. Name the woman's rights activist who popularized wearing pantaloons?

18. 22 months
19. Robinson Crusoe
20. 18 months

Eyes (Answers)

1. Superman
2. Mosche Dayan
3. Albert Einstein
4. "Eye of the Tiger"
5. Cyclops
6. Red and green
7. *The Eyes of Laura Mars* (1978)
8. E
9. Argus
10. Andre de Toth

Fashion (Answers)

1. Topless bathing suits and dresses
2. Alligator
3. Gabrielle "Coco" Chanel
4. Amelia Bloomer

5. What British dandy known for his flamboyant dress helped to influence the style of men's dress for years to come?
6. The first collection of clothing for men was introduced by what fashion designer?
7. This socialite's designer jeans have been a best-seller for girls. In 1982 she was the subject of a television movie. Name her.
8. Actress Gene Tierney was married to what fashion designer from 1941 to 1952?
9. On October 10, 1886, Griswold Lorilhard introduced this style of dinner jacket, at a club from which it got its name. Name it?
10. What French designer introduced the sack dress in the 1950s?

Fathers Of

Identify the men known by following epithets:
1. The Father of Existentialism
2. The Father of Medicine
3. The Father of the Constitution
4. Father of History
5. The Father of Psychoanalysis
6. The Father of Comedy
7. The Father of American Literature
8. The Father of Greek Tragedy
9. The Father of the Atomic Bomb
10. The Father of Baseball

Forts

1. What was the name of the fort captured by Ethan Allen and his Green Mountain Boys in 1775?
2. Fort Peck Dam appeared on the cover of the first issue of what magazine?
3. At what fort in Charleston Harbor, South Carolina, did the Civil War begin on April 12, 1861?
4. What Florida city is the annual site of a migration of college students who have fun in the sun?
5. What Revolutionary War general-to-be surrendered to the French at Fort Necessity on July 4, 1754?

5.   Beau Brummell
6.   Pierre Cardin
7.   Gloria Vanderbilt
8.   Oleg Cassini
9.   Tuxedo, introduced at the Tuxedo Park Country Club Ball
10. Christian Dior

Fathers Of (Answers)

1.   Jean-Paul Sarte
2.   Hippocrates
3.   James Madison
4.   Herodotus
5.   Sigmund Freud
6.   Aristophanes
7.   Washington Irving
8.   Aeschylus
9.   Julius Robert Oppenheimer
10. Abner Doubleday (although he wasn't really)

Forts (Answers)

1.   Fort Ticonderoga
2.   *Life*
3.   Fort Sumter
4.   Fort Lauderdale
5.   George Washington

6. What is the name of the largest fortress in Europe?
7. What well-known city did Fort York, Canada, become?
8. What is the old U.S. Army fort that is situated just below the San Francisco side of the Golden Gate Bridge?
9. What was the U.S. Cavalry fort that George Armstrong Custer and the 7th Cavalry departed from on May 17, 1876, on their way to the Little Big Horn?
10. Fort Dearborn changed its name, becoming what better known city?

Gravesites

1. What U.S. general is buried in a grave at Arlington National Cemetery with an enlisted man's marker, as he requested?
2. What heavyweight boxing champion, buried at Graceland Cemetery in Chicago, had his name misspelled on his tombstone?
3. In what capital city was Karl Marx buried in March of 1883?
4. President William McKinley is buried in the same town where the Football Hall of Fame is located. Where is it?
5. Admiral Richard Byrd took a stone from the grave of his pilot Floyd Bennett. What did he do with the stone on November 29, 1929?
6. Where was ex-heavyweight boxing champion Joe Louis buried in April 12, 1981?
7. Where is mystery writer Dashiell Hammett buried?
8. What Russian admiral is buried at the U. S. Naval Academy at Annapolis?
9. What American rock musician is buried in the Pére Lachaise Cemetey in Paris, France?
10. Both what poet and his Newfoundland dog Boatswain are buried at Newstead Abbey, where the dog has a larger monument?
11. Who is the only soldier to be buried at West Point under a foreign flag?
12. At whose mausoleum in Moscow does a clock nearby constantly read 6:50 P.M., the time of his death?
13. Who was the prime minister of a European country who was buried in Arlington National Cemetery?
14. What British playwright and poet was buried in a standing position in Westminister Abbey?

6. Kremlin (in Moscow)
7. Toronto
8. Fort Point
9. Fort Abraham Lincoln
10. Chicago

Gravesites (Answers)

1. General John J. Pershing
2. Bob Fitzsimmons (it was misspelled Fitzimmons)
3. London
4. Canton, Ohio
5. He used it to weigh down an American flag that he dropped over the South Pole when he flew over it in memory of Bennett.
6. Arlington National Cemetery
7. Arlington National Cemetery
8. John Paul Jones
9. Jim Morrison
10. Lord Byron (George Gordon)
11. David "Mickey" Marcus
12. Nikolai Lenin's
13. Ignace Jan Paderewski (prime minister of Poland 1919–1921)
14. Ben Joñson

15. What western outlaw was buried in the Old Fort Sumner Military Cemetery although he never spent time in the military?

16. Actresses Marilyn Monroe and Natalie Wood are buried in what small gravesite not far from Beverly Hills shopping district?

17. What two famous characters of the Wild West are buried at the Glenwood Cemetery in Glenwood Springs, Colorado?

18. Name the woman who was in love with "Wild Bill" Hickock and requested to be buried next to him at Mount Moriah Cemetery in Deadwood, South Dakota, when she died?

19. What is the name of the large cemetery in Glendale, California, where dozens of Hollywood personalities are buried?

20. Whose grave in Park Cemetery in Fairmount, Indiana, has become a mecca for cult followers and fans?

High School

1. Fairmount High in Fairmount, Indiana has produced two celebrities. One was Garfield's cartoonist Jim Davis; who was the other?

2. Name the alma mater of such celebrities as The Four Preps, Carol Burnett, and Rick Nelson.

3. What Southern California high school not only is situated on some of the most expensive land in the United States, but has its own oilwell too?

4. What Winnetka, Illinois, high school did the following all attend: Bruce Dern, Charlton Heston, Ann-Margaret, Rock Hudson, Ralph Bellamy, and Hugh O'Brian?

5. Name the high school in Waukegan, Illinois, that is named for a well-known entertainer?

6. On September 25, 1957, a 15-year-old black student, Elizabeth Eckford, attempted to enter what Southern high school in order to desegragate the school system?

7. Barbra Streisand and Neil Diamond are just two of a number of celebrities who attended what Brooklyn, New York school?

8. What Oakland, California, high school did both actor Clint Eastwood and the author of this book attend?

9. Neil Simon, Burt Lancaster, Richard Rodgers, and Robert Klein and a number of other celebrities attended what Bronx, New York high school?

10. What school provides the setting for the movie/TV series *Fame?*

15. Billy the Kid
16. Westwood Memorial Park
17. "Doc" Holliday and Kid Curry
18. Calamity Jane
19. Forest Lawn Memorial Park
20. James Dean

High Schools (Answers)

1. Actor James Dean
2. Hollywood High School
3. Beverly Hills High School
4. New Trier High School
5. Jack Benny High School
6. Little Rock Central High
7. Erasmus High School
8. Oakland Technical High School
9. DeWitt Clinton High School
10. The New York High School for the Performing Arts

Horses

1. Aethelnoth, which was named for the Archbishop of Canterbury, was the name of the horse upon which who rode naked through the town of Coventry?
2. Who beat the horse Julio McCaw in a 100-yard dash held in Havana on December 27, 1936? (The winner had been given a 40-yard head start).
3. What Spanish leader rode a horse named Babieca?
4. What was the name of Gene Autry's talented horse that he named in part after a rock 'n' roll group in 1958?
5. What breed of horses pull the famous Anhauser Busch beer wagon?
6. What is the name of the Arabian stallion that was brought to Britain in the early 1700s and of which approximately 90% of all thoroughbred horses are descendents?
7. What was the name of the horse that Tom Mix rode in films?
8. What was the name of Hopalong Cassidy's beautiful white horse?
9. What western writer owned a horse named Fritz?
10. What American Civil War general rode a horse named Traveler?

Hotels

1. What hotel chain was founded in Memphis by realtor Kemmons Wilson, in 1945?
2. Sirhan Bishara Sirhan shot and killed Presidential candidate Robert Kennedy in what Los Angeles hotel on the evening of June 5, 1968?
3. What popular TV and film comedian died at the Chateau Marmont Hotel in Los Angeles on March 5, 1982?
4. What British poet died of alcoholism in New York City's Chelsea Hotel on November 9, 1953?
5. The Beatles stayed in what famous New York City hotel when they arrived in the United States in February of 1964?
6. Shown on the cover of the Eagles album *Hotel California*, this Southern California hotel was built in 1912 and is nicknamed the Pink Palace. What is the actual name?

Horses (Answers)

1. Lady Godiva
2. Jesse Owens
3. El Cid
4. Champion
5. Clydesdale
6. Eclipse
7. Toni
8. Topper
9. William S. Hart
10. Robert E. Lee

Hotels (Answers)

1. Holiday Inn
2. Ambassador Hotel
3. John Belushi
4. Dylan Thomas
5. Plaza Hotel
6. Beverly Hills Hotel

7. On October 17, 1978, New York City's Chelsea Hotel became the site of the murder of Nancy Spungen, the girlfriend of what punk rocker who died of an overdose before he could be brought to trial?

8. In 1976 the Philadelphia Bellevue Stratford Hotel became the site of several deaths of some men who came from Bloomington, Illinois. What disease was associated with their deaths?

9. At age 71, on February 25, 1983, what Pulitzer Prize-winning playwright died of natural causes in New York City's Elysee Hotel?

10. What Mafia leader was shot and killed in the barbershop of New York's Park Sheridan Hotel on October 25, 1957?

Inspirations

1. The great Babe Ruth copied his famous swing from what other well-known major league player?

2. Travis Bickle, a character in a 1976 film, became the inspiration for what mentally depressed individual?

3. Harriet Beecher Stowe based what character of hers on the real-life slave Josiah Henson, who dictated to her his life story?

4. What actor is supposedly the subject of Carly Simon's 1972 hit song "You're So Vain"?

5. Who was the inspiration for the character of Sheridan Whiteside in George S. Kaufman and Moss Hart's play *The Man Who Came to Dinner,* played by Monty Woolley, in the 1941 movie?

6. What song was Katharine Lee Bates inspired to compose after she climbed Pikes Peak in 1893?

7. One Mr. S. K. Hicks was the real-life inspiration for what 1969 hit song by Johnny Cash, written by cartoonist Shel Silversten?

8. What Hollywood actor's face became the inspiration for the face of comic-book hero Captain Marvel?

9. What 1930 science fiction novel by Philip Wylie inspired writer Jerry Siegel and artist Joe Shuster to create *Superman?*

10. Hollywood western film star Jack Holt's face was used as the model for what Al Capp comic-strip character?

  7. Sid Vicious
  8. Legionnaire's disease
  9. Tennessee Williams
10. Albert Anastasia

Inspirations (Answers)

1. "Shoeless" Joe Jackson
2. John Hinkley, who attempted to shoot Ronald Reagan. (Robert DeNiro played Bickle opposite Jodie Foster in the movie *Taxi Driver*.)
3. Uncle Tom—the main character in her novel *Uncle Tom's Cabin*
4. Warren Beatty
5. Drama critic Alexander Woollcott
6. "America the Beautiful"
7. "A Boy Named Sue"
8. Fred MacMurray's
9. *Gladiator*
10. Fearless Fosdick

Material

1. Out of what material was Noah's Ark made?
2. What substance was the shoe that Charlie Chaplin ate in the 1925 silent film *The Gold Rush,* made of?
3. What was Thor Heyerdahl's vessel *Tigris*—in which he sailed from Safi, Morocco, to Barbados in 1970—made of?
4. When Secretary of War Henry Lewis Stimson selected the first draft number (#158) in November 1910, he did so blindfolded. What material made up the bandages that he used?
5. One of the age-old questions asked by trivia buffs concerns Superman: When he is disguised as mild-mannered Clark Kent, why doesn't he melt his glasses when he uses his X-ray vision?
6. When Tonto was helping ranger John Reid to recover, he made him a mask to wear, creating his secret identity as the Lone Ranger. What was the mask made from?
7. What new material was U.S. pole vaulter John Pennel's pole made of? (In 1963, he broke the World's Record several times with it.)
8. What are little girls made of?
9. When the Indianapolis 500 Speedway was first built in 1911, what material was used for the racetrack itself?
10. What material was Howard Hughes's *Spruce Goose* transport aircraft made of?

Messages

1. "Testing: The quick brown fox jumped over the lazy dog's back, 1234567890" was the first message ever spoken on what hot line?
2. "Air raid . . . this is no drill" was a message sent out where and when?
3. Elbert Hubbard's essay made what Cuban revolutionary famous?
4. What country sent and what country received the Zimmerman telegraph message of World War I?
5. Who invented the telegraph?
6. On the cover of Paul McCartney and Wing's 1973 album *Red Rose Speedway* album a message appeared in braille, stating, "We love you, baby." To whom was it addressed?

Material (Answers)

1. Gopherwood
2. Licorice
3. Papyrus
4. Cloth from the cover of a chair from Independence Hall
5. His glasses were made from the glass material from the windshield of the spacecraft in which he came to earth as a baby.
6. From the vest of his dead brother Captain Daniel Reid
7. Fiberglass
8. Sugar and spice and everything nice
9. Bricks
10. Birchwood and fiber

Messages (Answers)

1. The hot line between the White House and the Kremlin
2. Pearl Harbor, December 7, 1941
3. Calixto Garcia—*A Message to Garcia*
4. Germany sent, Mexico received
5. Samuel Morse
6. Stevie Wonder

7. What is the CB radio channel (27.065 MHz) allocated for emergency messages?
8. In an automobile race what color flag tells the drivers that the race has begun?
9. What color flag tells the drivers that they have crossed the finish line?
10. Every April 15th the international ice patrol sends out a radio message in honor of an event. What was the event?

Monkeys

1. On May 28, 1959, two chimpanzees were launched into space from Cape Canaveral and brought safely back to earth, becoming the first primates to return from space unharmed. Give their names.
2. What roller-skating chimpanzee appeared on several television shows in the 1950s, such as Howdy Doody's?
3. In films, what was the name of Tarzan's chimp?
4. To whom is the J. Fred Muggs award given by *TV Guide?*
5. What chimp appeared with Ronald Reagan in a 1951 film? (The chimp's name appears in the title)
6. What are the names given to the chimpanzees on the TV series "The Hathaways"?
7. What was the name of the first United States animal to orbit the earth on January 31, 1961?
8. What was the name of the chimpanzee on Dave Garroway's TV series, the "Today Show"?
9. What orangutan starred in his own short-lived TV series in 1983?
10. What don't the three little Japanese apes of Nikko do?

Museums

1. The Patton Museum, which houses General George S. Patton's memorabilia, also is the home for an Oscar. Whose Academy Award is kept there?
2. Shelley Winter's Oscar for Best Supporting Actress is kept at what museum in Amsterdam?

7. Channel 9
8. Green
9. Checkered (white and black) flag
10. The sinking of the Titanic ("RMS Titanic, 41°, 46″ north; 50° 14″ west, 15 April 12, Rest in peace")

Monkeys (Answers)

1. Abel and Baker
2. Zippy
3. Chita
4. "Those who excelled at making monkeys of themselves."
5. Bonzo (*Bedtime for Bonzo*)
6. Marquis Chimpanzee
7. Ham (Holliman Aerospace Medical Center)
8. J. Fred Muggs
9. C. J. ("Mr. Smith")
10. See no evil; hear no evil; speak no evil

Museums (Answers)

1. George C. Scott's Academy Award for Best Actor for the 1970 movie *Patton*
2. Anne Frank Museum

3. Who designed the Guggenheim Museum in New York City in 1943?
4. Who was the founder of the first museum in the United States? (Founded in 1786, it bears his last name.)
5. In what city can a tourist find piano virtuoso Liberace's museum, his piano, clothes, automobiles, and other assorted memorabilia?
6. The Hall of Mirrors is located in what museum?
7. What is the museum that has the largest art collection in the United States?
8. What scientific museum was created by a congressional act in 1846?
9. In what country other than Egypt can one find the most Egyptian relics located in museums?
10. In what state is the John Dillinger Historical Museum located?

Mythology

1. Who is the Roman God of love?
2. In Greek mythology what goddess is both sister and wife of Zeus and queen of the Olympic gods?
3. In Greek and Roman mythology who is the son of Zeus and Alcmene, known for his strength?
4. What is the name of the three-headed dog that guards the gates of hell?
5. In Greek mythology who helped Jason in his quest for the Golden Fleece?
6. Where is the home of the gods?
7. What is the drink of the gods?
8. In Norse mythology what is the name of the great hall where Odin lives?
9. What is the name of the Greek messenger god equivalent to the Roman god Mercury?
10. Who is the chief Greek god?

Ocean Liners

1. Where is the ocean liner *Queen Elizabeth* moored as a tourist attraction for Americans?

3. Frank Lloyd Wright
4. Charles Peale—The Peale Museum
5. Las Vegas
6. Versailles
7. Metropolitan Museum of Art in New York City
8. Smithsonian
9. Britain
10. Indiana

Mythology (Answers)
1. Cupid
2. Hera
3. Hercules
4. Cerberus
5. Medea
6. Mt. Olympus
7. Nectar
8. Valhalla
9. Hermes
10. Zeus

Ocean Liners (Answers)
1. Port Everglades, Florida

2. What ocean liner is moored at pier J in Long Beach, California, as a tourist attraction?

3. What unsinkable vessel sank on her maiden voyage in 1912?

4. What Cunard liner was torpedoed and sunk on May 7, 1915, by a German submarine?

5. What ocean liner held the record for the fastest Atlantic crossing time?

6. What happened at 12:10 A.M. September 24, 1967, for the very last time?

7. What French ocean liner was scrapped in 1959, after serving for 32 years?

8. What was the sister ship of the *Lusitania*?

9. What was the name of the passenger ship that burned off Asbury Park, New Jersey, on September 8, 1934?

10. What two ocean liners collided off Nantucket on the night of July 26, 1956?

Paintings

1. What 1872 painting, by James Whistler, is actually titled *Arrangement in Gray and Black No 1: The Artists Mother?*

2. What 1930 painting is Grant Wood's most well-known?

3. This painter of everyday American life designed the covers for hundreds of *Saturday Evening Post* magazines. Name him.

4. What British painter created *Blue Boy* in order to show art critics that the color blue need not be dull?

5. Which one of Norman Rockwell's paintings is the most reproduced painting in history?

6. What was the subject of Peter Hurd's 1967 painting that President Lyndon B. Johnson called the ugliest painting he had ever seen?

7. Who created the painting *Nude Descending a Staircase?*

8. What is the only painting that inspired a million-selling song?

9. What is the famous painting of the girl Sarah Moulton-Barrett by Sir Thomas Laurence?

10. Who painted the *Last Supper* and in what city was it painted on the refectory wall of a church?

2. *Queen Mary*
3. *Titanic*
4. *Lusitania*
5. *United States*
6. The eastbound *Queen Mary* passed the westbound *Queen Elizabeth* in mid-Atlantic.
7. *Ile de France*
8. *Muritania*
9. *Morro Castle*
10. *Andrea Doria* and *Stockholm*. The *Andrea Doria* sank.

Paintings (Answers)

1. *Whistler's Mother*
2. *American Gothic*
3. Norman Rockwell
4. Sir Thomas Gainsborough
5. *The Four Freedoms*
6. It was the official Presidential portrait of Johnson.
7. Marcel Duchamps
8. *Mona Lisa*
9. *Pinkie*
10. Leonardo da Vinci—Milan, Italy

Post Offices

1. Who was the first postmaster general in the United States?
2. Who was the first pilot to carry the U.S. mail across the Atlantic Ocean?
3. What zip code is used in first day of issue cancellations of stamps issued in Washington, DC?
4. Newton Falls, Ohio, has only one reoccurring number in its zip code. What is it?
5. What do the initials R.F.D. stand for?
6. What credo of the post office was created by Herodotus?
7. In what year was the U.S. postal service established?
8. What does the acronym zip mean?
9. The year 1963 saw what means of mail delivery in Alaska come to an end?
10. What went on sale from the U.S. post office on May 1, 1873?

Products

1. George J. French introduced what prepared food spread in 1904?
2. King Camp Gillette introduced what safety product in 1901, and two years later founded a company to manufacture them?
3. Joyce C. Hall's autobiography is appropriately titled *When You Care Enough*. What company did Joyce found in 1913?
4. In 1896, when Leo Hirschfield created a new candy, he decided to name it after his daughter Clara's nickname. What is the name?
5. Victor Kian was so impressed with a product that he bought the company, after which he made his own TV commercial for what product?
6. What breakfast cereal received a credit line in the 1978 movie *Superman?*
7. What do the initials B.V.D.'s in men's underwear stand for?
8. Brothers John and Will founded what food product company in Battle Creek, Michigan, which bears their last names?
9. In 1887, what company became the first to sell fresh milk in bottles?
10. What automobile tire manufacturer with the first name of Benjamin (Franklin) founded his rubber company in 1826?

Post Offices (Answers)

1. Benjamin Franklin
2. Admiral Richard Byrd
3. 20013
4. 44444
5. Rural Free Delivery
6. "Neither snow, nor rain, nor heat, nor gloom of night stays these couriers from the swift completion of their appointed rounds."
7. 1707 (August 12)
8. Zone Improvement Plan
9. Dog sleds
10. Penny postal card

Products (Answers)

1. Mustard
2. Safety razors. He founded the Gillette Safety Razor Company.
3. Hallmark Cards
4. Tootsie Roll (Clara was called Tootsie)
5. Remington Shaver
6. Cheerios by General Mills
7. Bradley, Vorhees, and Day
8. Kellogg's Cereal
9. Borden's Milk
10. Goodrich

Religions

1. George Fox founded what religious group in 1668, that was originally called the Society of Friends?
2. The founder of what religion nailed his 95 theses on the Wittenberg Church doors in 1517?
3. What religion is Mary Baker Eddy credited with founding in 1879?
4. What religious cult was founded by Jim Jones in the 1970s?
5. Who was the first ordained woman minister in the United States?
6. British social reformer William Booth founded what religious organization in 1878?
7. What is the book that encompasses the whole body of Jewish religious literature?
8. What consists of Brahma, Shiva, and Vishnu?
9. Who founded the Church of England?
10. Who began the Church of the Latter Day Saints (Mormons) in 1830?

Rules

1. Henry Chadwick wrote the first book of rules for what sport in 1858?
2. Harvard University passed a rule limiting senior theses to 40,000 words because one student submitted a 377-page thesis in 1950 titled "The Meaning of History." What was the student's name?
3. What is the maximum number of letters that a thoroughbred horse can have in its name?
4. Who published a set of rules for the card game of whist in 1742, which eventually lead to the publication of rules in other card games?
5. When groups hold meetings based on parliamentary procedures, what rule book do they use?
6. What is the Golden Rule?
7. Sir John Sholto Douglas, in 1867, established a code of fair play for pugilists. By what other name do we know Sir Douglas?

Religions (Answers)

1. Quakers
2. Lutheranism (Martin Luther)
3. Christian Science Church
4. People's Temple
5. Antoinette Louisa Blackwell
6. Salvation Army
7. Torah
8. The Hindu Trinity
9. King Henry VIII
10. Joseph Smith

Rules (Answers)

1. Baseball
2. Henry Kissinger
3. 14
4. Hoyle (Edmund Hoyle)
5. *Robert's Rules of Order*
6. "Do unto others as you would have them do unto you."
7. Marquis of Queensbury

8. Who created the Ten Commandments of the cowboys?
9. What simple rule tells us when to adjust the clocks to begin and end daylight savings time?
10. What is the only sport that has a rule against left-handed players?

Secret Identities

Name the individuals behind the following cover identities:
1. Diana Prince
2. The clandestine Watergate informant of the *Washington Post* reporter Bob Woodward, whom he met secretly in a garage in Washington?
3. Billy Batson
4. This nemisis of Batman and Robin's real name is Selina Kyle. Name her.
5. When Kal-El came to Earth what secret identity was he given?
6. Peter Parker
7. Steve Rogers
8. Britt Reid
9. Bruce Banner
10. Norrin Radd

Ships

1. Prior to the Trident class of nuclear submarines, the first of which was named the *Ohio*, after what animals were U.S. submarines named?
2. Name the nine U.S. battleships present at Pearl Harbor on December 7, 1941.
3. Who, as a young telegraph operator, relayed the news about the sinking of the *Titanic* in 1912? (He later founded the NBC radio network.)
4. On April 30, 1979, the vessel the *Ashdod* became the first Israeli ship to travel through what?
5. What was the name of the Japanese destroyer that rammed and sank *PT-109* on August 2, 1943, in Blackett Strait in the Solomon Islands? Also who commanded *PT-109*?

8. Gene Autry
9. Spring forward, fall back.
10. Polo (All players must hit right-handed.)

Secret Identities (Answers)

1. Wonder Woman
2. Deep Throat
3. Captain Marvel
4. Cat Woman
5. Clark Kent
6. Spider Man
7. Captain America
8. Green Hornet
9. The Hulk
10. Silver Surfer

Ships (Answers)

1. Fish
2. *Arizona, California, Maryland, Nevada, Oklahoma, Pennsylvania, Tennessee, Utah, and West Virginia*
3. David Sarnoff
4. Suez Canal
5. *Amigiri*. Lt. jg John F. Kennedy

6. On what British vessel did naturalist Charles Darwin travel between 1831 and 1836 in order to study animal life in foreign lands?

7. What is the only U.S. Navy warship named after a man who committed suicide?

8. What is the name of Jacques-Yves Cousteau's research vessel? (John Denver titled one of his songs after it.)

9. What was the name of the passenger liner that left Hamburg, Germany, on May 27, 1939, but couldn't find a port to disembark its escaping Jewish passengers?

10. What is the name of the largest German battleship built during World War II, which was sunk on May 27, 1941?

Sounds

1. What are the three noises that a horse makes with its mouth?
2. What is the sound of a thunderbolt in Johnny Hart's comic strip, *B.C.*?
3. In what key do the majority of American automobile's horns sound?
4. A rider who wants to tell a horse to make a right or left turn, says what two words?
5. How fast does sound travel at sea level at 32°F?
6. Columnist Walter Winchell once coined a word representing the sound of a marriage going flat. The word was used for the title of a 1954 movie. Name it.
7. What unit is used to measure sound?
8. Who recorded the "Sounds of Silence," and what 1967 film featured this song?
9. According to the *Guinness Book of World Records,* what is the loudest rock band?
10. What low-frequency audio effect, ranging from 16–20 cycles per second, can be heard in such films as *Earthquake* (1974) and *Midway* (1976)?

6. H.M.S. *Beagle*
7. Aircraft carrier *Forrestal* (named after James Vincent Forrestal)
8. *Calypso*
9. *St. Louis*
10. *Bismark*

Sounds (Answers)

1. Snort, neigh, and whinny
2. *Zot!*
3. F
4. "Gee" and "haw," respectively
5. 1,088 feet per second
6. *Phffft!*
7. Decibel
8. Simon and Garfunkel—*The Graduate*
9. The Who
10. Sensurround

Statues

1. In a story by Joel Chandler Harris, a statue of what character was erected in Eatontan, Georgia, in front of the courthouse?
2. Charlotte Beysser Bartholdi modeled for a statue that was sculpted by her son Frederick Auguste Bartholdi. What is the name of this statue?
3. In London's Trafalgar Square, there is a statue of what U.S. President?
4. A large statue of what naval hero is located 185 feet above ground in London's Trafalgar Square?
5. Enterprise, Alabama, is the site of a statue that was dedicated to what insect on December 11, 1949?
6. Pine Bluff, Arkansas, erected a $10,000 life-sized bronze bust of what controversial Washington, DC, figure?
7. What is the inscription on the famous statue of two young boys that stands in front of Boy's Town, Nebraska?
8. A 78-foot-high bronze reproduction by Felix de Weldon of what great incident overlooks Washington, DC, just outside of Arlington National Cemetery?
9. What statue by Edward Erickson sits at the water's edge in Copenhagen Harbor?
10. Who is the only American to have a bust at London's Westminster Abbey?

Telephone

1. In what New England city was the first pay telephone installed in 1899?
2. In what year did the transcontinental telephone line open for service?
3. What is Emma Nutt's claim to fame (she became employed on September 1, 1878)?
4. What three numbers does a person in Great Britain dial to get emergency help?
5. What Connecticut town introduced the first telephone directory in 1878?

Statues (Answers)

1. Br'er Rabbit
2. The Statue of Liberty
3. George Washington
4. Lord Nelson
5. Boll weevil
6. Martha Mitchell
7. "He Ain't Heavy, He's My Brother"
8. The U.S. Marine flag raising on Iwo Jima
9. *The Little Mermaid*
10. Henry Wadsworth Longfellow

Telephone (Answers)

1. Hartford, Connecticut
2. 1914
3. She became the first telephone operator
4. 999
5. New Haven

6. What number do you dial to get information?
7. What three digits are used by the telephone company for their own numbers? (The numbers are used on TV and in movies as a prefix when giving out a telephone number.)
8. Glenn Miller and his orchestra had a big hit with a telephone number in the late 1930s. Name the song.
9. The telephone number (202) 456-1414, is the number of what?
10. The letters *ABC* are accompanied by what number on a telephone dial?

Toys

1. This toy was the rage of Christmas 1983. There was such a demand for these items that they were being sold for $100 each. What were they?
2. In 1919, inventor George B. Hansburg introduced what bouncing toy, which is still selling today?
3. In 1927, Filipino busboy Pedro Flores introduced what toy to the United States?
4. Who is the father of the inventor of the toy construction set known as Lincoln Logs?
5. What San Gabriel, California, company introduced the Frisbee toy in 1957 and the Hula-Hoop in 1958?
6. A. C. Gilbert, a young athlete who represented the U.S. in the pole vault in the 1908 Olympic Games, later invented what popular toy construction set?
7. Joshua Cowen named his toy train company after his middle name, which he founded in 1902. Name it.
8. Binney and Smith have been producing what children's art supplies for years?
9. What toy was named for the President of the United States?
10. Luck, Wisconsin, was once called the yo-yo capital of the world. What manufacturer produced yo-yos there from 1946 until 1966?

Trains

1. Who lead the robbery of the Aberdeen Express train of $7 million in British currency on August 8, 1963? (The robbery has become known as The Great Train Robbery.)

6. 411
7. 555
8. "Pennsylvania 6500"
9. The White House
10. 2

Toys (Answers)

1. Cabbage Patch Dolls
2. Pogo Stick
3. Yo-yo
4. Frank Lloyd Wright (his son John created the toy)
5. Wham-O
6. Erector Set
7. Lionel
8. Crayola crayons
9. The teddy bear (named for Teddy Roosevelt)
10. Duncan

Trains (Answers)

1. Ronald Briggs

2. What are the three stops of the train called out by announcer Mel Blanc on the radio show "The Jack Benny Program"?

3. What American league batting champion was born on a train in the Panama Canal Zone on October 1, 1945?

4. In 1873, Eli H. Janney was responsible for what modern device used on all railroad cars and train engines?

5. What is the name of the passenger train that once ran between London and Edinburgh?

6. What was the name of Casey Jones's regular train on the Illinois Central Railroad? (It was, however, not the train on which he was killed on April 30, 1900.)

7. Chessie the Cat is the symbol of what U.S. railroad?

8. When the railroad that went up to Italy's Mount Vesuvius was opened in 1880, what song was composed for the occasion?

9. What was the name of the Confederate train locomotive hijacked by Union soldiers led by James J. Andrews in what has become known as the Great Locomotive Chase?

10. After 94 years of service, what luxury passenger train, that ran between Paris and Istanbul, ceased its run?

Trilogy

1. What three novels by Charles Nordhoff and James Norman Hall make up the *Bounty Trilogy?*

2. Who were the first three men to form the Roman governing board called the Triumvirate, founded in 60 B.C.?

3. For what three films did Walter Brennan win his three Academy Awards for Best Supporting Actor?

4. Name the three U.S. Presidents whose last names consist of only four letters?

5. What are the three novels that make up Isaac Asimov's *Foundation* trilogy?

6. What are the titles of the novels that make up James Jones's World War II trilogy? (He died in 1977 before he could finish the last work.)

7. What are the three types of ancient Greek columns?

8. What three books make up the *Lord of the Rings* trilogy?

9. Name the three musketeers.

10. According to the West Point Military Academy, what are the 3 D's of the fighting man?

2. "Anaheim, Azusa, and Cucamonga"
3. Rod Carew
4. Couplers
5. The Flying Scotsman
6. Cannonball Express
7. Chesapeake and Ohio Railroad
8. "Funiculi, Funicula" (after the Funicula Railway)
9. The General
10. Orient Express

Trilogy (Answers)

1. *Mutiny On the Bounty* (1932), *Men Against the Sea* (1934), and *Pitcairn's Island* (1934)
2. Julius Caesar, Pompey, and Crassus
3. *Come and Get It* (1936), *Kentucky* (1938), and *The Westerner* (1940)
4. Polk, Taft, and Ford
5. *Foundation, Foundation and Empire, Second Foundation*
6. *From Here To Eternity, The Thin Red Line, Whistle*
7. Ionic, Doric, and Corinthian
8. *The Fellowship of the Ring; The Two Towers; The Return of the King*
9. Athos, Porthos, and Aramis
10. Discipline, Decision, and Devotion to Duty

Typewriters

1. During the battle at Arnhem during World War II, what news reporter flew into the battle in a glider with his Olivetti typewriter in hand?
2. In what movie did Jack Nicholson type over and over again the single sentence "All work and no play makes Johnny a dull boy" on his Royal typewriter?
3. What brand of typewriter did Grantland Rice use for his newspaper columns? (The machine is on display today at the College Football Hall of Fame.)
4. On what brand of typewriter did Mark Twain type *The Adventures of Tom Sawyer* in 1875 (the first book ever to be prepared on a typewriter)?
5. George K. Anderson invented what additon to the typewriter in 1886?
6. What are the two standard kinds of type?
7. What brand of manual typewriter does Irving Wallace use to type his novels?
8. On what brand of typewriter did Margaret Mitchell type her huge novel, *Gone with the Wind?*
9. Which hand performs 56% of the typing?
10. His Woodstock typewriter (No. 230,099) helped lead to his conviction for treason. Name him.

Weapons

1. What did frontiersman Davy Crockett nickname his rifle?
2. Name the gunsmith who made the two custom long-handled pistols for Wyatt Earp?
3. What is the first name of the creator of the Bowie knife?
4. What was the name of the first atomic cannon (built in the United States in 1953)?
5. President Franklin Delano Roosevelt and his First Lady Eleanor both kept pistols under their pillows at night. What names did they give to these weapons?
6. What does BAR stand for?

Typewriters (Answers)

1. Walter Cronkite
2. *The Shining*
3. Underwood
4. Remington
5. Typewriter ribbon
6. Pica and elite
7. Underwood
8. Remington
9. Left
10. Alger Hiss

Weapons (Answers)

1. Old Betsy
2. Ned Buntline
3. Rezin, the brother of Jim
4. Atomic Annie
5. His and Hers
6. Browning Automatic Rifle

7. What was the name of the large cannon used by the Germans to bombard Paris during World War I?
8. Built during World War I by the British, the first modern operational model was named H.M.S. Centipede. What was it?
9. What German manufacturer of armaments was supplying over 40 countries with weapons by 1887?
10. What weapon did Richard J. Gatling invent in 1862?

Zeppelins

1. What was the first lighter-than-air ship to fly around the world in 1929?
2. What was the name of the German zeppelin that exploded and crashed at Lakehurst, New Jersey, on May 6, 1937?
3. What was the highly explosive gas that kept the *Hindenberg* afloat?
4. What gas was later used in zeppelins that was much safer, and why didn't Germany use it originally?
5. What U.S. tire manufacturer uses zeppelins to advertise its products as well as photographing interesting shots of sporting events?
6. What U.S. Navy zeppelin crashed off the New Jersey coast on April 4, 1933, killing 73 men?
7. The sister ship of the dirigible *Akron* crashed off the California coast on February 12, 1935, was named what?
8. What German-built U.S. dirigible (ZR-3) launched on October 15, 1924, was named for a West Coast city?
9. What heavy metal group was named, in part, for a zeppelin?
10. What West Coast U.S. Navy base still uses hangars that were built to house dirigibles?

7. Big Bertha
8. Tank
9. The House of Krupp
10. The maching gun

Zeppelins (Answers)

1. The *Graf Zeppelin*
2. *Hindenberg*
3. Hydrogen
4. Helium—the United States was the only source of the gas.
5. Goodyear
6. *Akron*
7. *Macon*
8. *Los Angeles*
9. Led Zeppelin
10. Moffett, NAS

Index to Categories